Lost Football Heroes
of the First World War

Jeff Williamson was born in Farnworth, Bolton. A former detective, he is now an investigator and football historian. His last book was published in 2015, *The Wonderful Wanderers, Bolton Wanderers 1874 to 1960*.

It was during his research on this book that he became interested in the First World War and the large numbers of footballers who signed up for the conflict, and more so of those who gave their lives, which number over 453 to date, serving with British, Canadian, Australian and South African Armed Forces. It covers all the players from the English, Scottish, Welsh and Irish clubs in their respective top-flight football leagues from 1914-15 to the end of the conflict in 1918. Over three years of research have gone into compiling this information.

There are many stories of bravery and sacrifice, as well as, of course, the statistics of the footballers themselves. Researching the events these men went through was a truly humbling experience. They are all heroes.

Book cover by (Art)-Susan Williamson

First Published in Great Britain in 2018 by DB Publishing,
an imprint of JMD Media Ltd

ISBN 978-1-78091-577-7

Printed and bound in the UK

Lost Football Heroes
of the First World War

Jeff Williamson

CONTENTS

West Ham United — 206

Sydney Frederick Hammond, William James Jones, William Kennedy and Edward Arthur James Stallard.

Wolverhampton Wanderers — 209

Walter Lovegrove Blunt and John Edward Shelton.

SCOTTISH LEAGUE TEAMS — 211

Abercorn — 211

Charles C. Jeffrey and Robert Gardner Houston.

Aberdeen — 212

Alexander Laing Halkett, Andrew Hamilton, Allan Lawrie, Angus Cameron McLeod, John Munroe, Herbert Murray, Charles Neilson, James Hadden Neilson, Roland Miller Neilson, William Neilson, Frederick Watson and Joseph Ellis Milne.

Airdrieonians — 216

Thomas Farrell, John Findlay and Robert Williams.

Albion Rovers — 218

Archibald Campbell (see Ayr), James Conlin (see Manchester City), Patrick Slavin (see Motherwell).

Arthurlie — 219

Thomas Gracie (see Hearts).

Ayr United — 219

John Bellringer, Archibald Campbell, Robert Capperuald, Samuel Herbertson and Archibald McMillan.

Celtic — 222

Peter Johnstone, Donald McLeod, William Strang, John Young, John McLaughlin and Robert Downie.

Clyde — 225

Charles Clunas, Robert Milligan and William McAdam Sharp.

Clydebank — 227

No players listed.

Cowdenbeath — 227

Charles Penman Scott.

Dumbarton — 228

Henry Gildea.

Queens Park   257

James Alexander, John Barbour, James Bryce, Macdonald Cameron, Robert Main Christie, John Clarkson, Walter McFarlane Coulter, William Eadie (Prince), Harry Middleton Fletcher, Edwin Freeland, Edwin Stanley Garvie, Thomas Haydock, George Legge, John Buchanan Monteith, Andrew Bowie McCrae, Alex McLean, John James Ormiston, John Stevenson, John Wilkinson and James Gilmour Wilson.

Raith Rovers   268

Thomas Cranston, James Burton Gibson, George McLay, James Scott and James Colin Todd.

Rangers   271

Alexander Barrie (see Kilmarnock), David Murray (see Leeds), James Spiers (see Bradford City), Walter Tull (see Northampton) and John Clarke

St Bernards   272

Frederick James Albert, John Ferguson, John Fleming, John Frail, James Hastie, Gordon Hossack, Alexander Kay and David Brunton McDougall.

St Johnstone   277

David McWalter, Thomas Fletcher Moncrieff, Bertram Sampson, John Cameron, William McPherson and Charles Scott.

St Mirren   279

James Rae Armstrong, James Brannick, George Elmore, Thomas Alexander Jackson and Archibald McLardie.

Third Lanark   282

James Blyth Galloway and George Gibb.

Vale of Leven   284

John Wilson.

LEAGUE TEAMS FROM WALES   285

Barry Town   285

James Wightman.

Cardiff City   287

Wally Stewart and Thomas William Witts.

INTRODUCTION

This book is a factual narrative of the many brave footballers who gave their lives in a dreadful conflict. They may be lost to the earth but let their memory live on.

Today we live in a relatively safe world, and football is the number-one sport, top-flight players being amongst the highest paid people of any profession. Turn the clock back to 28th July, 1914 and it was a far different world. A Britain run by the affluent political elite and still gripped by the iron fist of Edwardian society. We were about to enter one of the bloodiest wars in world history. Between 1914 and the official end of the conflict on 11th November 1918, over 8.9 million British Empire and Commonwealth personnel either volunteered or were conscripted into the armed services. In total, worldwide some 20 million people died, with military casualties estimated to be in the region of 10 million from all countries. British and Allied Imperial Forces suffered over 1.1 million deaths and more than 2 million were wounded; this does not include over 14,000 Merchant Navy casualties.

This was a devastating event for this country, taking many years after its conclusion to recover due in the main to a whole generation being lost. It left many families and communities shattered and heartbroken. This was to be 'the war to end all wars'. Perhaps the worst pre-conflict quote in history.

At that time, the upper classes and bureaucrats seemingly controlled football, in addition to the country. There were over 5000 registered footballers at the outbreak of war, with tremendous pressure put on these prominent athletes to join the armed forces. Most professionals were contracted to their club, mainly on a one-year basis, with the clubs eventually allowing them to sign up. This was after campaigns by public figures backing the Government and Lord Kitchener in December 1914, including people such as Sir Arthur Conan Doyle and politician and academic C.B Fry, who had himself played football at first-class level. One article condemned the football league, stating '*It was far from the right thing for men to be kicking a football around when others were dying in places like France and Flanders, assisting in the defence of these countries against the German invasion.*' Over 2000 players answered the call, once the frivolous red tape and contract rules had been relaxed, though many footballers supplemented their careers with jobs such as mining, a reserved occupation in itself.

The now famous Sportsman's Battalion 17th Middlesex Regiment came into being thanks in the main to William Joynson-Hicks MP. It had as one of its officers Major Franklin Charles Buckley, born in Urmston, Manchester (1882-1964), the former Derby County and England player. He was an honest no nonsense disciplinarian, though highly respected. Buckley received serious wounds in 1916 at Delville Wood, France, and was discharged after lifesaving surgery, his football career over due to the injuries. He was later successful in management at Wolves and Leeds, amongst others. His one England appearance was in 1914, prior to the war.

Major Buckley was a man of great integrity, he deeply respected his men and kept records of all those serving under him. He later wrote *'with great sadness, of the 600 who served, over 500 were killed or died from the wounds they received in action'*.

The 16th Royal Scots; 'McCrae's Battalion,' also equally famous, was formed by politician Sir George McCrae. Born in 1860 in Aberdeen, he was an ardent football follower, director and backer of the Heart of Midlothian club. The 16th Scots suffered many casualties too; McCrae himself was invalided and sent home with a number of illnesses including exhaustion in November 1916.

The battalion suffered 70 percent casualties on the first day of the Somme alone. Total 4th Army forces casualties on this day were over 57,000, of which over 19,000 were deaths.

Within a week of enlisting in November,1914, The Scotsman News reported *'McCrae has secured the enlistment of over 1,350 players and supporters mainly from clubs in Edinburgh and Borders, the Lothians, Linlithgowshire and Fife'*.

He was immensely popular, and a superb orator and motivator of people. His call to arms speeches motivated the entire Midlothian area, spreading throughout the rest of Scotland in general, many other football club players, supporters and the general public following suit. A great number paid the ultimate sacrifice. Over 75 professionals initially signed, and influentially one of the most highly publicised in Scotland were the eleven players from the Heart of Midlothian club, thus creating their legacy.

Colonel McCrae (D.S.O.) was idolised by many. The funeral after his death on 27th November 1928 is reportedly one of the largest attended in Scotland. As one article read, *'You would have thought the King had died,'* with estimates of over 100,000 people lining the route in silent respect. The book *'McCrae's Battalion'* gives a wonderful and sometimes graphic account of his and their journey through the conflict.

The Irish also rallied to the cause, even though the long running political troubles of the country where boiling over and about to escalate. Of the 1.2 million recorded men in Ireland, over 200,000 enlisted.

The order of the day seemingly had their way, after much controversy on the morality of professional football's continuance during war, the English league coming to a halt shortly after the 1915 FA Cup final. The debate, however, did not quite end there. There was a backlash from the public, football fans and the sporting press. One quote exclaimed, *'This is nothing less than an attempt by the ruling classes to stop the recreation of the masses. They do not care for the poor man's sport'.* It went on to describe them as 'Virulent Snobs'. A further report stated, *'the common man in general, not just the sporting personality was being used merely as cannon fodder, like innocent lambs to the slaughter'.* The military generals were seemingly testing their theories of warfare with scant regard for men's lives. All this worried the authorities, but the public was by now answering the call. The campaign against footballers was, after much thought, debate and provocation, used by the Government and Minister for Sport to their advantage to enlist others alongside their heroes. Some would say a calculated publicity stunt. Recruitment drives were commonplace and successful at football grounds throughout the country. They were used to better effect in Scotland, as their league carried on throughout the war. This was after the Scottish Football Association had agreed its continuance in a reduced format.

The recognised top-tier football leagues involving English, Scottish, Welsh and Irish teams were in a much different format to that of today, but with the public still looking up to players in much the same way as present day. The game was tough and physical, but of an exacting standard. Players, in general, had a hard time, with most having to subsidise their profession with other employment to make ends meet. There was no golden handshake or lucrative pension at the end of their careers; life, like the game, was tough.

Most of those enlisting or conscripted endured terrible events on the battlefield; many would never return home or were severely wounded, physically, mentally or both, thus ending their careers. What started out as an adventure for some, turned into an unimaginable hell. Furthermore, the medical and personal assistance afforded today did not exist. It is distressing to know that those suffering from shell shock or nervous disorders, known today as Post Traumatic Stress Disorder (PTSD), ended up as patients in asylums. If deemed to have recovered sufficiently they returned to the battlefield.

In 1916 voluntary enlistment ended and conscription regulations were introduced as the war escalated and casualty numbers grew; there were simply not enough volunteers to cover the losses. The Military Service Act 1916 now meant that from 2nd March 1916 all males up to 41 years of age had to answer call up regulations. This was changed in May 1916 to include married men, and amended further in 1918 to include all men up to age 51 years.

The players in this book are from teams listed in football league tables after the call for suspension of football during the 1914-15 season. I have covered as many players as possible from researched information and they, in the main, are listed under the club they had the most appearances with, though as you will see there are cross-references with other listed clubs.

(Note: 1. Football League tables 1914-15 referenced are at the end of the book for information. 2. War time player appearances in general are not included. 3. They are referenced for the Scottish League as this continued throughout the war. 4. The Irish League continued on an unofficial basis after 1915-16).

It was also a time when a number of players, or ex-players,

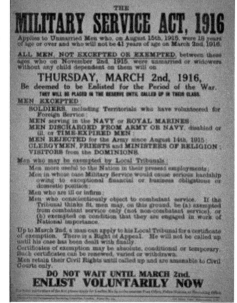

Pictured is a copy of the Military Service Act rules and regulations.

18

1915 – The 17th Middlesex Battalion football team.

left our shores to try a new life in other commonwealth countries. They served with armed forces from Canada, Australia and South Africa.

It must be emphasised that many other league and lower league footballers throughout the British Isles and Ireland, as well as other sportsmen, armed forces and essential service personnel gave their lives for this country. The latter two continue to do so to this day, as we know all too well, through present day conflicts,

Frank Buckley *(left)*
He is also in the team photograph pictured above, seated in the middle, second from left. Along with Bell (Victoria Cross – Bradford Park Avenue – killed), extreme left, Foster (Reading – killed). back fourth from right, and McFadden (Military Medal – Leyton Orient – killed), front middle on the ground

19

16ᵗʰ Royal Scots - Battalion Football Team, October 1915

Back: Cecil Neill (Killed), Jimmy Todd (died of wounds), Alfie Briggs (severely wounded), Pat Crossan (severely wounded, gassed)
Andy Henderson (wounded, gassed), Alex Henderson (wounded), Annan Ness (wounded), George McLay (Killed), Fred Muir
Middle; Jimmy Boyd (killed), Harry Wattie (killed), John Fowler, Sir George McCrae (invalided),
Cuthbert Lodge (killed), Bobby Wood (wounded), Jimmy Scott (killed)
Front; Duncan Currie (killed).

terrorism and the everyday protection of society. I reiterate, the main aim is to prick the conscience of humanity and reignite the stories of the fallen heroes, to enable their memories to live on. There are many in this chronicle, some of whom are truly inspiring, some heart breaking and emotional. It shows what a great nation we had and I believe still have today. After all, does the responsibility for history not lie with ourselves?

These men had unquestionable integrity, they stood shoulder to shoulder with each other, without division, to retain our precious bonds and galvanise these Isles as one. War and evil still affects many people's lives and I hope that the book will assist in heightening the awareness for those who have fallen, as well as the bereaved of those unfortunate enough to have lost their life and those who continue to protect us. The following quote from King George V on Armistice Day 1922 epitomises the effects of this devastating conflict:

Sir George McCrae.

20

'We can truly say that the whole circuit of the earth is girdled with the graves of our dead.

In the course of my pilgrimage, I have many times asked myself whether there can be more potent advocates of peace upon earth through the years to come, than the massed multitude of Silent Witnesses to the desolation of war.'

(**Note:** If you feel the need to contribute, the Royal British Legion are one of the main charity for those who served or sacrificed their life protecting us. They have a specific project for the 100th anniversary of the end of the First World War. Their website is britishlegion.org.uk.

Pictured below are two other regiment football teams:
1. Royal Welsh Fusiliers. 2. 9th Royal Irish Fusiliers, 1917.

Courtesy: "Blacker's Boys", Nick Metcalfe

Poetry and its influence

Lieutenant Colonel John McCrae was a Canadian Military Doctor, who penned his poem after conducting the funeral of Lieutenant Alexis Helmer, as the regiment Chaplin was away on other duties. He wrote these now famous words 'In Flanders Fields' that same evening. The date is believed to have been 2nd May 1915. He died of pneumonia during active service on 28th January 1918 in France, age 45 years.

The Poppy Appeal was started in 1921 by American Moina Belle Michael and Madame Ann Guerin of France, known as 'The Poppy' and 'French Poppy' ladies respectively. They started the charity out of respect for those who died. McCrae's poem inspired this. Michael herself wrote 'The Poppy' poem 'We shall keep the faith' in 1918.

Below are two of the strongest and most influential poems of the era.

In Flanders Fields

In Flanders fields the poppies blow
Between the crosses, row on row,
That mark our place: and in the sky
The larks, still bravely singing, fly
Scarce heard amid the guns below.

We are the Dead. Short days ago
We lived, felt dawn, saw sunset glow,
Loved and were loved, and now we lie,
In Flanders fields.

Take up our quarrel with the foe:
To you from failing hands we throw
The torch: be yours to hold it high.
If ye break faith with us who die
We shall not sleep, though poppies grow
In Flanders fields.

We shall keep the faith

Oh! You who sleep in Flanders Fields,
Sleep sweet – to rise anew!
We caught the torch you threw
And holding high, we keep the Faith
With All who died.

We cherish, too, the poppy red
That grows on fields where valour led;
It seems to signal to the skies
That blood of heroes never dies,
But lends a lustre to the red
Of the flower that blooms above the dead
In Flanders Fields.

And now the Torch and Poppy Red
We wear in honour of our dead.
Fear not that ye have died for naught
We'll teach the lesson that ye wrought
In Flanders Fields.

The following maps and images will give you a perspective of some of the places and conditions that soldiers endured during the war, and there were many more.

The Somme and map of the area.

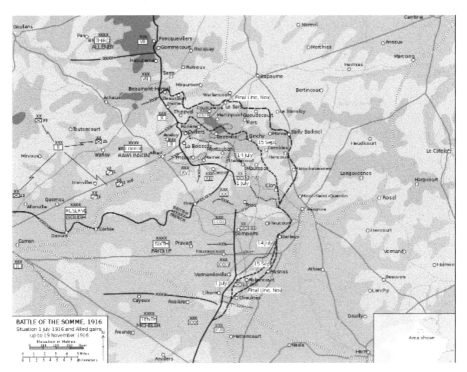

Picture and map of Ypres.

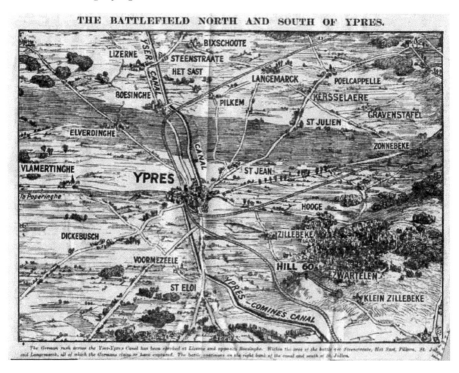

Picture and map of Passchendaele.

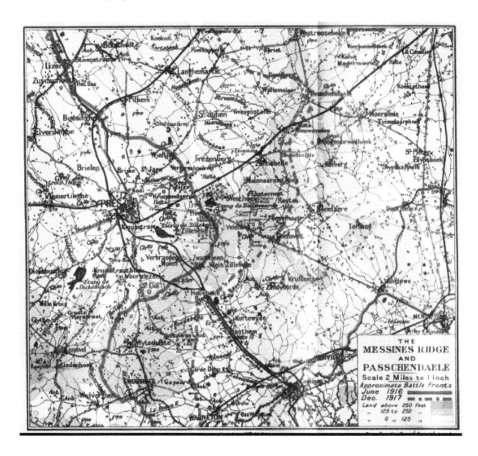

Picture (Helles) and map of Gallipoli campaign.

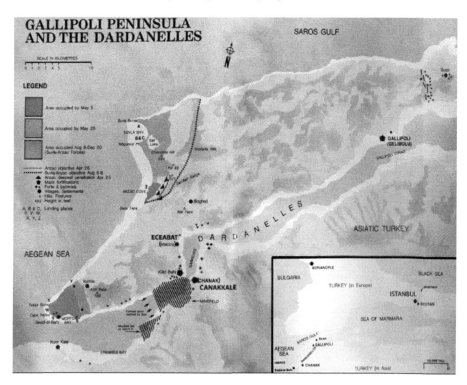

ENGLISH LEAGUE TEAMS

The English league was structured into Division One and Two, with two lower divisions, Southern League One and Two. The winners of Southern One either qualified for promotion or applied for election into the upper tier, the same rule applying to the runners-up.

Woolwich Arsenal/Arsenal FC after 1914, Division Two

(League position: fifth)

Albert Benjamin 'Bert' Beney was born in Hastings on 21st February 1883. He was an inside forward who played for Hastings & St Leonards United FC from 1906-09, prior to signing for Arsenal in 1909-10 for £200, by which time he had scored a superb tally of 148 goals in three seasons. He made 17 appearances with 6 goals for Arsenal, also scoring 18 goals in 20 reserve games. In 1910 Beney was briefly on Carlisle's books before moving to Bury FC in the 1910-11 season, playing four games for them. His playing career movements are unknown after this.

He joined the 1st/2nd Field Company Royal Engineers stationed in France and Belgium, attaining the rank of Corporal. He was badly injured in action on 20th April 1915 at West Flanders, dying later from his wounds. He was buried in the Poperinghe Old Military Cemetery (Ref: I.I.M.45.). Bert was 32 years old. (Other websites show him as being born in 1887, but birth and cemetery records confirm it was 1883).

John Thomas 'Pat' Flanagan was born on 20th September 1889 in Aston, Birmingham. He was described as a pint-sized inside forward, full of energy. He began at Stourbridge, signed for Norwich then Fulham in 1909-10. Arsenal then took him in 1911, where he played 121 games and scored 28 goals by 1915. Before enlisting in 1917, he had retired through injury, though continued to play in the London Combination. Flanagan had enlisted in 1915 under the Derby Scheme. He was at that time in reserved occupation as an artillery shell machinist but decided to sign up.

John died after contracting dysentery on 31st August 1917 at the 52nd clearing station. He had been serving with the 816th Mechanical Transport Company in Mingoyo, German East Africa. Age 27 years, he was buried in Dar Es Salaam War Cemetery, Tanzania (Ref: 5.J.4.).

Hugh Lachlan McDonald was born in 1884 in Kilwinning, Ayrshire. He was a goalkeeper who initially played in Scotland but signed for Arsenal in 1905 from Beith FC. He played for Arsenal until 1913-14 in three spells. He played at Brighton in 1906, Oldham in 1910 and Bradford Park Avenue in 1911. Making 103 appearances for Arsenal, he was a highly respected keeper. McDonald then moved to Fulham in 1914, then Bristol Rovers in 1915, before enlisting for the services and war effort with the Royal Scots Fusiliers.

He did survive, though his health was badly affected after being gassed. After 1918 he managed the Melbourne Arms in Plumstead, London, less than a mile from the Highbury football ground. Hugh eventually succumbed to his war injuries on 27th August 1920. He was buried locally, and he was 36 years old.

Charles Edward Randall was born in 1884 in Burnopfield, Durham. Charles played for Arsenal on 44 occasions, scoring 12 goals as an inside forward from 1911-13. A phenomenal amateur goal scorer locally, he was initially spotted and signed by Newcastle from 1908-11, before moving to Arsenal for £400. His other clubs were Huddersfield Town (loan), Castleford Town and finally North Shields, where he lived with his wife Mary.

WOOLWICH ARSENAL F.-C. 1912-13

He was killed in action on 27th September 1916 serving with the Coldstream Guards, aged 32. He was buried in the Dantzig Alley British Cemetery, Somme, France (I.D. 6).

Aston Villa FC, Division One

(League position: 14th)

William James Bowker was born on 15th June 1890 in Aston, Birmingham. He was signed by Aston Villa during the early stages of the war but did not play in the first team due to enlisting.

Bowker joined the Royal Garrison Artillery during the 1915-16 season. Wounded on the western front in March 1918, war records show he died on 23rd March 1918 near Arras, at just 27 years old. He was buried in Duisans British Cemetery, Etrun, France. (VI.E.48).

Henry Arthur Dobson was born on 1st April 1893 in Chesterton, Staffordshire. He had played for Aston Villa from 1912-15, joining after an amateur career with Chesterton Foresters and Audley as a half back. Dobson made seven appearances for the first team. He later guested for Rotherham County in 1917.

Serving with the North Staffordshire Regiment near Calais, France, in January 1918, he was involved in the Battle at St Quentin on 21st March 1918. The Germans fired over one million shells in the first five hours.

Wounded in the retreat, Henry died from his wounds, aged 25 years, on 29th March 1918. He was buried in Premont Cemetery, France (III.AA.9.).

William Webber Walter 'Billy' Gerrish was born in 1884 in Bristol, one of 10 children. Playing as a forward, his best football was with Aston Villa, with whom he won the First Division title in 1909-10, scoring 14 goals in 36 games after signing from Bristol Rovers in 1909. Injuries hampered his career, although he managed over 55 games before moving to Preston North End in 1912 and finally onto Chesterfield Town.

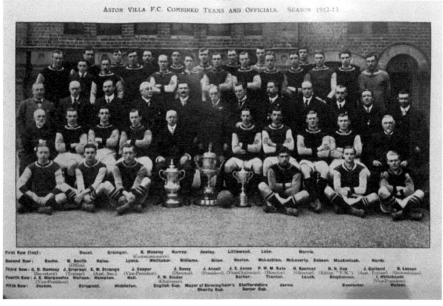

Gerrish joined the Footballers' Battalion, Middlesex Regiment in 1915. He died on 8th August 1916 at the Somme after suffering horrific injuries, losing both legs when a shell exploded next to him in one of the worst battles recorded at Delville Wood. A friend later reported that Billy just lay there calmly smoking a cigarette until the stretcher bearers arrived, but he died soon after; he was 32 years old. Major Frank Buckley stated he was '*a splendid soldier, most willing and brave*'. He was commemorated at the Thiepval Memorial, France. (Pier and Face 12D and 13B).

Barnsley FC, Division Two
(League position: third)

Charles Henry Wilfred 'Will' Bartrop was born on 22nd November 1887 in Worksop, one of seven children. He played for Worksop, Barnsley and ended his career at Liverpool. His main career was at Barnsley, for whom he played over 150 games. He played in two FA Cup finals, once in 1910, losing to Newcastle 2-0 after a 1-1 draw, and also in the legendary Barnsley side of 1912, when they beat West Brom. This final also went to a replay after a 0-0 draw, Barnsley finally winning the game 1-0.

Bartrop enlisted in 1918, joining the Royal Field Artillery as a Gunner, serving in Belgium. He was wounded in the leg and chest by shrapnel from an exploding shell on 7th November 1918. A colleague stated, '*He just said I'm hit in the leg, the next thing he was dead*'. He is commemorated in the Warcoing Cemetery Churchyard, Belgium. (Northwest of the churchyard, near the entrance). He was 30 years old, and married to Ruby Bartrop. (A biography about Bartrop entitled 'Swifter than the Arrow' gives a detailed account of his career).

Harry Joseph Dennis was born in 1894 in Barnsley, Yorkshire. An inside right, Dennis was on the books for Barnsley before the war. He enlisted with the 2nd Battalion Duke of Wellington West Riding Regiment, attaining the rank of Lance Corporal.

He was killed in action on 31st August 1918 in Northern France, aged 24 years, and buried in the Ligny St Flochel British Cemetery, Pas de Calais (III.C.7).

Samuel Lyon is listed in war records as being born in 1891, which contradicts the Hull City site details which say he was born in 1890. He was born in Prescot, then part of Lancashire.

Lyon is believed to have played for Prescot before signing for Hull City in 1912-14 as a centre forward, playing in six games and scoring one goal. In 1914 he moved to Barnsley, playing eight games and scoring three goals before the outbreak of war.

He enlisted with the 2nd Middlesex Regiment, fighting in France. Reports state he was, '*killed in action in France on the 1/7/1916*, age *25 years*'. It was not until 1948 that a report in the *Hull Daily Mail* clarified he was alive. At the time of the 1916 report he was in a French hospital recuperating from injuries.

Barnsley FC, 1914.

The West Riding Senior Cup Winners 1913/14

Insets, R Downs, W Bartrop
J Hastie (Manager), J Bethune, J Cooper, J Tindall, W Norman (Trainer), F Barson, P Bratley, G Utley, C Donkin, C Travers, J Morton, H Tufnell, J Moore.

Birmingham City FC (previously Small Heath), Division Two

(League position: sixth)

Benjamin Haigh Green was born on 23rd February 1883 in Penistone, Yorkshire. He was an inside forward, beginning his football career in 1901 at Barnsley before joining Small Heath from 1903-09. He played over 200 games in total for them as Small Heath and after they were renamed Birmingham City, scoring the first ever goal at the St Andrews ground in 1906, for which he was gifted 'a piano'. Green's other clubs were Burnley, Preston and Blackpool, where he resided before enlisting.

He joined the King's Own Royal Lancashire Regiment on 11th December 1915 and was in action from 1916. Killed at Arras on 26th April 1917, Benjamin was only 34 years old. He was married to Mabel Green, and is commemorated at the Arras Memorial, France. (Bay 2).

James Moles was born in Tottenham, London, in 1883. A wing half, he was initially at Leyton, then Tottenham in 1909, before he signed

for Birmingham City in the same year. He played 33 games before moving back to Leyton in 1911. He was signed by City as cover for Frank Buckley.

Moles was an aggressive player and this ultimately cost him his place in the side, prompting his return to Leyton, where he lived with his family.

He joined the 11th Battalion Middlesex Regiment and was an Acting Lance Corporal. He fought in France and lost his life near Calais on 7th November 1915. He is commemorated at the Lillers Communal Cemetery, Pas de Calais. (IV. D.38). James was 32 years old when he died, and married to Wilhelmina Mary Moles.

William McCourty was born in 1888 in Morpeth, Northumberland. He was a coal miner who played amateur football as a left half for North Seaton before

Birmingham players and officials before the start of the 1913-14 season. Back row (left to right): W.George (trainer), G.Robertson, J.Smith, A.Evans, F.C.Hodges, A.Stanton, A.Arnold, R.Fairman, A.Jones, J.Stevenson, H.Crossthwaite. Third row: Mr F.Richards (secretary), Mr T.Turley (director), E.Gardener, R.Gibson, G.Darby, W.Jones, Mr H.Cant (chairman), W.Morgan, J.Roulson, A.R.Smith, Mr S.Newey (director), Mr W.Hart (director). Second row: Mr R.McRoberts (team manager), Mr H.Rawson (director), F.Womack, A.McClure, W.Ball, C.Duncan, J.Bumphrey, A.Reed, Mr C.Muddyman (director), Mr F.Lattimer (director). Front row: J.Eccles (assistant trainer), R.O.Evans, J.Ballantyne, J.H.Hall, W.Hastings, E.Edwards. Inset above: A.W.Smith, Mr S.Richards (assistant secretary), A.Tinkler.

signing for Birmingham City in 1909-10. He only played one first team game before moving back to the north to play for his last known team Ryton, in the Tyne and Wear area.

William served with the 119th Siege Battalion Royal Garrison Artillery in West Flanders. Killed on 10th December 1917, age 29 years, he was married to Emily McCourty. He was buried in the Ypres Reservoir Cemetery (IV.B.6).

Joseph 'Joe' Enoch Smith was born in 1889 in Kilnhurst, Yorkshire, one of 5 children. He was a coal miner by trade who signed for Birmingham as a half back in 1912 from Hickleton, a local club.

A FALLEN HERO.

The late Joe Smith.

He played 8 games then moved to Chesterfield Town in 1914 where he resided with his wife. Chesterfield played in the Midlands League, and Smith played over 30 games for them before the war.

Joe joined the Footballers' Battalion in 1915 and attained the rank of Sergeant Major. He was killed at Serra on the last day of the Battle of the Somme on 13th November 1916, aged

27 years. (He is mentioned in dispatches for continuing to attack the enemy whilst wounded.)

He was buried in the Serra Road Cemetery, France (I.G.19).

Walter 'Wally' Smith; See Bury FC

Blackburn Rovers FC, Division One
(League position: third)

Edwin Gladstone Latheron was born in April 1887 in Brotton, Carlin Howe, North Riding. He was one of eight children. He played football locally in Yorkshire before joining Blackburn from Grangetown Athletic in 1906 as a striker, and he had a very successful career there, winning the league title twice. A huge favourite with the crowds, he played over 300 games for them, scoring 120 goals. He was capped by England on two occasions in 1913-14, scoring one goal.

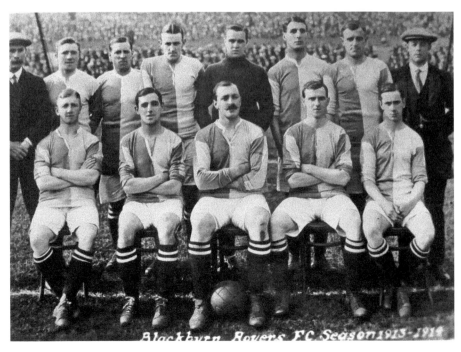

Latherton married Bertha Livesey in 1910 and they had one son.

He joined the Royal Field Artillery in 1917 and was killed in action at Passchendaele on 14th October 1917 by splinters from an exploding shell. Edwin was 29 years old. He was buried in Vlamertinghe Cemetery, Belgium (XI. F2.).

Blackpool FC, Division Two
(League position: 10th)

Arthur Thomas Evans was born in Horwich, Bolton, circa 1884. He played for Blackpool and Exeter City as a half back, playing over 43 games for Blackpool between 1909 and 1912. A brief spell at Manchester City followed before he moved to Exeter City in 1913 until 1914-15, making 20 appearances before enlisting.

He served in the 24th Royal Fusiliers in France and attained the rank of Sergeant. During fierce fighting, he lost his life at the Somme on 31st July 1916. He was commemorated on the wall of the missing at Thiepval, France. (Pier and Face 8C and 9A, 16A). Arthur was 32 years old.

William 'Tommy' Fiske was born on 7th August 1885 in Beccles, Suffolk. He was initially an inside forward and played for his county, Suffolk. He then joined the Norfolk Regiment and served in South Africa. At some point he was scouted by Norwich City and bought out of the services in 1906. By this time, he had switched to goalkeeper. His main career though was at Blackpool from 1907-14, where he played 224 games. He was described as a cat-like keeper. He then moved on to Nottingham Forest in 1914.

Fiske signed up again for the 1st Battalion Norfolk Regiment in 1914 and was wounded in action during fighting. After treatment, he returned to France, attaining the rank of Sergeant. On the 27th May 1918 at Marne the German Army had pinned

Blackpool FC, 1914.

down his unit, near to the river of the same name. Reports state: '*Fiske last seen rolling up his sleeves and going back over the top to attack the enemy*'. He was commemorated at the Siossons Memorial, France (Border Regiment Panel). Tommy was 32 years old and married to Bessie Fiske.

Bolton Wanderers FC, Division One
(League position: 17th)

Herbert Lewis Bithell was born in 1893 in Holywell, Wales. He is believed to have been with Bolton around 1914-15, but joined up before he had opportunity to play for the club, in May 1915. His other clubs had been Atherton and Macclesfield. Bithell moved to the Bolton area with his parents and siblings, where he was employed at Denmark Mill, Farnworth. Bithell lived on Longcauseway, Farnworth, with his wife Edna who he married in October 1915. He also taught Sunday School at Farnworth Baptist Church.

He was killed on 18th March 1918, serving with the Welsh Regiment as a Sergeant. He was commemorated at the Merville Communal Cemetery, Nord, France (I.C.61), and he was 25 years old when he died. Sadly, Edna never saw Herbert again after he returned to France in 1915 as he remained on the western front until his death.

Jabez Cartwright was born in 1883 in Holbeach, Lincolnshire, and a Mr and Mrs Smith in Peterborough then adopted him. He began his football career for Mapperly and then Grantham Town in 1912 as a

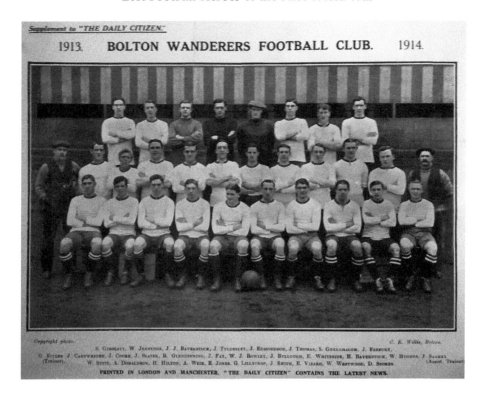

right back. He signed for Bolton not long after this for £110, yet he failed to break into the first team, playing mostly for the reserves. In 1914 he signed for Merthyr Town, making one appearance, and at the end of that season he returned to Grantham Town.

Cartwright joined the war effort, fighting with the Lincolnshire Regiment 1st and 8th Service Battalion. Killed in action on 4th October 1917, he was 33-34 years old. He is commemorated at the Tyne Cot Memorial, Belgium (Panel 35 to 37 and 162-162A).

Harold Greenhalgh was born in 1893 in Egerton, Bolton. He was listed as a full back with Bolton sometime during 1915-16, though club records do not have an entry for him. Percy M. Young's book published in two versions, 1961 and 1965, mentions him briefly. It refers to Greenhalgh as a Bolton player and being a victim of the war.

War records show Harold enlisted in Bolton with the Royal Field Artillery 'A' Battery 164th Brigade. He was killed in France on 27th June 1916, aged 23 years, and buried in the Bouzincourt Communal Cemetery Extension (II.C.13). He is remembered at the Walmsley Christ Church, Turton, Bolton.

James Arthur Greenhalgh was born in 1889 in Daubhill, Bolton. A *Manchester Evening News* report gave details of his death being near Voilaines, France, on 22nd October 1914. It stated he was a good amateur player who assisted the Wanderers when required, possibly as a reserve player. He represented Manchester University, from where he had graduated.

Commissioned as a Lieutenant to the Cheshire Regiment in August 1914, he took command of his unit on 19th October 1914, when his superior officer was wounded. Captain Lewis later wrote to the parents of James after his death expressing his gratitude for the bravery of his actions, along with 84 of his comrades who died with him trying to capture La Bassee Canal.

Reports state, *'it took another four years to achieve that goal, no one else got as near as they had before 1918'*. This epitomises their bravery and the difficulty of the task they attempted. He is commemorated at the Touret Memorial, France (Panel 13), and is also remembered on the Manchester University and Bolton Church Memorials. James was 25 years old.

William Wallace, see Manchester City.

Bradford City FC, Division One
(League position: 11th)

George Draycott was born on 1st December 1887 in Newhall, Derbyshire. He began life as a colliery horse driver supporting his family, as his father had died when Draycott was 13. He played for Gresley Rovers and was signed in 1913 for £150 by Bradford. He played in a testimonial against Leicester Fosse and was reported to be ready to break into the first team at the outbreak of war.

Draycott then joined the Leicester Regiment. In 1918 he was with the 7th Battalion Lincolnshire Regiment. Wounded on 18th September 1918 at the Battle of Epehy, he died later that day. George was 30 years old and married to Maggie Draycott. He was buried in Gauche Wood

Cemetery near Villers-Guislain, France (Grave 21) and remembered on the Gresley War Memorial.

Ernest Goodwin was born in Bradford on 7th April 1894, and he is listed as playing part-time for Bradford. He worked for a local wool merchant, who was at that time chairman of the club. Goodwin lived in South Parade behind Bradford's ground.

He enlisted in the West Yorkshire Regiment and went to France in 1915 as a Corporal; he was later promoted to Sergeant, serving at Ypres and then at the Somme. The company lead the attack on Thiepval Wood and suffered many casualties, in which Goodwin was initially reported missing. A letter to his parents sometime later from his friend and colleague informed them of the circumstances. Wounded by shrapnel in the arm and leg, they moved Ernest to a hospital in Etaples. He died from these injuries on 16th December 1915, aged 21 years. He was buried in Etaples Military Cemetery, France (XIV.C.2A).

Gerald Kirk was born on 14th July 1883 in Headingley, Yorkshire, the son of a wealthy landowner. He was public school educated and worked for the family estate. A good all-round sportsman, he excelled at football and cricket. Described as a most genuine character, he was highly respected in the community. He captained Ingleton FC and signed for Bradford City in 1905, establishing himself as the centre half. Kirk played over 40 games in total in two spells at the club, scoring two goals. He transferred to Leeds City in 1906 but returned the following season as stated, then played mainly in the reserves. Kirk went back into amateur football with Ingleton in 1908; he was still only 26 years old.

He joined up on 1st September 1914 and is described as one of the gallant 200 in the local papers. He gave up his position as 'a gentleman' and enlisted as a private in the Lancaster Regiment, initially stationed in England. He was commissioned as Second Lieutenant and then stationed in France during 1915. His battalion were initially at Neuve

Englise then the infamous Ypres Salient in front line trenches on 12ᵗʰ April 1915, losing 14 with 44 injured in five days. They lost 26 in total with 102 wounded. On 22ⁿᵈ April 1915, another sustained attack took place on Weiltje, led by Kirk, with Mustard Gas used against them. This, along with sustained machine gun fire, made the situation a hopeless one. They were wounded as they tried to hold their position and taken to Poperinghe casualty site. His Colonel had tried to persuade command to allow a retreat, but they refused. Gerald had bullet wounds to the chest. He died from his injuries on 24ᵗʰ April 1915, aged 31 years. He was buried in Poperinghe Old Military Cemetery, France (II.K.28).

Evelyn Henry Lintott was born on 2ⁿᵈ November 1883 in Godalming, Surrey. A talented half back, he initially played for Woking, scoring over 50 goals for them from 1899. In 1905 he moved to Exeter and St Lukes College for teacher training studies, though he maintained his connections with Woking. He played for Plymouth during his time at college and represented England amateur side on five occasions, the first in a 15-0 victory against France.

In 1907 he moved to London to be a teacher. Signed by QPR, he played 35 games for them and was their first player to represent England at professional level in a 3-1 win against Ireland. In 1908 Bradford signed him and he combined football with teaching. He played 53 games scoring six goals, though he missed the 1911 FA Cup final victory because of injury. He moved to Leeds in 1912-13, playing 43 games for them. Lintott was now aged 30 and he decided to retire, returning to teaching. He had played over 120 professional games and gained seven full England caps.

He was one of the first to sign up in 1914 for the West Yorkshire Regiment also known as the Leeds Pals. Commissioned to Lieutenant in December 1914, he became one of the first professional footballers to attain this rank. Initially sent to Egypt then France in March 1916. Lintott was in the Serra town offensive for the Somme on 1ˢᵗ July 1916, the Battle of Albert. He was one of many casualties on that day, the first of a long bloody campaign. Struck in the chest by machine gun fire, the report states, '*He was gallant and struggled on after being hit twice, continuing to attack firing his weapon but the third hit felled him'*. He was 32 years old.

Evelyn has no known grave. He is commemorated at the Thiepval Memorial (Pier Face 2A. 2C. and 2D).

Note: Records show that almost 20,000 British personnel were killed and casualty numbers totalled over 57,000 on that fateful first day at the Somme. In all, there were over one million casualties of the Somme offensives from all sides.

Harry Potter was born on 24th November 1884 in Bradford. He was mainly a reserve-team player from 1906-10, though he was part of the team that won Bradford's first competition, the West Riding Cup, in 1906, winning 1-0 against Heckmondwike. He found chances in the first team difficult as Bradford were becoming a first-class outfit. He moved to Lincoln City in 1910 to better his chances of first-team football but found this just as problematic. He had worked as a dyer's labourer, then for a fur company to make ends meet.

Potter joined the West Yorkshire Regiment then later transferred to the 2nd/4th Lincoln Regiment in 1917. They were involved in the assault on the Hindenburg Line, suffering heavy casualties. There was no respite and other bloody battles, such as Cambrai and Bourlon Wood, France, followed, to name but two. The 1st/4th and 2nd/4th Lincolns had now merged due to casualty numbers.

On 22nd March 1918, after a massive offensive by the Germans, the regiment were at Vraucourt by the village of Mory during the Battle of St Quentin. The battle lasted for almost a day and continued into the night. Harry lost his life during an enemy assault when the Lincolnshire's were in retreat. The regiment suffered 75 per cent casualties.

He is commemorated at the Memorial of the Missing Faubourg-d'Amiens Cemetery, Arras (Bay 3 and 4). Harry was 33 years old and left behind a wife and 7-year-old daughter.

James Hamilton Spiers M.M. was born in Govanhill, Glasgow, on the 22nd March 1886 as one of six children. In what was then a strong mining community, he worked as a clerk. He was soon involved in

football, playing locally for Annandale then Maryhill FC as a forward. Glasgow Rangers took an interest in him during 1905. After signing aged 19 years, he played 62 games scoring 29 goals. Clyde FC then took him on in 1908, where he scored 10 goals in 20 games. It was during his time at Clyde that he won his only Scotland cap.

In 1909 Bradford stepped in, and he enjoyed his best spell in football here playing over 96 games, and scoring 33 goals, winning the FA Cup in 1911. Spiers not only captained the side, but he also scored the only goal in the replay at Old Trafford against Newcastle. In 1912 Herbert Chapman of Huddersfield and Arsenal fame signed Spiers for Leeds City for a large signing on fee of £1,400, where he made 78 appearances scoring 32 goals.

In 1915 he moved back to Glasgow to enlist in the Cameron Highlanders, though he would have been exempt at that time due to being married and having two small children, but he signed in any case and trained in Inverness. He had played over 256 professional games in total for his clubs.

By 1916 Spiers was a Corporal in France, stationed near the Somme. Wounded in the elbow on 8th September 1916 during fighting, he returned to action after treatment. He was awarded the Military Medal for bravery during the Battle of Arras in spring 1917. After promotion to the rank of Sergeant, he had a short period of home leave in June 1917 before returning to his unit in July. He died on 20th August 1917, killed by heavy machine gun fire when his unit had made an assault on German positions near Pommern Redoubt, Passchendaele.

Initially reported missing, it was hoped he had been captured, but this was not to be and he was officially reported missing presumed dead. It was another year before his wife was informed his body had been found where he had fallen. This was near to Iberian Farm, during the Battle for Passchendaele. He was buried in the Dochy Farm Cemetery, near Zonnebeke (VI.E.15). James was 31 years old. In 2007 the War Graves Commission rectified an error on his headstone, replacing it with the correctly spelt surname. There were over 500,000 casualties during three bloody months at Passchendaele, of which an estimated 325,000 were British and associated allied forces.

(James's FA Cup medal sold at auction in 2003 for £26,210).

Robert 'Bob' Torrance was born in 1888 in Kirkintilloch, Scotland. He played locally for Kirkintilloch Rob Roy FC before signing for Bradford in 1907 for just £5, before making his debut in 1908. He was initially a full back but moved into central defence where he excelled throughout the rest of his career at the club, playing 161 games for them up to 1914. He was regarded as one of the finest players in the country and was man of the match in the 1911 FA Cup final win.

Torrance played in two international trial matches for Scotland in 1913-14 and continued playing for the Bradford club up to 1917 whilst working in munitions.

Bradford City, 1914.

During March 1917 Torrance joined up with the 162nd Brigade Royal Field Artillery. In April 1918 they were involved in the Battle of Merville, France, and on 22nd April 1918 were supporting the West Riding Division on the Reninghelst-Poperinghe Road. Two days later, on 24th April 1918, they were at Hallebast crossroads west of Kemmelbeck when they came under intense fire. Robert was seriously injured and lost an arm. There are conflicting reports about the exact date of his death, after a colleague found some of his papers on the battlefield. There had been much shelling, which included a direct hit on a field hospital. Research shows that if he is in an unmarked grave it is at Klien-Veirstraat Cemetery. His name is now on the Tyne Cot Memorial (Addenda Panel), Ypres. Robert was 30 years old, and married to Mary Torrance.

Bradford Park Avenue FC, Division One
(League position: ninth)

Donald Simpson Bell V.C. was born on 3rd December 1890 in Harrogate, Yorkshire. He was a grammar school student, later going on to Westminster College, a Methodist teacher college, he chose over St John's in York because of his religious beliefs. A noted sportsman who excelled at all sports and especially football, he had connections with Crystal Palace when he was at college and later Newcastle United. He was a superb sprinter, running 100 yards in 10.6 seconds, and he played rugby and cricket for the college. After finishing his studies in 1911 he returned to Yorkshire to become a teacher at Starbeck College. He played for Bishop Auckland and Mirfield United before signing professionally for Park Avenue in

1912, being proficient in both defence and midfield roles. Bell had played 6 games by 1914, helping them gain promotion to the First Division, when he asked them to release him so he could sign up for the war effort.

He joined as a Private in the Yorkshire Regiment in November 1914 and was then commissioned to 2nd Lieutenant with the 9th Battalion known as the Green Jackets. By 1915 he had married, but in August he departed with his battalion to France into the Somme region. It was on 5th June 1916 at Horseshoe Trench that Bell showed extreme bravery with two colleges. The report reads, *'pinned down by heavy machine gun fire, he attacked the German post and destroyed it saving many lives'*. He was awarded the ultimate honour, the Victoria Cross, later stating *'that god must have been with me'*. It was, however, only five days later on 10th June 1916 that he met his end from machine gun fire on open ground near the village of Contalmaison, dying where he fell. His men laid him to rest in the area, now named 'Bells Redoubt'. (Later reinterred at Gordon Dump Cemetery. Row A. Section 4); he was 25 years old. In September 1916 the *London Gazette* announced the award of the Victoria Cross, King George V presenting it to Donald's wife Rhoda in a private ceremony.

In 2000 the PFA erected a memorial at Bells Redoubt in his memory. In 2010 they purchased his Victoria Cross for £210,000. It is on display in the National Football Museum, Manchester.

William James Cox was born in 1880 in Liverpool. He was a centre forward who began his career at Rossendale, before signing for Bury in 1903-04, only making four appearances. He then signed for Argyle in 1904-05, playing 14 games and scoring five goals.

Cox then moved to Leicester in 1905, playing three games, before going on his travels around Lancashire, playing for Accrington, Oldham and Preston.

He then had a change of fortunes as he tried his hand in Scottish football, signing for Dundee before moving to Hearts in 1907, making nine appearances and scoring four goals. Into the 1907-08 season, he moved to his final club before retiring, Bradford Park Avenue, making 15 appearances and scoring five goals.

After retiring, he was a stonemason in the Blackpool area, where he had settled. He enlisted with the King's Own Royal Lancaster Regiment stationed in Turkey. He was wounded at Dardanelles and was also suffering from dysentery. He was shipped home and admitted to hospital in Birmingham. Cox died on 6th November 1915. His brother was the famous Liverpool and England player Jack Cox, and he organised his funeral in the Blackpool area. It was a well-attended send-off conducted with full military honours. Buried in Layton Cemetery (K.708), Blackpool, Bill was only 35 years old and married to Lena Cox.

Bradford Park Avenue FC 1914-1915

James 'Jimmy' Smith was born in 1889 in Stafford. He was a centre forward and prolific goal scorer. He played locally for Hanley PSA and Swifts before signing for Brighton and Hove Albion in 1911, scoring 40 goals in 65 games.

Smith signed for Park Avenue in 1912 for £735 plus a player exchange (Bobby Simpson). He played over 90 games for Bradford, scoring 49 goals before the war stopped his career.

He enlisted as a gunner with the Royal Artillery on the western front. He was killed in action on 8th October 1918, age 29 years, weeks before James was due to be married. He was buried in Ramicourt British Cemetery, Aisne, France (Row A.10).

Brentford FC, Southern League Division Two
(League position: third)

William George Allwright was born in 1880 in the Brentford area and was on Brentford's books as a left back prior to the first war, in around 1900, where he had played in the Southern League, though not as a regular as he played only five games scoring one goal. He was one of three brothers to play for Brentford.

He enlisted in the army in 1902. During the war he was with the Royal Field Artillery in France as a Bombardier in the 5th Reserve. Badly injured at Mons,

BOMBDR. W. G. ALLWRIGHT.

A former member of the Brenford F.C. has passed away in the person of ex-Bombardier W. G. Allwright, R.F.A., who before the war frequently figured with ability at left back. Present at the Mons' retreat, he was subsequently invalided from the Service on account of shell shock, the effects of which proved fatal last week. The ex-Gunner was 37 years of age.

1900-01

he also suffered from shell shock and was discharged on 16th September 1916. William died on 12th April 1918 from these related injuries, aged 37 years. He was buried in South Ealing Cemetery (H.P.21), where there is a memorial to the fallen. He was married to Alice Jane Allwright and had one daughter.

(I could not find a photo of William. On the previous page is an unnamed Brentford squad from 1900-01, when he was at the club.)

Patrick 'Paddy' Hagan was born in Edinburgh in 1880. He joined Hibernian in May 1905 from Belfast Celtic and could play in midfield or as a forward. He had one season at Easter Road in 1905-06 where he played 25 league matches, scoring five goals. He spent the next year and a half at Brentford, where he made 49 appearances, scoring 11 goals in the Southern League. Hagan then re- joined Hibernian during season 1907-08, making another nine appearances and scoring three goals before moving on to Port Glasgow Athletic, where he was a regular in the side (57 appearances and 11 goals).

Hagan was a Sergeant in the 11th Royal Scots and had previously served in the Boer War. He was killed at the battles on the Somme on 14th July 1916 when he was 36 years old. Patrick has no known grave.

He is commemorated on the Thiepval Memorial (Pier and Face 6D and 7D). He was married with two young children.

George William Kennedy M.M. and D.C.M. was born in Dumfries

on 12th March 1882 and began his football career as a half back at amateur level with Maxwell Town Volunteers, who were later to become Queen of the South. In 1906 he joined Lincoln City, staying for two seasons. Chelsea signed him in 1908 and he played 12 games for them. In 1909-10 George did not make a single Chelsea first-team appearance, so in the summer of 1910 Brentford FC's manager Fred Halliday secured his services. He went on to play in the Southern League from 1910-13, appearing 73 times and scoring two goals. He

also made an additional five appearances in the FA Cup. The 1911 census shows that he lived at 33 Adelaide Road, Brentford, as a 'boarder', but later he was recorded as a plasterer. George returned to Scotland after Brentford released him and Dumfries signed him in 1913-14.

On 23rd May 1914 George emigrated to Canada and arrived in Montreal on 1st June 1914. He went alone and was listed there as a plasterer by trade.

As Canada is a British Colony, they came on board with the war effort, and Kennedy went to a Montreal enlistment station and signed up to the 42nd Battalion Royal Highlanders, Quebec Regiment, in March 1915, serving in France and Belgium. Decorated for bravery, he was then promoted to Company Sergeant Major of 'D' Company (25th February 1916). The *London Gazette* reported the award of the Military Medal in October 1917. He then received the Distinguished Conduct Medal in February 1917 for '*Conspicuous gallantry and devotion to duty.*' (Military Medal pictured).

On 16th November 1917 George Kennedy received wounds to the face during fighting at Passchendaele, the third battle of Ypres. He was taken to No.9 Canadian Field Ambulance where he died from these wounds aged 35 years. Recorded as '*a soldier of great standing*', George is Brentford's most decorated player.

He was buried in Lijssenthoek Military Cemetery, Ypres (XXII. DD.12A), Belgium.

George Albert Littler was born on 21st June 1888 in Hulme, Manchester. He enlisted in the King's Royal Rifle Corps (The Green Jackets) before the First World War and was a renowned footballer in the area. In the 1911-12 season he played for the very successful 1st Battalion team in their fourth-round FA Cup tie against Brentford FC. A news report of the match stated:

'The weather on the day was atrocious and a crowd of just 1,475 saw Brentford surprisingly held to a 1-1 draw. The soldiers wanted the replay to take place on their ground in Aldershot, but the FA refused and Brentford duly triumphed 4-1 at Griffin Park before another poor crowd of 2,600.'

George caught the eye, Brentford signing him for the 1913-14 season as a forward, though he was mainly used in the reserves. Another report from the Rifle Depot 1st Battalion's records refer to the loss of Littler: *'We were at the beginning of the season 1912-13 and have been greatly handicapped by losing two of our best players Corporal Kemp and Rifleman Littler'.*

During the 1912-13 season Littler had represented the Rifle Depot. Knocked out of both the Army Cup and the Amateur Cup, the Depot team were still top of the South Hants League at the half-way point in the season.

On 7 December 1912 he played for the South against the North in an England amateur trial held in York, scoring in a 4-0 win. Because of his performance, he earned a call-up to the England amateur team and on 24 March 1913 represented the England amateur international team in a friendly match against the Netherlands first team. He played in Den Haag [The Hague] in front of 20,000 people. England lost 1-0. The war then ended his footballing fortunes and he returned to his regiment where he attained the rank of Sergeant in 1915.

George Littler died on 11th May 1915, aged 27, due to wounds received while serving with the 2nd Battalion, the King's Royal Rifle Corps, at the Battle of Aubers, Neuve Chapelle, France. He was buried in Bethune Town Cemetery, Pas De Calais, France (III.C.27). In the *Manchester Evening News*, dated 11th May 1915, George's mother, Ellen, and his brothers and sisters paid for an obituary to be included on the 'In Memoriam' page, with the following poem, in memory of George.

'Though nothing can the loss replace, Our dear brother taken from our side, Yet in sadness we rejoice, To think twas nobly that he died, Life's highest mission he fulfilled, And bravely answered duty's call, Give unto him eternal rest, O Lord.'

Henry George Purver was born in Isleworth in 1891, one of seven children. He was with Brentford during the 1911-12 season, playing as a half back or forward. He only played two first-team games but was a regular reserve-team player. Purver had also played for Oxford City, and he had a reputation as a goal getter in amateur football. He was a reporter by occupation for *The Times* newspaper.

Purver signed up for the war effort and served in France with the 14th Battalion (Sportsmen's) Royal Fusiliers. He was killed in action on 31st July 1916 at the Battle of Delville Wood, Somme. Henry was 26 years of age and married to Margaret Purver. He has no known grave. He is commemorated on the Thiepval Memorial (Pier and Face

8C. 9A and 16A) and Bridget's Church, Isleworth.

Notes: John Frederick 'Fred' Alborough was born in 1892 in Battersea, London. He enlisted and served with the 2nd Signals Royal Engineers. He played three war games for the club in 1918 as a right winger. He died from Spanish Flu on 31st October 1918, just five days after his third game for Brentford. He was buried in the Brookwood Military Cemetery, Surrey (XIII.A.4B). He was 26 years old.

Henry John Gould was born in 1894 in Brentford and was a reserve player for the club. He enlisted with the 8th Royal Fusiliers and died in Colchester, Essex, on 7th September 1914 during his initial training, age 30 years. It is listed that he was suffering from a heart condition. He was buried in his home town, Isleworth.

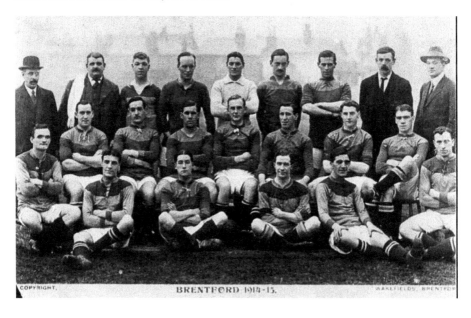

BRENTFORD 1914-15.

John Michael Hendren was born on 17th January 1893 in Chiswick, London. The brother of Brentford player Patsy Hendren, he is believed to have assisted the club during the war years. Both men were also established cricketers with the Middlesex CC. John is listed as killed in action on 27th July 1916, serving as a Lance Corporal with the 23rd Battalion Royal Fusiliers in the Somme area near Delville Wood, age 23 years. He is commemorated on the Thiepval Memorial.

Brighton and Hove Albion FC, Southern League Division One
(League position: seventh)

Jasper Matthews Batey was born in July 1891 in South Shields, Durham, one of five children. His pre-war football career commenced with a stint for South Shields FC in the North Eastern League, in addition to short periods with Coventry City and Portsmouth's reserve teams. While playing for the Portsmouth team against Brighton's reserves on Boxing Day 1912, he scored a hat trick and Brighton signed him. Described as 'an enthusiastic and popular player', he was popular with the crowds, gaining the nickname 'Ginger, after the popular ginger beer drink. Batey played in a number of positions: centre forward, half back and finally, in 1914, as a left half. He made 40 appearances scoring four goals for Brighton.

Jasper enlisted in London, originally into the Footballers' Battalion Middlesex Regiment, in 1915. He was killed in action in France on 23 October 1916, aged 25 years, while serving in the 11th Battalion, Army Cyclist Corps. He was buried in the Cambrin Military Cemetery (G30).

James Francis Brennan was born on 10th September 1884 in Templemore, Ireland. In 1903 he was in Liverpool, on their books as a forward and eligible for matches with them, though he played for local amateur club African Royal, for whom he scored goals on

a consistent basis. In 1906-07 his tally was 32 goals as they secured the West Cheshire League and the Liverpool Shield. Still an amateur, he signed for Bury in 1907-08 and was registered for one first-team game.

The 1908-09 season saw him with Brighton, making 18 appearances in total, scoring three goals. After 1910 he returned to amateur football in the North West.

Brennan enlisted with the King's Own Liverpool Regiment, 1st/8th Irish Battalion and was then a Corporal with the 1st/5th Lancashire Fusiliers, serving in France and Flanders. He is recorded as killed on 6th September 1917 in Belgium at the third battle at Ypres. He is commemorated on the Tyne Cot Memorial (Panel 54-60 and 163A). James was 32 years old.

Charles 'Charlie' Dexter was born in Crewton, Derbyshire, in 1889 and played for Brighton prior to the war, making 36 appearances as a full back. He had settled at the club, living in the area when war broke out.

He joined up with the 17th Battalion Duke of Cambridge Regiment, serving in France. He was gassed in 1916 and invalided home with septic poisoning. His condition deteriorated and he was discharged completely in April 1916. Charles died on 27th June 1916.

He was buried in Derby at the Nottingham Road, Cemetery (3421.C). He was 27 years old. Sadly, his brother Harold was also a casualty of the war.

Julius Reginald Gregory was born in Romiley, Stockport, on 4th July 1881. A former Manchester Grammar School pupil, Gregory began his football career at local side Unsworth before joining First Division club Bury in 1902. After establishing himself as a reserve-team regular, Gregory made his senior debut in December 1903 in a goalless draw with Wolverhampton Wanderers at Gigg Lane. Over the next two seasons, Gregory made 14 appearances for the Bury first eleven and was a regular fixture with the club's second team.

In May 1905 Gregory took the decision to leave Gigg Lane to sign for Manchester City, where he made his debut in a 2-0 defeat at Preston North End in October 1905. He subsequently struggled to establish himself at Hyde Road and after playing just two further matches he left at the end of the 1905-06 campaign to join Brighton and Hove Albion.

PROMINENT FOOTBALLERS.

!. GREGORY,

BRIGHTON & HOVE ALBION.

After making his debut against Leyton in September 1906, Gregory soon established himself as the first-choice fullback at the Goldstone Ground. He did have a temper though and had a number of disciplinary problems on the pitch. In November 1906 the Football Association heavily sanctioned him. He was found guilty of an 'under violence' charge against an opponent during a match at Northampton Town. The incident sparked disorder among the home supporters, leading to a review on ground safety. He was banned for a second time less than 12 months later, when he was found guilty of misconduct following a tempestuous 3-2 defeat at Southampton. Despite these disciplinary problems, he enjoyed a largely productive two-season stay at Brighton and had played a total of 86 games scoring two goals by the time he left the club to join Luton Town at the end of the 1907-08 campaign. Gregory then went on to make a further 26 league appearances in one season at Kenilworth Road before finally calling time on his playing career.

He joined the 20th Battalion of the Royal Fusiliers (Third Public Schools) in late 1914 and underwent initial training near Leatherhead. After joining the 98th Brigade, 33rd Division at Clipstone Camp, Mansfield, the battalion moved to Tidworth in August 1915 before landing in France three months later. After transferring to the 19th Brigade and spending time in the Givenchy sector he moved to the Somme on 10th July 1916. On 20th July 1916 the battalion took part in the attack on High Wood and suffered significant losses during fierce hand-to-hand fighting. Going into action in the early hours, the Fusiliers helped clear the area to the south east of the wood but had sustained

390 casualties by the time they were withdrawn from the frontline at midnight. Among those killed during the attack was Julius Gregory, whose name is now among more than 72,000 listed on the Memorial to the Missing on the Somme at Thiepval, France, the largest memorial in the world (Pier and Face 8C 9A and 16A). He was 35 years old.

Joseph Arthur Hulme was born in Leek, Staffordshire, on 18th December 1877. He signed for Lincoln in 1897 as an inside right or right back, playing 29 games and scoring 12 goals. Following that he had spells at Gravesend, Wellingborough and Bristol Rovers. He signed for Brighton from 1902-09, playing over 174 games and scoring seven goals. He retired in 1909 and returned to his home town as a trainer for Leek Town.

Hulme signed up and served with the Royal Sussex Regiment, where he was a Corporal. He was one of the many men who lost their lives at the Somme. He was killed at Gueudecourt on 3rd October 1916, aged 38 years. He was commemorated at the Thiepval Memorial (Pier and Face 7 C.) and the Nicholson Memorial in Leek. Joseph left a wife and three small children, who resided in the Tunstall area, near Stafford.

Clement Henry 'Charlie' Matthews was from Falmer, Sussex. Born in 1889, he was initially a bricklayer in Horsham. He was on Brighton's books, mainly as a reserve player, though he did play 12 games for the first team up to 1914 as a half back.

He joined the 1st/4th Battalion Sussex Regiment stationed in Turkey for the Gallipoli campaign. A Turkish sniper shot him on 15th August 1915 at Sulva Bay. He is commemorated at Green Hill Cemetery, Turkey (F6). Charlie was 26 years of age.

Ernest Victor Townsend was born in 1895 in Sussex and is in football records as being on Brighton's books before the outbreak of the war. He also played for Hove FC. He is not shown as having any first-team appearances, though he is in the 1914 squad team photo of Brighton for that

year. Apparently, a number of the Townsend family members were associated with the club.

He enlisted with the Royal Sussex Regiment and fought in Belgium. Recorded as killed in action on 20th September 1917 and commemorated on the Tyne Cot Memorial (Panel 86-88). Ernest was 22 years old.

Robert 'Pom Pom' Whiting was born on 6th January 1884 in West Ham, one of seven children. He was a goalkeeper who signed for Chelsea in 1905 as a successor to the famous Willie Foulke and helped them to promotion in 1906-07. He had a reputation as a long kicker of the ball and teams used this to their benefit, which is how he got his nickname. He moved to Brighton in 1908 and became their regular, playing over 320 games for them.

Whiting enlisted in the 17th Middlesex in 1914 and was later promoted to Lance Sergeant, stationed in France by 1915. In horrendous conditions, after contracting scabies, he returned home and was hospitalised in 1916. His wife was pregnant, so Whiting went AWOL for 133 days.

BRIGHTON & HOVE ALBION 1913/14
Top Row: F.Sparkes, F.Partlett, W.Miller, J.Robson (Mgr), C.Webb, W.Hodge, R.Whiting.
Second Row: A.Nelmes (Trn), A.Needham, J.Woodhouse, D.Parkes, J.Leeming, G.Whittington, M.Bridge, T.Higham, F.Coles (Ass.Trn).
Seated: A.Longstaff, R.Simpson, W.Brown, W.Booth, F.Spencer, C.Matthews, H.Lowe.
Front: E.Townsend, W.Spooner, J.Batey, A.Tyler, G.Moore.

Once captured he was found guilty and sentenced to nine months imprisonment. However, this was short lived, as men were drastically required for the Arras offensive in 1917. Bob returned to the front but was demoted back to Private. On 28th April 1917 he was one of 462 men killed in the village of Oppy, near Calais. Bob was 33 years old and married to Sarah Nellie Whiting. He is commemorated at the Arras Memorial (Bay 7).

Bristol City FC, Division Two
(League position: 13th)

Edmund Burton was born in 1893 in Dunston on Tyne, County Durham. He was a forward signed by Bristol City from Shildon Athletic in 1913, where he had established a good reputation as a solid performer. He made the last of his 19 appearances on 24th April 1915 in a 1-1 draw at Birmingham City. He had scored seven goals for the club.

Edmund enlisted with the 14th Durham Light Infantry, stationed in France. He was killed in action on 13th August 1916, aged 23 years. He was buried in Englebelmer Communal Cemetery, France (I.C.4).

Thomas 'Tommy' Ware was born on 16th October 1885. A local lad, he was signed by Bristol City in 1911 as a back-up goalkeeper for the long-serving Harry Clay. He was at that time in the Army with the Scots Rifles as a musician, stationed in Colchester. He had represented the Army at football and they allowed his discharge, though he remained on the reserve list. Ware made his debut in the same year and soon established himself, becoming a popular player with the supporters, playing over 58 games for the club, as well as in the Gloucester Cup finals in 1913 and 1914.

At the outbreak of war, Tommy re-joined the army as a Gunner in the 367th Royal Field Artillery. He was wounded in action on or around 25th April 1915 at the second battle of Ypres in the Zonnebeke district and removed to a field hospital. He died from his wounds on 1st May

City pictured before the start of the 1913-14 season. Back row (left to right): F.Bacon (director), Harris, Broad, Young, Ware, J.Jones, Howling, Moss, Kearns, E.Jones, R.Batten (assistant trainer), G.Bacon (director). Middle: W.Pont (vice-chairman), G.Hedley (manager); Shortt, Harrison, Fuge, Wedlock, Tasker, Chapple, Nicholson, J.Palmer (trainer), E.Murdock (chairman). Front: Henry, Irving, Burton, Batey.

1915, aged 29. He was buried in the Poperinghe Military Cemetery, Belgium (II.L9).

Bristol Rovers FC, Southern League Division One

(League position: 17th)

John Alfred Hardman was born in 1889 in Miles Platting, near Ancoats, Manchester. Oldham signed him in 1910 as a defender, where he made two first-team appearances. He then moved to Pontypridd in 1912, followed by Derby County in 1913-14, playing 15 games for them as they won the Second Division title. The following season he was at Rovers, playing 27 games in total. Prior to the war he was living in Bristol with his wife Mary.

There is little information on him after this, but he is believed to have served as a Sergeant in the army during the war. Some information states that he was killed in action in February 1917 in France, aged 27 years. (This information is contained in Bristol Rovers FC records, but nothing in Derby County, Oldham or CWGC records.)

Harry 'Henry' Phillips was born in 1887 in Bristol and played his early football career with Greenbank, before signing for Rovers in

1908 as a half back, playing mainly in the reserves. He made his first-team debut in 1910, playing over 63 games and scoring two goals for the club, staying till after 1913, when he joined Treodyrhiw Stars, Wales. Harry enlisted with the Gloucester Regiment 12th Battalion for the hostilities after 1914. He was killed in Belgium on 2nd October 1917, aged 30 years, and he was married to Blanche Edith Phillips. He is commemorated on the Tyne Cot Memorial (Panel 72-75).

William Howell Powell Westwood was born in 1882 in Langley Green, Worcester. A coal mine pony rider by occupation, he played for clubs in the Yorkshire area, such as Thornhill, Denaby United and Mexborough Town. Not to be mistaken with William 'Bill' John Westwood, William was at Bristol Rovers around season 1912-13 and is in the first-team squad photograph for that season, though he did not play in first-team league games.

At the end of season 1914-15 he was at Mexborough, in Doncaster.

Bristol Rovers, 1914.

It was from here that he joined up with several of his teammates in Strensall, Yorkshire.

He served with the 2nd and 5th King's Own Yorkshire Light Infantry, ranked as a Corporal. He was killed in action at the second battle of Bullecourt, Northern France, on 3rd May 1917. William was 34-35 years old, married to Annie Westwood and had four children. He is commemorated at the Arras Memorial (Bay 7).

John William 'Bill' Westwood was born in Sheffield in 1886, and he played for the club as a half or full back from 1909-15. He is listed on some sites as killed during the Great War. He does not appear in War Records or in the club's historical information as killed. He played 98 times for Rovers. This may stem from confusion with the above William Westwood. (John is middle row, third from right in team image above.)

Burnley FC, Division One

(League position: fourth)

Jonathan Brown was born in Clayton le Moors, Lancashire, in 1889 and signed for Burnley from Great Harwood in December 1913. He was a half back and played mainly as a reserve, with one senior game in 1915 for Burnley, replacing the injured Billy Watson at left half. They won the game 2-1 against Aston Villa at Turf Moor. Brown was a regular in the Burnley reserve team that finished fourth in the Central League in 1914-15 and was in the Clarets reserve side that overcame Blackburn Rovers reserves 2-0 in the final of the East Lancashire Charity Cup in April 1915, played at Turf Moor.

Brown enlisted with the 1st Lancashire Regiment stationed in France. He was killed in action on 6th November 1918 ans was buried in Maubeuge-Centre Cemetery, Nord, France (D.1.). Jonathan was 29 years old and married to Hannah Brown.

John Thomas Heaton was born in Padiham in March 1894 and played for Burnley in trial matches in 1914 as a left winger, but did not get a chance of a first-team game because of the war.

John enlisted with the 1st Coldstream Guards and fought in France. He was killed in action on 16th August 1915 near Lens, aged 21 years. He was buried in Vermelles British Cemetery, near Lens, in Northern France (Plot I.E.18).

Edward 'Teddy' Hodgson was born in Chorley in 1885 and was one of Burnley's most influential and popular players. He was a late arrival into league football, moving to Turf Moor from Lancashire Combination club Chorley in 1911 at the age of 25.

He was a first-team regular almost immediately and his intelligent inside forward play was a key factor in Burnley's promotion back to the First Division in 1913. He scored 17 goals during the Clarets' 1913-14 campaign, including five in the FA Cup run that saw Burnley lift the trophy. Teddy laid on the match winner for Bert Freeman against Liverpool at The Crystal Palace.

Hodgson's consistency led to his selection for the Football League, although his only representative honour ended in a 3-2 defeat by the Scottish League He played 137 games for Burnley and scored 62 goals.

As the war began to escalate, he joined the 52nd Manchester Regiment in 1915, although he did turn out for Burnley and Clapton Orient in the wartime leagues whenever possible. After surviving the conflict, in 1919 he returned to Germany to serve with the Allied Army of occupation and was by now an Acting Sergeant. After developing a kidney infection, he was transferred to hospital back in England where his condition rapidly deteriorated. He passed away on 4th August 1919. Teddy was 33 years old and married to Bessie Hodgson. He was buried in Burnley Cemetery (Screen Wall 2268).

William Johnson was born in Aldershot in 1890 into a military family; his father had been in the army for more than 20 years and had served in the Boer War. His brother was also a serving soldier. After living in India, the family eventually returned to England and settled in Burnley.

Johnson, an all-round sportsman, excelled at football and cricket. He was at Burnley FC in November 1911 and signed professional terms in

April 1912, usually playing at half back. He played regularly in the Central League over the next few years and was a member of Burnley's reserve side that finished third in their league and won the Burnley Hospital Cup in 1913.

When war broke out it was inevitable that William signed up again and enlisted with the 4th King's Own Liverpool Regiment, serving in Belgium. He was killed in action on 20th November 1917 aged 27 years. He was buried in Dochy Farm New British Cemetery, Langemark-Poelkapelle, West-Vlaanderen, Belgium (I.V. C4).

Alfred 'Alf' Lorimer was born in Longridge, Lancashire, in 1892. He worked as a tailor in Burnley and played in the Burnley Tuesday League before playing in a trial match for the Burnley reserve team in February 1914.

He had previously played for Preston's reserves but appeared in his first Central League game for Burnley. Playing on the right wing, they won 2-1 against Southport Central. Lorimer made a good impression and was offered a professional contract. Described as fast with excellent ball control, he was showing signs of becoming a top professional player before he enlisted for the war.

Alf joined the 240 Royal Army Medical Corps (2nd East Lancashire Ambulance) and completed his training in 1915. Sadly, he never got the chance to fulfil his potential and died in Egypt on 1st February 1915, after a trench collapsed on him. Alf was 23 years old. He was buried in Ismailia War Cemetery in Northern Egypt (A113 A).

Philip Smith was born in Newcastle-Under-Lyme on 1st January 1885. He was from good footballing stock, as his brother was the legendary Joe Smith of Bolton Wanderers fame from the famous 1923 FA Cup final. He was also the Blackpool manager when they won the FA Cup in 1953. Joe also served in the forces during the war.

Philip was initially at Burslem Port Vale and then Crewe. Chelsea signed him for £250 in 1909 as a centre forward, the same position as his brother.

He only played one game for them before moving to Burnley in 1910, playing seven games there, but never emulating Joe's success. He is in the Blackpool FC team photo from 1914-15, so it is likely he was on their books or at least guested for them before serving abroad. His other club was Stalybridge Celtic.

Philip served with the 282nd Brigade Royal Field Artillery in France. He was killed in action on 29th September 1918, aged 33 years. He was buried in the Windmill British Cemetery, Pas-de-Calais (II.H.5).

William 'Billy' Pickering was born in Glasgow in 1894 and joined Burnley from a Glasgow junior club in August 1912. He was a centre forward and a prolific scorer in Burnley's reserve team in his first two seasons at Turf Moor, and he made his First Division debut against Liverpool at Turf Moor in March 1914. He replaced the great Bert Freeman at centre forward and made an excellent impression, scoring in a 5-2 victory. It was just six weeks before the teams would meet again in the FA Cup final at the Crystal Palace, with the Clarets again victorious after a 1-0 win, although William did not play in the final, much to his disappointment.

In December 1914 Burnley reached the final of the Lancashire Senior Cup after victories over Manchester United (5-0), Liverpool (5-1 at Anfield) and Blackburn Rovers (2-1). Pickering played in all these ties, scoring one goal against United. Prior to the final against Rochdale at Hyde Road, Manchester, the manager stated that Bert Freeman would play at centre forward; however, Freeman insisted that William Pickering should lead Burnley's attack and the young man stepped in and seized his chance, scoring twice in a 4-1 victory. He appeared in 14 League and FA Cup games for Burnley, scoring six times. His final goal for the Clarets came in the very last League match played at Turf Moor before the suspension of the Football League, a 2-1 victory against Sunderland in April 1915. He then returned to Scotland and played five games for Morton FC, scoring four goals, before enlisting with the 1st Seaforth Highlanders.

He was killed in action at the Battle for Tikrit in Mesopotamia, Iraq, after being shot in the head on 9th November 1917, aged 23 years. His

mother wrote to the Burnley secretary informing them of Billy's death. He was buried in Baghdad North Gate Cemetery, Iraq (III.E.4).

Wilfred 'Wilf' Toman was born in Bishop Auckland in 1874. He was a teacher by profession and started his football career in Scotland with Victoria United, Aberdeen Strollers and Dundee before moving to Burnley in 1896.

A centre forward, he played over 60 games for them, scoring 30 goals. Although top scorer at the time, he moved to Everton in the 1899-1900 season. He also played for Southampton, Everton for a second spell, Stockport, Oldham and Newcastle. He was quite injury prone and retired after 1907, a leg break from which he never fully recovered ending his career. He then returned to live in Scotland, although in 1911 he was living in a shared residence in the Liverpool area. He was described as an electrifying player with great footwork.

During the war, he enlisted in the King's Regiment, Liverpool, and was a Lance Corporal. He was fatally wounded by shelling on the trenches at the western front, France, on 2nd May 1917. A friend heartfeltly recalled, *'although Wilf put up a brave fight the injuries were too severe and he sadly died a short time later'*. He was buried in the Erquinghem-Lys Churchyard Extension, France (II.B.23). He was 43 years old.

BURNLEY 1913-14.

Halley. Lindley. Boyle. Bamford. Freeman. Dawson. Hodgson.
Watson. (Captain) Taylor. Nesbitt. Mosscrop.

Phot's Lofinga's Weekly

Bury FC, Division Two

(League position: 11th)

Edward 'Teddy' Bullen was born in Warrington in 1884 and lived in Altrincham. Bury signed him from Altrincham FC in 1906. He made his first-team debut the following year, and by the outbreak of the war he had made 188 first-team appearances as a wing half. He would have made more but for bad luck with injuries, but he was still very much part of the Bury team of that time, a strong First Division outfit. He also ran the Rose Inn, Sankey, Warrington, with his wife Bertha, who by this time was pregnant. She continued to run the pub even after his death.

Bullen joined up following suspension of the Football League programme with the Royal Horse Artillery and then the Royal Field Artillery. He was killed in action on 11th August 1917 at Vaulx, Vraucourt, in northern France. He was buried in the Vraucourt Copse Cemetery (II.A.9). Teddy was 32 years old. He did not get to see his daughter.

Frederick Marginson 'Fred' Collinson was born in Bolton in 1873, one of six children. The family later moved to the Bury area. He was firstly a soldier, although he had gained a good reputation as a footballer. Fred added three years to his age to join the 1st/5th Lancashire Fusiliers on 15th April 1889, Bury being the regiment's home since its formation in 1881.

In 1892 Collinson appeared fleetingly with Everton FC, playing full back for Everton's Combination team in a 7-0 thrashing of Gorton Villa, whose local rivals in Manchester were St Mark's, later to become Manchester City. He also played as a wing half, but his stay at City was a short one.

There is a tribute to Fred Collinson in the Lancashire Fusiliers Museum in Bury. Signed for a £10 fee by Bury in 1893 he scored one of six goals on his Bury debut against Small Heath, now renamed Birmingham City. Fred's Bury career appears to have peaked in the mid-1890s; he then went on to play for Ashton and Darwen. At this time Bury were entering their golden era. They joined the Football League in 1894 and immediately won the Second Division title; this was after a play-off against Liverpool. At the turn of the 20th century, they excelled in the FA Cup, winning it twice in quick succession in 1901 and 1903. Collinson, however, re-joined the colours in 1900 and sailed for South Africa, where the second Boer War was not going well for the British. He gained campaign medals from his tour of duty there.

Fred then returned and resettled in Bury with his wife Mary and two children. He kept up the pretence about his real age on the census form, describing himself as 34 and not 37. He was working as a meter inspector for the local gas works while his wife worked in the wool mills.

When war broke out in August 1914, Collinson appears to have volunteered very quickly, enlisting as a Private with the 1st/5th Fusiliers Battalion in Egypt. His age was clearly not a problem; as an old soldier with experience of action, he was a very valuable asset, serving in Gallipoli, Turkey. Unfortunately, he was killed in action on or about 15th May 1915 at the infamous Gully Ravine. He has no known grave. Second Lieutenant Horridge gives an account of the incident surrounding Fred's death:

'Eventually we got to the trench behind the front line. Next to me was an old soldier, called Collinson. We got out of the trench and had to go at the double because the fire was very heavy. The bullets were hissing round swish, swish, swish, swish, swish. We ran halfway then got behind a mound. I said to Collinson "Look we've got to go on," and off we set again. I wasn't too bad a runner, I outstripped Collinson, and I eventually leapt into the front line trench. I am sorry to say that Collinson, in the last ten yards, got hit through the chest or stomach. We got him in but he died later.'

Note: Collinson's date of death is an estimate, due to his body being unrecovered. He is commemorated at the Helles Memorial, Turkey (Panel 58 to 72 or 218-219). He was 41 years old.

Walter 'Wally' Smith was born in 1885 in Bootle, Liverpool. An inside forward, he was on Liverpool's books in 1908 as a reserve player. He listed with a number of clubs, including Chester City who he had reasonable success with from 1910-12. Other clubs include Darwen and Birmingham City from 1914-16. His was at Bury from 1911-13. Smith guested for them and

Season 1912/13
Back: Fenner, Marsh, McDonald, Millington, Humphreys, Goldie.   Front: Connor, Peake, Kay, Smith, Duffy

Rochdale during the war. After 1916 he was at Altrincham. There is no information on him being a victim of the conflict.

The other footballing Wally Smith that enlisted during the war played for Lincoln City, and he died in 1958.

Chelsea FC, Division One
(League position: 19th)

George Andrew Lake was born in 1889 in Eastham, Wirral, Liverpool. He was a reserve-team player at Manchester City in 1912 as a wing half. He also played for Chelsea from 1913, making one senior appearance. The First World War then brought his career to a premature end, Lake enlisting in the British Army and serving on the western front before losing his life just one week before the Armistice on 6th November 1918. (The ex-Manchester City player Paul Lake was shocked to discover George was his great-uncle after research by his wife.)

George enlisted in the army in mid-1915 and was posted to the 66th (2nd East Lancashire) Divisional Cyclist Company. This unit remained in Britain throughout the war, and Lake transferred to the 2nd/4th Battalion

CHELSEA FOOTBALL CLUB, 1913-14.

Back Row— Foord, Whitley, Logan, Molyneux, Bridgeman, Bettridge, Denoon, McLeod, Turnbull
Second Row— Wright (Trainer), Walker, Essery, (Asst Trainer), Hunter, Steer, Taylor, Sharp, Macfarlane, Ford, Andrews, Brown (Asst Trainer), Clark (Groundman).
Front Row— Douglas, Brown (W.), Calderhead, Marshall, Downing, Freeman, Fairgray, Harrow, H. Livesey
Whittingham, Brown (J.)

of the Hampshire Regiment overseas. The battalion was in India after the declaration of war before moving to Egypt in May 1917 to join the 233rd Brigade, 75th Division. In June 1918 they moved to France, attached to the 186th Brigade, 62nd (Second West Riding) Division.

Lake then took part in the Hundred Days Offensive, which saw the allies push German forces back across ground that had been lost in March 1918. He was among troops tasked with crossing the Sambre Canal near the village of Frasnoy on 4th November 1918. It was during this action that Lake sustained his wounds, near the village of Cognaux, in wooded orchards. He died two days later on 6th November 1918. His brother received a letter of condolence from Chelsea manager David Calderhead. It read:

'Dear Sir, I am in receipt of your note recording the Death of your brother George. All the people at Chelsea beg to express to you and your family their very sincere sympathy in your great sorrow, he was very greatly respected by both Players and Officials of the Club and we were in the hope that after the War he would again have played for us. He is the only Chelsea player who has fallen. I again beg to express our Sympathy. Yours faithfully D. Calderhead.'

George Lake's grave is in Frasnoy Communal Cemetery alongside 41 other British soldiers who fell during the attack (Plot A.33). The

First World War ended just five days later. Six months after his death, George's mother, Elisha, received his effects, totalling £18 8s 6d, from the army. George was 29 years old.

Clapton Orient FC
(Leyton Orient after World War Two), Division Two
(League position: ninth)

The club provided 41 players and staff for the war effort. They were also the first English club to sign up to the Footballers' Battalion. The club has had a number of name changes since its inception but finally settled on the current name in 1987.

James Greechan was born 1883 in Glasgow and first played for Petershill in Glasgow as an inside forward, before signing for Hibernian in 1903. He only managed 4 first-team games before transferring to Bo'ness.

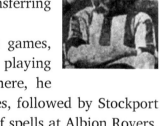

After a short spell at Brentford with 12 games, Greechan moved to Clapton Orient in 1907, playing 30 games and scoring eight goals. From here, he moved to Glossop in 1908, playing 19 games, followed by Stockport in 1909, playing 16 games. He then had brief spells at Albion Rovers, Carlisle and finally Bathgate.

James signed up for the conflict in Glasgow as a Private with the 12th Battalion Highland Light Infantry and served in France from 1915. He was killed in Belgium on 25th August 1917 serving with the 46th Brigade, age 34 years and buried in the Lijssenthoek Military Cemetery (XVIII. A9).

William Jonas was born in Cambois, Blyth, Northumberland, in 1890. He began his career with Jarrow Croft. Jonas joined Clapton Orient from local side Havanna Rovers in 1912, after scoring 68 goals for them as a midfielder, but he could play just about any position, even in goal. He went on to score 23 goals in 74 games for Orient before the First World War. He was a good looking athlete, adored by the Clapton fans, especially the females. Jonas was a charismatic individual who attracted so many female admirers that the Orient club printed a note in a match programme informing fans that he was happily married to Mary Jane Jonas. His best friend was fellow teammate Richard McFadden.

When football was suspended they joined the Footballers' Battalion, Middlesex Regiment, stationed in France. They were the first two professional footballers to do so.

Reported information from this time states, *'These were public idols, strong men and long-term friends now engaged in a conflict on one of the bloodiest arenas, the Somme, enduring gassing, constant shelling, machine-gun fire, and the interminable lice that bred on their bodies.'* This put into context the horrors they and many others had been encountering.

The battalion were under orders to clear Delville Wood, Somme, of Germans. The fighting inched back and forth for three weeks after General Haig launched the offensive. Pinned down in a muddy trench on 27th July 1916, McFadden and Jonas were far from safety. They decided they had to make a break for it.

McFadden takes up the story: *'"Goodbye Mac," Jonas said. "Best of luck, special love to my sweetheart Mary Jane and best regards to the lads at Orient."'* McFadden's sorrowful letter then explains what happened next. *'Before I could reply to him, he was up and over. No sooner had he jumped up out of the trench, my best friend of nearly 20 years was killed before my eyes. Words cannot express my feelings at this time.'*

What makes this even more tragic is that by the time the letter was circulated back home, McFadden himself was also dead.

Private William Jonas was 26 years of age, his body lost where it fell. He is commemorated on the Thiepval Memorial to the Missing (Pier and Face 12D and 13B).

Richard McFadden M.M. was born in 1889 in Cambuslang, Scotland. He was a striker who started his career with Blyth in 1910 then Wallsend Park Villa, before signing for Clapton in 1911, playing over 140 games for them with in excess of 60 goals, breaking the goal scoring record in his first season. He also represented the Southern League side.

He had been instrumental in the signing of his friend William Jonas. McFadden was a hero both in his civil life as well as during his military service. Before the war, he had saved a man from a burning building and on another occasion, whilst on a training run along the River Lea near to the Orient ground in east London, he saved a young boy who was drowning by jumping in to rescue him.

He joined the Middlesex Regiment after suspension of the league and his life-saving exploits continued in northern France, when he ventured out into no-man's land to rescue wounded comrades, during which he received wounds himself. Awarded the Military Medal for his bravery, McFadden was about to be offered a commission as a Warrant Officer. He had now attained the rank of Company Sergeant Major.

McFadden had witnessed the death of his friend Jonas in July 1916, which had affected him deeply, yet he remained positive.

On the 22nd October 1916 Richard was seriously wounded in action near Serre, France, and died the following day, aged 27 years. He was married to Isabella and is buried in the Couin British Cemetery (III. B19).

Norman Grey Riddell M.M. was born in 1887 in Blyth, Northumberland. A left back, he played locally for Blyth Spartans and Morpeth Town before Rochdale signed him, where he made 25 appearances before signing for Orient in 1911-12, playing 12 games. After 1912 he was back in Lancashire at Rossendale United where he finished his career.

Norman served with the 11th Service Battalion Northumberland Fusiliers, ranked as a Colour Sergeant serving in Italy. He was killed in action on 15th June 1918 in the Vicenza district when he was 31 years old. (He was awarded the Military Medal for bravery in the field prior to his death.)

He was buried in the Magnaboschi British Military Cemetery (Plot 3. Row E. Grave 4).

George Scott was born in Sunderland on 29th September 1885, one of five children. He played his football locally before signing for Orient as a midfielder

CLAPTON ORIENT FOOTBALL CLUB. 1913-14.

in 1908, as a centre half or half back. He played over 200 games for the club with 33 goals. He also represented a London select eleven against a Paris team in France.

Scott joined the Middlesex Regiment with a number of Clapton players, seeing action at the Somme. George died from his wounds in a German Military hospital at Saint-Quentin, Aisne, on 16th August 1916 aged 30 years. He was at the time technically a prisoner of war. He was buried in the St Souplet British Cemetery, Le Cateau, France (II.AA.19) and was married to Margaret Ann Scott and had two children.

Coventry City FC, Southern League Division Two

(League position: fifth – elected to Division Two proper in 1919-20)

David Claud Graham Davies was born in 1892 in Llanrwst, Conwy district of Wales according to Llandudno Parish Records. He was better known and referenced as Claude Davies. His father, a doctor, died in 1897, his stepfather when his mother remarried was Hungarian by birth and a tailor. Davies was educated at the John Bright School then Bangor

University College, where he excelled at athletics and football, before graduating in engineering. He played as an outside left for the University and Llandudno Town. Davies is shown on the books of Coventry City, where he played two games in 1910-11. This was probably whilst he was at University.

Thereafter he was employed at British Thompson Houston Electrical Laboratories Limited in Coventry, at which time he was living in Rugby.

He was commissioned as a 2nd Lieutenant in the 1st Siege Battalion Royal Garrison Artillery and served in France. He was wounded by shrapnel leading his men in an offensive at Bethune in Northern France and taken to hospital.

David died from his wounds on 15th May 1915, aged 23 years, in the 24th Field Hospital, and was buried in the Bethune Town British Cemetery, Pas de Calais (II.G.15).

(Note: War records show him as 33 years old, but the Parish and other birth records seem to be more credible.)

William 'Bill' Hanson was born in 1887 in Rushall, Walsall, West Midlands. He was a left back who started at Aston Villa in 1907, although he never played a first-team game. He moved to Coventry in 1908-10, playing 53 games. From here, he moved to Bradford Park Avenue in 1910-11, though he only managed one first-team game.

There is some information that states he was a victim of the war, but there does not appear to be a record of this and there is no mention on any of his former clubs' sites, or in football records.

Stephen Jackson M.M. and D.C.M. was born in 1890 in Smethwick, Birmingham. He signed for Coventry City in 1911 as a full back and went on to play 13 games over three seasons.

He enlisted in September 1914, becoming a Sergeant in the South Staffordshire Regiment, serving in the 7th South Staffordshire Regiment in the Dardanelles. He was wounded there, but he recovered sufficiently to return to his regiment. He then transferred to the 1st Battalion in France and was awarded the Military Medal for his conduct during fighting at Bullecourt in April 1917. Promotion to Acting Company-Sergeant-Major in 'B' Company followed, with a further award of the Distinguished Conduct Medal during a raid in the Bullecourt sector. His citation, published in the *London Gazette*, described the circumstances of the award:

'For conspicuous gallantry and devotion to duty during a raid. Although not taking part in it, he went out under heavy fire at a critical moment, having learnt that the raid was making very little progress owing to the considerable opposition. He reorganised the parties and led them forward, afterwards personally conducting stretcher-bearers up to the enemy's firing line and clearing No-Man's Land of wounded. His fearlessness and splendid initiative at a trying time proved invaluable to the success of the operation.'

He was killed on 26th October 1917 during his battalion's attack on a fortified mound south-west of Hamp Farm, in front of the village of Gheluvelt. Jackson's grave is in the Perth Cemetery, China Wall, Ypres, Belgium (V.F.4). He was 27 years old.

Walter John Kimberley was born on 1st May 1886 in Aston, Birmingham. He was a defender and played seven games for Aston Villa from 1906 after signing from Aston Manor, though he moved on to Coventry in 1912 and was more successful here, playing 24 games and scoring one goal, before finishing at Walsall prior to the war.

Wounded in action during heavy fighting at the Battle of Marne, France, he was serving as a Lance Corporal for the Coldstream Guards. Captured by the Germans, he spent two years in captivity and contracted pulmonary T.B, through which he lost his voice permanently and became terminally ill so was allowed repatriation in 1916 before his death. He died in Birmingham on 22nd April 1917, aged 32 years. Walter was married to Ada Kimberley and was buried in Witton Cemetery, Birmingham (Sec 82 Grave 13233A).

Jack Speare Tosswill was born in Eastbourne in 1890. He was a good footballer and cricketer. His football career started at Eastbourne Borough before moving on to nearby Hastings and St. Leonards, Aberdare Athletic, Tunbridge Wells Rangers in 1909 and then Maidstone United as a half back or forward. Bigger clubs then followed and he joined QPR in 1912, playing three games and scoring one goal. He then moved to Liverpool in 1912-13 playing 11 games for them, before Southend

United stepped in. He then finally settled at Coventry in 1913, where he made 18 appearances, scoring one goal. Tosswill was partially deaf, which caused some amusement on match days, as he could not hear the whistle, and he carried on playing until someone attracted his attention.

Tosswill nevertheless still enlisted despite his shortcoming, joining the Royal Engineer Signals in Eastbourne during 1914. He showed great enthusiasm, reaching the rank of Corporal. Jack became seriously ill whilst with his unit at Southampton in September 1915 and died following an operation on 28th September 1915, aged 25 years. He was buried in Eastbourne Cemetery (Grave UA.250). (Details of his illness are not recorded.)

George 'Tubby' Warren was born on 6th March 1881 in Burton-on-Trent, Staffordshire. George had earlier played for numerous local clubs before signing for Leicester Fosse in 1903-04. He then spent four seasons with Coventry as a forward from 1907-11, playing 109 games and scoring 56 goals in all competitions. He was a member of the FA Cup giant-killing teams of 1908 and 1910, scoring two of City's goals in the famous 3-1 third-round win over Nottingham Forest in 1910. His last major club was Stockport in 1911. He had the nickname of 'Tubby', due to his rotund physique. Warren was still playing

Coventry City 1914-15

BELOW: The last get-together before the war, 1914-15 — back row: T. Shields, A. Robinson, A. Craig, W. Fulljames, J. Orchard, R. Roberts, J. Preston, T. Casey, J. Meunier, S. Blake, R. Barnacle, W. Bennett, J. Oxenham, H. Harbourne, R. Scott-Walford, J. Enright; middle row: J. Tosswill, A. F. Collingbourne, T. Morris, F. Scott-Walford (Manager), D. Cooke (Chairman), G. Harris, J. Harkins, S. Day, W. Turrall, A. Holmes) front row: J. Beaufoy, H. Dobson, R. Alderson, T. Lowes, J. Doran, J. Allen, H. Welch, R. Turner.

locally in the Midlands for Hinckley then Nuneaton Town before the war.

George enlisted in Leicester in February 1917 with the 2nd Battalion York and Lancaster Regiment. He was killed in action in France on 16th May 1917. Buried in the Philosophe British Cemetery, Mazingarbe, France (I.P.20). He was 36 years old and married to Lily Warren.

(Note: There is mention of an Alf Edwards killed in the conflict, but there is no personal information to narrow down the search and check this. (An Edwards with no initial is listed at the club from 1904-07.))

Croydon Common FC, Southern League Division One

(League position: 19th – did not apply for re-election after the war and dissolved in 1917)

Thomas Henry Jack Ellison was born on 26th January 1891 in Woolwich. He began his career with Colchester Town, for whom he played 48 games with an impressive 49 goals from 1910-13. Ellison is also on the books of Croydon from 1912-14 as a centre or inside forward, playing six games and scoring two goals. He also turned out for Grays  Athletic. Ellison was a soldier, as was his father. This is the reason he moved to the Grays club, to be nearer to his barracks.

A trumpeter with the 134th Royal Field Artillery from 1911, he was based in Hampshire, which may account for his lack of appearances. A gunner in the 32nd Field Artillery during the conflict, he was killed in action near Neuve Eglise, France, on 20th October 1914, aged 23 years. His medical card shows that he died from wounds.

Buried in the Bailleul Communal Cemetery, his headstone simply states, *'buried in this graveyard'* (B.4.). This is due to German shelling of the site in 1918, destroying many of the graves and headstones.

Frank James Hesham was born in 1879 in Gorton, Manchester. Playing as a forward, he began his career at Manchester City in 1897. He played for numerous clubs including Crewe, Accrington Stanley, Stoke, Clapton Orient, Oldham Athletic, Hyde and finally Newton Heath Albion in 1913. His main success was at Croydon from 1909-11. He played 55 games and scored 27 goals.

Frank signed up with the 21st Siege Battery Royal Garrison Artillery in 1914 as a gunner, serving in Belgium. He was killed in action on 17th November 1915, and was buried in the La Clytte Military Cemetery, Heuvelland, Belgium (I.C 17). He was 36 years old and married to Jenny Hesham.

Crystal Palace FC,
Southern League Division One
(League position: 15th)

Joseph Bulcock was born in 1880 and was the son of a Burnley cotton weaver. He initially played reserve-team football for Burnley and then Aston Villa, before going on to appear for Bury and Exeter City. He then spent five seasons with Crystal Palace from 1909-14, playing 146 games and scoring two goals. He gained the reputation as one of the best full backs in the Southern League. He was part of a representative England squad the FA sent to tour South Africa in 1910, playing one game and selected as a reserve for the other.

Bulcock then joined Swansea Town late in the 1913-14 season and went on to captain them on a number of occasions, including their famous 1915 FA Cup match victory over Football League champions Blackburn Rovers. He was a favourite both on and off the pitch. After professional football ended in the summer of 1915, he resided in Llanelli, working as a plumber's mate.

He joined the 9th Battalion Welsh Regiment as a private in December 1915 and served in France in September 1917. Joseph died on 20th April 1918 after receiving head wounds at the fourth Battle of Ypres, Watten, Flanders. He was 38 years old and was buried in Haringhe (Bandaghem) Military Cemetery, Poperinge, Belgium (V.C.21).

PROMINENT FOOTBALLERS.

H. HANGER.

Harry Hanger was born circa 1885 in the Kettering district. He was a half back and began his career at Kettering Town. Hanger (no initial shown) is then listed with Northampton Town in 1903, playing five games before returning to Kettering. Hanger played 79 games for Bradford City in 1906-09. The other Hanger from this period is Percy Hanger, his brother, who also played for Kettering and later with Leicester Fosse. He was a centre half, listed as still playing football after 1920-21. (There are no other players named Hanger listed as professional footballers and Harry is not in records again after the conflict.)

Harry moved to Crystal Palace where he played from 1909-15 making 177 appearances and scoring seven goals. He captained Palace for a number of seasons, described in the following press report: *'No player has shown greater ability to retain possession of the ball; his passes are invariably accurate, reaching the forward so the latter can make rapid headway'*

Hanger is believed to have enlisted towards the end of December 1914, with, as it was reported, the Footballers' Battalion. This is where the confusion begins. A Harold (nickname Harry) Hanger of the 5th Royal Irish Lancers, Household Cavalry, serving in France, was killed in action on 23rd March 1918. He is commemorated at the Pozieres Memorial to the missing (Panel 3 – age unknown). He was born in Market Harborough and enlisted before 1914. Therefore, it appears they may be different people and Bradford City historians point this out. This name appears on the Kettering War Memorial. There are no other persons named Hanger listed as killed during the conflict from Northamptonshire. There is no information regarding what happened to our Harry Hanger after the war, if they are not one in the same, which it seems they may not be. If he did survive, he would have been 33-34 years old and most likely have retired from professional football. To ere on the side of caution and respect, this entry remains.

Richard 'Dick' Harker was born on 20th May 1883 in Wardley, Gateshead, one of two children. Initially he played for Swalwell FC before joining Newcastle in 1903-05, playing in the lower tier sides, though he did make one first-team appearance. This was a class Newcastle outfit, winning the league in 1905, so he found opportunities in the first team difficult.

He moved to Palace in 1905 where he made more of an impact in his role as an inside forward. He then transferred to Hibernian in 1907-09, followed by a spell at Hearts until 1911, playing over 68 games and 81 games respectively, scoring over 50 goals in total.

Harker returned to Palace in 1911-12 before finishing his career at Darlington FC prior to enlisting.

In all he played over 83 games for Palace, scoring 28 goals.

He joined the Northumberland Fusiliers and fought in France. He was reported missing in action/killed on 9th April 1917 and is commemorated at the Arras Memorial (Bay 2 and 3). Richard was 33 years old.

John 'James' William Williams was born in Buckley, Flintshire, Wales, in 1885. He was nicknamed 'Ginger'. A prolific scorer in junior football, he played for Bury (not professionally), Atherton, Accrington Stanley then Birmingham City after a trial. Williams signed for them in August 1908 and made his debut in September at home to Bradford. Given a decent run of games in the starting eleven, he failed to impress, returning to Accrington Stanley in February 1909.

In the 1909 close season he moved to Crystal Palace, where he played in his favoured position, centre forward, though he was capable of playing any forward role. He was described as *'an eager, neat and busy little footballer who possessed a snappy tackle and plenty of enthusiasm and determination'*. He scored 58 goals from 149 appearances in all competitions, including scoring five in one match against Southend United. He remained for five seasons, winning two caps for Wales in 1912. In February 1914 he joined Millwall.

John served in the 17th Battalion Middlesex Regiment, serving in Northern France after 1915. Listed as missing presumed dead on 5th June 1916. He is commemorated on the Arras Memorial (Bay 7) and at Millwall FC's ground. He was 30 years old and married to Sarah Ellen, and he had one son.

Ernest 'Ernie' York was born in the Moulton area, Northamptonshire, in 1886. He was a versatile player who could feature as either a half back or a forward. He also played for Kettering and other local sides, winning numerous medals

Crystal Palace, 1914.

in cup and league competitions in the Northamptonshire leagues. He scored six times for Palace in 58 southern league matches between 1912 and 1915 and played three games in FA Cup competitions.

Ernie joined the 7th Royal Berkshire Regiment around 1915 after enlisting in the Reading area. He was killed in action two years later on 24th April 1917 aged 30 years, whilst involved in the Salonika Campaign, at Dorian Lake, Eastern Europe, Greece. He is commemorated at the Doiran Memorial, Greece.

Derby County FC, Division Two
(League winners 1914-15)

George Harold Brooks was born in Radcliffe, Lancashire, in 1887. Brooks made his senior debut for Manchester City in a 1-1 home draw against Aston Villa on 18th February 1910 as a wing half, but he would find further opportunities few and far between, making two appearances, scoring one goal. Brooks left City in March 1910 for Bury FC, again only managing two games. In 1911-12 he moved to North Eastern League side South Shields, having better success there. Signed by Derby County in 1914, he went on to enjoy the most productive season of his career. In a season that saw County finish top of the

Football League Second Division, he played 34 games. His final competitive first-team appearances came in a 2-0 home victory over Preston North End on 24th April 1915.

Brooks enlisted in 1915 with the York and Lancaster Regiment and was with the 2nd/4th Hallamshire Battalion. By late 1918 he had been appointed as Lance Corporal, and his regiment was involved in fighting around the French and Belgian border, south of Mons. He was wounded three days before Armistice Day on 8th November 1918. George died at the 5th Casualty Clearing Station, aged 31 years. The time was around 11.00 hours. (He was one of the last footballers killed during the war.) He was buried in Maubeuge, Sous-Le-Bois Cemetery, France (D.D.3) and was married to Sarah Ellen Brooks and had two children.

Reginald Henry Callender was born in 1892 in Bishopton, Stockton-on-Tees, Durham. The Durham Cricket Club records have him as born on 31st August 1892. He was an accomplished footballer, playing for them in the Minor Counties League in 1914.

LIEUT. R. H. CALLENDER.
9th Durham Light Infantry.

As a scholar, he attended St Johns College, Cambridge, qualifying as a teacher. He represented the Corinthians football team and his position was usually on the wing. He was also a Cambridge Blue, playing for the England amateur side on five occasions. He is in football records with one appearance for Glossop FC in 1912, and in 1913 he was with Derby, making five appearances.

Callender enlisted in the Durham Light Infantry 9th and 17th Battalions in France and Flanders as a Second Lieutenant. He was killed on 5th October 1915 when a grenade exploded accidently. He was buried in Cite Bonjean Military Cemetery, Armentieres, Northern France. (X.D.16). Reginald was 23 years old.

Douglas Scott Hardcastle was born in Worksop in 1886 and was one of seven children. He was a Stove Grate Pattern Maker by trade and well known in the area, playing football for Worksop Town FC.

He was signed in 1905 by Derby County as an inside forward, playing five games and scoring one goal. His signing on fee had been £100, though he eventually returned to play for his favoured club Worksop.

Hardcastle signed up for the conflict with the Sherwood Foresters and served in France and Belgium, attaining the rank of Lance Corporal. He was wounded and it was hoped he had been taken prisoner. However, news eventually came through that Douglas had died on 9th May 1915. His family did not find out for definite until September 1915. He is commemorated on the Ploegsteert Memorial Belgium (Panel 7). Douglas was 29 years old.

James Stevenson was born in 1876 in Paisley, Scotland. He began his career with Ashfield before joining Clyde FC in 1894. The following season he moved to Derby as an inside forward and stayed for five seasons, playing 73 games and scoring 31 goals, playing in the losing FA Cup final side of 1897-98.

1913. DERBY COUNTY FOOTBALL CLUB. 1914.

Copyright Photo.]   [Teeble, 76, East Street, Derby.

METHVEN   HARDMAN   BLOOMER   ATKIN   SCATTERGOOD   BARROUR   BETTS   LATHAM
(Manager)   GRIMES   BAGSHAW   BUCKLEY   RICHARDS   WAUGH   (Trainer)
             WALKER   LEONARD   BARNES   NEVE

A P Co. Ltd.   **THE BEST NEWS IS "DAILY CITIZEN" NEWS.**

Note: Frank Buckley is in the middle row.

He then moved to Newcastle for two seasons, followed by Bristol City and Leicester Fosse. He finished his career back at Clyde, making over 30 appearances for them in total, scoring nine goals.

James enlisted with the Highland Light Infantry in 1915. He was killed in action at Flanders on the third day of the Battle of the Somme, 3rd July 1916, aged 39 years. He is commemorated at the Thiepval Memorial (Pier and Face 15C).

Everton FC, Division One

(League winners 1914-15)

James Roy was born in 1890 in West Lothian, Scotland. He was signed by Everton in 1913 from Broxburn FC for an initial fee of £60, but he was mainly used as a reserve-team player. They had a very strong squad, making it difficult to play in the first eleven.

Roy enlisted with the 6th Cameronian Scottish Rifles in 1915 and was involved in fierce fighting with his Regiment between Fontaine and Bullecourt, and then attacks on the Hindenburg line. He was killed on 23rd April 1917 and his remains were then lost and he has no known grave. He is commemorated at the Arras Memorial (Bay 6). James was 27 years old.

Harry Fitzroy Norris was born in 1884 in the Bolton/Bury area. His father was Thomas Fitzroy Norris, a former footballer with Nottingham Forest and the Bolton Wanderers secretary and then manager in 1887.

Harry is on Everton's books around 1905 as a reserve player, though he was loaned out to Tranmere Rovers in 1906.

He served with the 9th and 11th King's Own Liverpool Regiment, serving in France and Belgium.

EVERTON FOOTBALL CLUB, 1914-15.
C. McFadyen, S. Chedgzoy, J. Maconnachie, A. Grenyer, Wm. Brown.
H. Cook (Asst. Trainer), F. Jefferis, W. Kirsop, S. Challinor, James Galt (Captain), L. Weller, R. Thompson,
J. Taylor, W. Wareing, Jas. Roy, J. Elliott (Trainer).
J. Houston, T. Nuttall, J. Clennell, G. Harrison, Tom Fern (Goal), L. Johnson, F. Mitchell, W. Palmer, R. Simpson.
R. Parker, Wm. Wright, T. Fleetwood.   Richard Brown, Photo.

He was killed in action on 26th August 1915. He was buried in Ypres Reservoir Cemetery, Belgium (XI.C.20). Harry was 30 years old.

Exeter City FC, Southern League Division One
(League position: 11th)

(Exeter City, although a small club, are famous for their tour of South America during 1914, mainly in Argentina and Brazil. Exeter are the first team the Brazil side played in a competitive match, which they lost 2-0.)

Frederick Henry Bailey was born in 1895 in Exeter. He was an athlete of great promise and on the books of Exeter city, described as having tremendous physique and speed. He played locally as a centre forward for Friernhay and Exeter City reserves.

The outbreak of war stopped everything in its tracks before he got his chance with the clubs first eleven and he enlisted with the 24th Royal Army Field Medical Corps, Wessex Regiment, serving in France from the autumn of 1914. Wounded by a bullet in the arm, he received treatment in England before returning to France.

Frederick was killed on the first day of the Battle of the Somme on 1st July 1916, attempting to recover a wounded college when a shell exploded over him. He is commemorated at the Ribemont Communal Cemetery Extension (IV.E.8) and Exeter War Memorials; he was 21 years old.

Spencer Thomas Bassett was born in 1885 in Blackheath, London. A strong determined halfback, he played for a number of local clubs before signing for Maidstone United in 1903, where he played centre half. He realised one of his dreams when Arsenal signed him from 1906-10, but he was disappointed to be mainly a reserve player, with only one recorded first-team game.

He reluctantly decided a career move to Exeter City was his best option and this proved the right choice. From 1910-13 he played 81 games and scored three goals, mainly as a half back or centre half. Swansea Town then secured his services in 1913-14, where he made 32 appearances for them.

In 1914-15 another move followed, this time to Southend United, but with the war intervening the league was suspended.

Bassett enlisted as a Gunner with the Royal Garrison Artillery, the 140th Siege Battery, and they eventually joined up with the 15th Heavy Artillery Group in France. He was appointed as an Acting Bombardier on 27th December 1916. On 11th April 1917 they were being used to provide heavy artillery support near the village of Bullecourt, Artois, near Arras, assisting the 5th Army. Injured during German counter offensive strikes and evacuated to safety, Spencer unfortunately died from his injuries later the same day.

He was buried in the Pozieres British Cemetery, Ovillers-La-Boisselle (II.J.35); he was 32 years old.

Edwin Clarke was from Exeter, born in 1889. He was mainly a reserve-team player with Exeter City. He was in the main squad in the 1912-13 season. He was a steady reliable player, listed as a half back

and known in Devon circles as one of the best amateurs in the district. He lived locally and was married to Ethel Clarke.

Clarke enlisted with the Royal Navy during the war as a carpenter serving on HMS *Vivid*. Reports state he was accidently wounded and paralysed, dying from his wounds on 6th November 1917. He was buried in St Mary's Churchyard and commemorated at the Exeter War Memorial. Edwin was 28 years old.

Frederick Thomas Hunt was born in 1890 in Exeter. He was on Exeter's books as a defender in the 1914 team squad.

During the war he served with the 2nd/4th Devonshire Regiment in Israel and Palestine, attaining the rank of Sergeant. He contracted pneumonia and died on 4th November 1918. He was buried in the British Jerusalem Memorial site, the Gaza War Cemetery (XIX.G.4). Frederick was 28 years old.

John Addems Webb was born in 1889 in Exeter and played his football locally for Friernhay and in the Plymouth league team. Just before the war he had trials in the Exeter reserves under George White's captaincy and was described as one of the best finds of the season, a centre half of great stature and athleticism.

Although from Exeter, he enlisted in the Sherwood Foresters, Nottingham, as a Private in the 1st/7th Regiment in October, 1914. He had moved there earlier in the year as a lithographic artist, which hindered his chances with the Exeter club. He served in France then Belgium and died during fighting at Ypres on 18th April 1915; he had

been there two months. His comrades buried John on site, but the grave was lost. He is remembered at the Lindenhoek Chalet Military Cemetery, near Ypres (Row I.B.15). He is also on his parent's headstone in Exwick Cemetery, Exeter, and the club's memorial. John was 26 years old.

George Thomas White was born in Exeter in 1883-84 and became the reserve-team captain before the war, after also captaining the Plymouth district side. He was responsible for a number of players coming to the club, such as Webb, mentioned previously. A defender, he was highly though of by the Exeter club and had great presence on the field. He only lived a short distance from the St James Park ground with his wife, Ada Rose. George White enlisted with the 1st Devonshire Regiment in August 1914, and served in France, attaining the rank of Sergeant. In October that year he was involved in an attempt to recapture Neuve Chapelle, in the Pas-de-Calais region, which the Germans controlled.

He was wounded and removed to a field hospital on 30th October 1914, where he died. Ironically, this was in the presence of one of his Exeter teammates, Fred Bailey of the Medical Corps. He too lost his life in 1916. George was the first Exeter player killed. He is commemorated at the Le Touret Memorial, Calais, and the plaque at the St Sidwell Community Centre, Exeter. He was 30 years old. (There is a Thomas Henry

White, an outside forward, listed in Exeter club records in the 1907-08 season, playing 22 games, having signed from Carlisle before moving on to Watford the following season with his brother Charles. He had also played for Stockport County. He was born in Tring, Hertfordshire. This is not the same person. George White was a local amateur player.)

Percival Seymour Worner was born in 1884 in Exeter. Educated at St Sidwells, Exeter, before teacher training at St Lukes, he then returned to Sidwells as a teacher. He had played for the college alongside his

good friend Evelyn Lintott (Bradford City), but Worner remained an amateur after Lintott turned professional. Worner then played for St Sidwells United, a club of which he was a founder member. He went on the books of Exeter City after 1904, though mainly as a reserve half back. He did, however, turn out for the first team in the Plymouth and District League, making 14 appearances.

EXETER CITY FOOTBALL TEAM. 1913 - 14.

TOP ROW.   J. LAGAN, J. FORT, R. PYM, S. STRETTLE, W. SMITH, A CHADWICK (MANAGER)
2ND ROW.   H. HOLT, F. LOVETT, F. WHITTAKER, H. McCANN, F. MARSHALL
3RD ROW.   C. BROOKSBANK, J. RIGBY, GOODWIN.

When war broke out he initially enlisted with the Public Schools Corps, then the 9th and 524th Devonshire Regiment, as a 2nd Lieutenant. Whilst in France he was informed his friend Lintott had been killed on 1st July 1916. Percival then lost his life on 4th September 1916 at the Somme, aged 32 years. He was laid to rest in the Bernafay Wood British Cemetery, Montauban (J.32). Just prior to his death, he had written to the club asking for a football, as he had wished to start a football team. His family received the news that both Worner, his friends Lintott and former Exeter player Spencer Bassett, who had lodged with him during his time at the club, were all dead. Worner's medals and the cross from his grave are on display in the Dorchester Museum.

Fulham FC, Division Two

(League position: 12th)

William Barr Borland was born in 1888 in Darvel, East Ayrshire. Playing his football locally, he then joined Fulham in 1910 as a centre half. He played seven games for the first team, but he was mainly captain of the reserve side. In 1912 he returned to Scotland, playing for Galston and Dumfries.

Borland enlisted at the outbreak of war and served with the Cameron Highlanders from October 1914.

He served in France from July 1915 and was then involved in the fierce fighting on the first day of the battle at Loos, where the British suffered heavy losses. Killed in action here on 25th September 1915, he was laid to rest where he fell.

The body was later lost due to the fighting and persistent shelling. His name is on the Loos Memorial, at Dud Corner Cemetery (Panel 119 to 124). William is one of over 20,000 British and Commonwealth soldiers killed during this battle with no known grave. He was 27 years old.

Frank 'Francis' Docherty was born in 1888 in Jarrow. A shipyard labourer, he played locally for Jarrow and Willington Quay. Shown as being approached by Everton around 1910 after their 1910 South American tour, he turned them down in favour of Fulham, allegedly because they got his surname wrong. Failing to break into the first eleven, he returned north around 1912, after suffering a knee injury. He enlisted in Newcastle with the 25th Tyneside Irish, Northumberland Fusiliers. It is reported that he was killed at the Somme on 1st July 1916.

Commemorated at the Thiepval Memorial (Pier and Face 10B, 11B and 12B), Frank was 28 years old. His brother William had lost his life on 12th January 1916, serving with the Northumberland Fusiliers in Northern France. He was buried in Cite Bonjean Military Cemetery, Armentieres IX.D.93, aged 34 years old.

William Henry Maughan was born in July 1894, in West Stanley, County Durham. He initially played for West Stanley and then Easington Colliery before Fulham signed him in 1913-14 as a wing half. He made 24 appearances scoring one goal before the war. He also played six wartime games before going overseas with the Durham Light Infantry, part of the Northumberland Division as a corporal.

Maughan enlisted in 1915 and was in France, seeing action at Ypres. Worse was to follow after the regiment had sustained heavy losses, as they were then engaged in action on the Somme. Wounded whilst involved in fighting at the Transloy Ridges on 1ˢᵗ October 1916, William died from his wounds in the field hospital at Dernancourt the next day, aged 22 years. He was buried in the Dernancourt Communal Cemetery Extension (III.D.15).

Patrick McLaughlin was born in Jarrow, Northumberland, in 1883. A much-travelled centre forward, he began his career at Jarrow Hibernians aged 14 years, then at senior level with Blaydon United and Hebburn Argyle. He then spent a short spell at Chorley FC, Lancashire, before returning to Hebburn. Other spells followed at Blyth Spartans and South Shields Adelaide.

In 1909 he moved to Fulham, playing two games for them before returning north to Wallsend Park Villa. A short spell at Southend followed, but again he could not settle and moved back north playing for Jarrow Caledonians then Scotswood. He had worked at the Palmer Shipyard, Jarrow, before enlisting.

McLaughlin joined the Northumberland Fusiliers in 1914 and after training was in France by December of the same year with the 1ˢᵗ Battalion.

During March 1915 he attained the rank of Sergeant in a short space of time. Wounded in July though not seriously, he was then promoted to Company Sergeant Major. In March 1916 as part of X Company he was involved in heavy fighting near St Eloi.

The British had placed mines at the German lines to take out the defences and barbed wire, the offensive taking place after this without success. McLaughlin was part of a team that had taken a

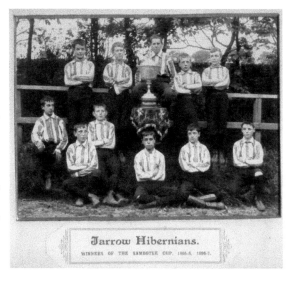

Seen here in his youth, in the 1897 cup-winning Jarrow Hibernian side. (Third from left front row.) (Photograph courtesy of Godric Page.)

Jarrow Hibernians.
WINNERS OF THE SAMBOTKE CUP, 1895-6, 1896-7.

trench. When the Germans made a counter offensive, they suffered large casualties with 50 killed and 150 wounded. They were unable to recover or bury the bodies. Patrick was one of those killed, a witness seeing him take a bullet that killed him instantaneously. Officially recorded as missing, he was killed in action on 27th March 1916. He is commemorated at the Menin Gate Memorial (Panel 8 to 12) and the Palmer Shipyard Memorial, Jarrow. Patrick was 33 years old and left a wife Helena.

Horace 'Harry' Osborne Robotham was born in 1879 in Heath Town, Wolverhampton. He was a wing half who played for Wolverhampton Post Office, Redshaw Albion, and Ossett. He then won the West Yorkshire League and Cup with Hunslet. Wolverhampton Wanderers signed him in 1901-03, where he played seven games and scored one goal.

He then moved to Fulham in 1903-05, playing 39 games, this being his longest spell at any of his clubs. In 1905-06 it was Brentford, playing 21 games; during 1906-07, Glossop, playing 26 games and scoring four goals; 1907-08 New Brompton, playing 33 games; and finally Wellington Town in 1908-09, playing 33 games.

After 1910, having retired, he was working as a window cleaner in the Wolverhampton area.

He joined the Middlesex Regiment, 2nd Footballers' Battalion, in 1915. After training, they were in Aldershot as part of the 123rd Brigade, 41st Division. They then landed in France in May 1916 and were subsequently involved in the Battle at the Somme. He was killed on 12th September 1916 in a subsidiary battle at Flers-Courcelette and is commemorated on the memorial to the missing at Thiepval (Pier and Face 12D and 13B). Harry was 37 years old and married to Jessie Gertrude Robotham.

Edward William Thompson was born in 1894 in Prudhoe, Northumberland. He worked as a Stoneman at Emma colliery in Durham. A talented footballer, he played locally for Spen Black n' Whites. Fulham came in for him in 1914-15 and he signed professionally, but after one game a knee injury forced his retirement from professional football, so he returned to his old job.

Thompson enlisted with the 2nd Battalion Scots Guards in 1917 subsequently serving in France. He was killed in action on 6th November 1918 at the Somme, just six days before the Armistice. Buried in the Bermeries Communal Cemetery, Nord, France (II.B.15), Edward was 24 years of age. His brother Charlton lost his life on 10th April 1917, serving with the Durham Light Infantry in Northern France.

Frederick Waterson was born in 1877 in Burton-on-Trent. He was a labourer and  railway worker who spent most of his career at Burton Swifts, later Burton United. Described as a tough, hard-working full back, he played over 178 games for them in total, scoring four goals. In 1903-04, after a dispute over wages, he moved to Fulham, spending the next six seasons there, before finishing his career at Doncaster Rovers in

1913.   FULHAM FOOTBALL CLUB.   1914.

Back Row   T Payne   Lea   Gray   Coquet   Templeton   Mavin   Bowering   Bowker   Collins   Nixon   Perks
Second Row   T S. Hamilton   Mr Clark   Reynolds   Marshall   Rickards   Houghton   Forrest   Charlton   Butler   Champion   Christie   Tom Walker
Third Row   J. E. Norris   Smith   Russell   Pearce   Curtis   Mr. Allen (Chairman)   Wood   Torrance   Burns   Garvey   Mr. P. Kelso (Sec. Manager)
Front Row   Coleman   Stuart   Nicol   Taylor   Walker   White

THE "DAILY CITIZEN" FOOTBALL REPORTS AND SKETCHES ARE THE TALK OF THE FOOTBALL WORLD.

1909-10. He played 14 first-team games for Fulham. Highly thought of, he captained the reserves and prior to leaving was given a benefit game on Boxing Day 1908 for his services.

Waterson enlisted with the Durham Light Infantry, stationed in France. In July 1918 he was with the 41st Brigade, 14th Division as a Corporal. Later that year, during one of the allied forces' final advances, he died from wounds in the clearing station at Hazebrouck on 12th October 1918. Buried in the La-Kreule Military Cemetery, Hazebrouck, Nord, France (IV.B.1), Fred was 41 years old.

Gillingham FC (New Brompton before 1911), Southern League Division One
(League position: 20th – not relegated due to war)

Frederick John Griffiths was born on 13th September 1873 in Presteigne, Wales. A large well-built reliable goalkeeper, he began his football career in 1894 in Lancashire with South Shore FC and was on Blackpool's books, becoming their first player to win international honours. He also played in the first-ever league match for them at Bloomfield Road. Other clubs he played for in the area were Clitheroe and Stalybridge Rovers. His best period was the early 1900's when he won two caps for the Welsh international side, against Scotland and England.

In 1900 the well-thought-of keeper moved to Millwall, but did not really settle there. In fact, he did not really settle at any one club in particular. His other clubs were Tottenham, Preston and then a good spell at West Ham, before moving to New Brompton in 1904-06, making over 50 appearances for them. Now in his thirties, Fred moved on to Middlesbrough in 1906, but did not play in the first team. He seems to have finished his career in amateur football playing for Moores Athletic in Derbyshire. After retiring, he became a miner in the area and coached football locally.

In 1915 he enlisted in the Sherwood Foresters (Notts and Derby Regiment, 15th Battalion), reaching the rank of Sergeant. By 1917 the unit was part of the 35th Division. Fred was engaged in fighting at Passchendaele and reported killed on 30th October 1917 with four other colleagues during manoeuvres. He was buried in the Dozinghem Military Cemetery, Belgium (XIII.D.11). He was 44 years old, married to Elizabeth Griffiths and had six children.

Andrew Mosley was born in 1885 in Sneinton, Nottingham, one of four children. A right back, he began his career at Sneinton before signing for Notts County from 1906-09, making 11 appearances. He married Annie in 1907, before they moved south when he signed for New Brompton in 1910-15. He played over 178 games for them before suspension of the league, and was described as a solid reliable defender.

Mosley enlisted with the South Wales Borderers and served in Belgium. He was killed in action in West Flanders at Passchendaele on 3rd August 1917. He is commemorated at the Ypres Menin Gate Memorial (Panel 22). Andrew was 33 years old, he left his wife and a daughter named Grace, aged 8 years.

John 'Jock' Taylor was born in 1886 in Elgin, Scotland. He was an inside forward who began his career at Peterhead before moving to Hull in 1907, making 12 appearances and scoring three goals. He then moved briefly to Tunbridge Wells Rangers, before signing for New Brompton in 1909-13. He played over 130 games and scored 37 goals for them. His last registered club was Leith Athletic.

GILLINGHAM FOOTBALL CLUB 1913-14

Taylor enlisted with the Northumberland Fusiliers, serving in France. He was killed on 15th September 1916, aged 30 years. He is commemorated at the Thiepval Memorial (Pier and Face 6D and 7D). John is also on the memorial to the Northumberland Fusiliers at Barras Bridge, Newcastle upon Tyne.

Glossop FC, Division Two

(League position: 20th – not re-elected after the war)

Harold Walley 'Harry' Bamford was born in October,1886 in Sculcoates, Yorkshire, but his parents then moved to Southampton. He was a pay clerk on the docks in Hampshire, then a schoolmaster. He played county football for amateur side Bitterne Guild. Signed by the Saints in 1907-11 as a half back, he made 11 first team appearances. In 1912 he signed for Glossop FC and although he was he mainly used in the reserves, made 15 first-team appearances as a centre half.

Bamford enlisted with the 1st Battalion King's Shropshire Light Infantry and was a Second Lieutenant. Wounded during fighting at Proven, Ypres, Harold died three days later on 26th November 1915 of septicaemia in Le Touquet hospital.

He was buried in Etaples Military Cemetery, Pas de Calais (I.A.15); he was 29 years old.

Thomas Clifford was born on 14th August 1875 in Kilbirnie, Ayrshire. He was a half back who began his football at Annbank, then in 1896-97 he played at Newton Heath FC, Manchester, though mainly in the reserves. In 1897 he made 10 appearances scoring four goals for Ayr. He then moved back to England, signing for Glossop FC in 1899-1900, making 44 appearances in two seasons, scoring one goal. He then went on his

travels to Luton, Celtic and Beith, then he made 16 appearances for Motherwell in 1904-05.

Clifford then appeared at Nottingham Forest in 1905 and is mentioned playing on their tour of South America in a match against Britanicos. Forest thrashed the local side 13-1, Clifford netting one goal from the penalty spot. He made six appearances for them after signing from Motherwell and got good reviews, but soon after sustained a knee injury and did not play again.

He enlisted for the war effort with the Royal Scots Fusiliers in 1916, involved in fighting at the Somme. He was killed on 19th January 1917, his body reported lost. Clifford was 42 years old and married to Jane Young. He is commemorated at the Thiepval Memorial (Pier and Face 3C).

John Costello was born on 15th May 1890 in Blackley, Manchester. A full back, he played his football in the Lancashire area at Altrincham, Rochdale and Stockport County, as a reserve player. He was at Glossop FC in 1913, playing seven games.

Costello enlisted with the Royal Navy Marines Light Infantry in Plymouth and after training he served at Gallipoli in 1915, ranked as a Sergeant. He died of wounds received at the Dardanelles on 24th June 1915. This was during the Balkans Theatre Campaign. He is commemorated at the Plymouth Naval Memorial (Panel 7); he was 25 years old.

Harold Chadwick Meadowcroft was born in 1889 in Workington, Cumbria. He then lived in the Manchester area and played football locally for Whitworth then Rochdale before signing for Glossop in 1912 as a right half, though he could also play on the wing. He played 10 games for them before moving to Bury in 1913, making five appearances.

Meadowcroft joined the Manchester Regiment for the war effort and was a Corporal. Harold was killed on the first day at the Somme – 1st July 1916 – at Danzig Alley. He was buried in the Danzig British Cemetery, Mametz, France

(III.F.10). He is also remembered in St Pauls Church, Kersal, Salford. He was 27 years old.

Edward Murphy was born in 1881 in Staffordshire and played most of his football career as an outside forward, mainly on the left. He played for a number of clubs including Bristol Rovers, Bury, Gainsborough and Swindon Town, whom he played 37 games for and scored six goals in 1906-07. He played for Glossop from 1902-04, playing 91 games and scoring 23 goals.

Murphy enlisted with the North Staffordshire Regiment for the conflict. He was repatriated to his home town, but he died on 25th May 1916 from wounds received in France. He was buried in Tunstall Cemetery, Staffordshire (FA.NC.7); he was 35 years old.

Charles Neil Newcombe was born on 16th March 1891 in Great Yarmouth, but moved to Matlock, Derbyshire, with his parents. He went to Chesterfield Grammar School and was head boy there. In 1913 he was playing football locally at amateur level as an inside left and was notably on Rotherham Town and Chesterfield Town's books. He then signed for Manchester United, playing for their reserve side. In 1913 Glossop signed him and he has two registered games with them.

Newcombe was a good all-round sportsman and in 1910 was with Derbyshire Cricket Club as an all-rounder.

He enlisted with the Yorkshire Light Infantry in 1914, ranked a Second Lieutenant. He was killed at Fleurbaix, France, on 27th December 1915, leading his men when a sniper shot him. He was buried in the Y-Farm, Military Cemetery (K.13); he was 24 years old.

Harold Sparkes was born in 1896 in Glossop. He was a plumber's apprentice, but Glossop used him in 1915 in an attempt to rejuvenate their failing fortunes, where he made three appearances as a centre forward.

Then aged 19 years he enlisted with the 11th Battalion Royal Scots for the war in October 1915. After this, he served in France, the battalion

suffering heavy losses during the Battle of Loos.

Sparkes survived this unscathed, only to sustain a number of wounds, the most serious of which was a gunshot wound to the head, during fighting near the Belgian village of Ploegsteert on 12th May 1916. Admitted to the 24th General Hospital at Etaples, three days later, on 15th May 1916, he returned to Britain on the Hospital Ship HMS *Brighton* and was admitted to the 4th Northern General Hospital in Lincoln on 29th May 1916, where he spent 100 days having treatment until early September 1916.

In today's world, he would most likely have been retired from service or at least removed from front-line duties. Unfortunately, this was a tough regime and as he was deemed to have recovered sufficiently, Sparkes returned to the 3rd Reserve Battalion of the Royal Scots on 30th November. On 12th December he transferred to the 16th Royal Scots, McCrae's Battalion and posted to 'D' Company.

The battalion was already battle scarred and saw further action during the first and second Battle of the Scarpe and the Battle of Arleux during the Arras offensive in April and May 1917.

Sparkes lost his life during these offensives on 2nd June 1917, aged just 21 years. He was buried north of the village of Fampoux, 3.5 miles north east of Arras on 3 June 1917. His personal belongings comprised a disc, letters, photographs, pocket book, cards, certificates and a razor. The Machine Gun Corps returned these to his widowed mother. He is commemorated on the Arras Memorial in Faubourg-d'Amiens Cemetery, Arras (Bay 1 and 2). Harold's body was lost after initial burial. He is also remembered at the Hadfield War Memorial.

Grimsby Town FC, Division Two
(League position: 17th)

Thomas Kelly was born in 1884 in Tunstall, Stoke-on-Trent. He began his football career at Glossop in 1906 as a halfback, playing 23 games and scoring one goal. He then moved briefly to Denaby United in the Sheffield League, before signing for Grimsby in 1908-09, making 26 appearances and scoring three goals.

He then moved to Silverwood Town, Yorkshire, before ending up at New Brompton in 1911-12, playing 16 games. Prior to the war, he was living in Stockport, working at the local Gas Factory.

In 1915 he joined the North Staffordshire Regiment with his brother. After training he was stationed in Turkey and was involved in the Gallipoli campaign.

On 9th April 1916, after an earlier encounter, the regiment came under tremendous and sustained machine gun fire from the Turks in no man's land near Sannaiyat, the 'Siege of Kut', with no means of defence. They were helpless and the scene was described as carnage; it was not until midnight under cover of darkness that they were able to retreat to safety. Forty-four of the battalion died, including Thomas.

Gallipoli was a particularly bloody and later reported pointless campaign with over 200,000 dead or wounded, with numerous casualties succumbing to disease. With thousands of bodies left where they fell, it further exasperated the problem of disease.

The battalion Chaplin, in what he described as a hell-like situation, wrote to Thomas's widow: *'It was late in the evening and his brother had been working tirelessly bringing in the wounded, when he came to me and told me Thomas had been killed. It was the completion of my cup of sorrow, my heart overcome with attending to the wounded all day long. I could see how keenly his brother felt it, yet he bore it with sublime resignation and went on with his work. Your husband had said goodbye to me the evening before, each of us hoping to meet again. He had been to mass and communion that day. I am sure he died the holiest and most perfect of deaths.'*

He is commemorated at the Basra Memorial, Iraq (Panel 34); he was 30 years old and married to Mary Ann Kelly.

William Lee McAllister Miller was born in 1875 in Dumfries, Scotland. He was a picture framer by trade who played his football locally for Dumfries Hibernians then St Bernards FC.

He signed for Grimsby in 1903 as a centre forward, making four appearances.

Miller enlisted with the King's Own Scottish Borderers and was a Sergeant. On 13th August 1915 he was on board the troop ship HMS *Royal Edward* in the Aegean Sea, when U-Boat 14 torpedoed it. He was recorded as missing presumed dead. He is remembered at the Helles Memorial (Panel 85 to 93) and on the Dumfries Memorial. He was 40 years old and married to Margaret Miller. William's brother Thomas, aged 37 years, had lost his life in France on 29th June 1915.

Ralph Motson Thompson was born in 1892 in West Hartlepool. He was the son of the Grimsby chairman and played 12 games as a winger for the club in 1914-15, before joining the war effort. Prior to this, he played locally for a number of teams including Grimsby Rovers and Heycroft Rovers.

After joining the Lincolnshire Regiment, Grimsby Chum's, Footballers Unit, he served in France. Thompson was killed on the first day of the Battle of the Somme on 1st July 1916.

He is commemorated at the Thiepval Memorial (Pier and Face 1C); Ralph was 24 years old.

Sidney Wheelhouse was born in July 1888 in Bishop Auckland, County Durham. A talented full back, he began his career at Bishop Auckland then Shildon Athletic, before signing for Grimsby in 1907, having turned down Sunderland.

A superb professional who gained the captaincy of the club, he played over 244 games and scored three goals. He was regarded as a very reliable and influential team member and stayed with them until 1915 when he joined the forces for the war.

He enlisted with the 17th Middlesex Footballers' Battalion in February, and during his training he was allowed to play at weekends. He also represented the Footballer's side and was in the team that beat Cardiff City at Ninian Park in October 1915.

Wheelhouse served overseas with the regiment, continuing to represent them in arranged football tournaments. He was stationed

Grimsby Town FC, 1914.

near Loos, France, but was allowed a short period of leave back home in May 1916. He played his last match for Grimsby at Blundell Park in a charity game in aid of the victims of a German Zeppelin attack at Cleethorpes, when 31 soldiers from the Manchester Regiment billeted in the Baptist Church perished. The Zeppelin was destined for London but developed engine problems and dropped its bombs there on its revised route home.

Having returned to his battalion as a Lance Corporal, Wheelhouse was involved in heavy fighting at Delville Wood between 27th and 29th July 1916, during which time they sustained significant casualties. The company then took part in further heavy fighting near the village of Guillemont some five days later.

On 18th September 1916 he was part of a work party that had been shoring up a collapsed trench parapet throughout the previous night. They came under heavy enemy mortar fire and attempted to take cover, but the Germans then blew a mine under their position. Unprepared and overcome by poisonous gasses, they evacuated to the rear. Reports suggest that Sid had walked unaided to the first aid station, though within 24 hours the entire working party was dead.

Sid Wheelhouse was 27 years old. He was married to Agnes Wheelhouse and had three children. He was buried in Couin Military Cemetery (III.A.14), which is located near Doullens, Northern France.

Huddersfield Town FC, Division Two
(League position: eighth)

John 'Jack' Cameron was born in Dornoch, Sutherland, Scotland. Historically there is not much information relating to him and personal details or his career. He was on Huddersfield's books in 1911-12, making two first-team appearances and scoring one goal as a centre forward. His footballing movements thereafter are unknown.

He enlisted with the Cameron Highlanders and the only information available states that John Cameron died in France in early 1916.

Sidney James, also listed as Sydney, was born in 1891 in Sheffield, one of four children. He began his football career at amateur level with Tinsley Church and the local pub team 'The Bird in Hand'. In 1913 he signed for Huddersfield on a contract for £2.10 shillings a

week. When war broke out, he was working at the local steelworks, which was a reserved occupation. This was to keep him in the Huddersfield team, as the club had organised the job. Angered when handed a white feather in the street, James enlisted for the cause. He had played over 12 games for the first team.

James joined the 9th King's Own Yorkshire Light Infantry, serving in France. He was killed on Easter Monday, 9th April 1917, the opening day of the Battle of Arras, aged 26 years.

He was buried in the Cojeul British Cemetery, Arras (D.9). His mother received his ID bracelet and treasured it for the rest of her days. When news filtered back to his home town of Sid's death, the people there realised that the war was not the glorified adventure it had been portrayed as and no one could have predicted that it would last almost five years. The 'white feather brigade' hung their heads in shame.

George Ernest Kenworthy was born in 1888 in Matlock, Derbyshire. He was a teacher educated at All Saints School, Matlock, and Peterborough Training College. Kenworthy played locally for Matlock and was associated with a number of other clubs, including Heckmondwike, and in 1906-08 he made two appearances and scored one goal for Bradford City. He signed for Huddersfield in 1909-10 as an inside forward, making 20 appearances with six goals in the Midlands League. He scored two goals in an 11-0 thrashing of his former club Heckmondwike

in the FA Cup, which still stands as the club's record win. At the end of the season, Huddersfield gained entry into the Football League. Unfortunately, an injury forced his retirement from the game and he returned to teaching, where he was eventually deputy headmaster at Matlock School.

Kenworthy enlisted in Matlock with the 135th Siege Battery, Royal Garrison Artillery, as a Gunner, serving in Belgium. On 10th November 1917 he was killed in action when a shell exploded near to him. He was buried in the Coxyde Military Cemetery (I.V.L.1.).

George was 29 years old, married to Annie Kenworthy and had a son. He is also remembered on the Matlock War Memorial.

Larrett Roebuck was born on 27th November 1889 in Jump, near Barnsley. One of three children, they had a difficult upbringing as their father died in 1902. With money scarce, Larrett was only 13 years old when he began working down the pits. In 1904 he served one month in prison for theft of a watch. On release, aged 16 claiming he was 18, he enlisted in the York and Lancaster Regiment to better himself, though he did not disclose the conviction.

He served in India in 1906-07, before being stationed in Limerick and attaining the rank of Lance Corporal. (He was demoted in 1910 after a misconduct charge.)

After 1910 and now out of the forces, he worked at Silverwood colliery, joining their football team. He had gained a good reputation as a solid full back and the team were a reputable side, regularly making the qualification stages of the FA Cup. Roebuck signed for Huddersfield in 1913, followed a few months later by his amateur teammate Harry Linley.

He made 19 appearances before being recalled to the services in September 1914. At that time, he was on £2 per week wages, rising to £3 in the 1914-15 season.

Once back with the York Regiment he served in St Nazaire, France. They reached Courcelles in very heavy rain early on the morning of 20th September to learn that the battalions, which had been engaged in the Battles of the Marne and Aisne, were much weakened and exhausted; the 16th Brigade was required to relieve them.

Roebuck and his comrades now faced the grim reality of immediate action. With both sides digging in, the 'race for the sea', as it was stated, had begun as each opposing army moved northwards to try to outflank the other. In terrible and foggy conditions, the British Expeditionary Force was looking to capture Menin when, on 18th October, Roebuck, now a Lance Corporal, was again one of 40 men listed as killed or missing in action near Beaucamps-Ligny, following an attack on an enemy position.

The regiment's record states: *'On the 18th October a reconnaissance force was ordered, which was brilliantly carried out. The Buffs and the York and Lancaster's on the right captured Radinghem without much opposition and advanced across a small plateau, 300 yards in width, towards the woods in which stands Chateau de Flandres. Here they came under a heavy crossfire of machine guns and shrapnel and were counter-attacked and driven back. Major Bayley's company of the York and Lancaster's, which had worked around on the left and threatened the flank of the counter-attack, which thereon withdrew, however, saved the situation. The York and Lancaster's suffered considerable casualties in this action.'*

His mother, who ran the Britannia Inn in Rotherham, hoped he would be found safe, but her other son eventually broke the news to her that he was officially reported missing presumed dead during the attack near Radinghem, the date was 18th October 1914. Larrett was 25 years old and married to Frances Walker. He is commemorated at the Ploegsteert Memorial, Belgium (Panel 8). He was the first English player killed in the conflict.

Hull City FC, Division Two
(League position: seventh)

Patrick Lavery was born in 1884 in Northumberland. He began his football at Gateshead FC before joining Hull City in 1905-06 as a defender, playing four games in total, though Patrick found it difficult to get a regular place, so they released him. He moved to West Stanley FC in 1906.

Lavery fought with the Highland Light Infantry, 10th Service Battalion, during the conflict. He was killed in France on 25th September 1915. He is commemorated at the Loos Memorial (Panel 108 to 112); Patrick was 31 years old.

Douglas 'Doug' Morgan was born on 8th June 1890 in Inverkeithing, Fife, Scotland. He played for Inverkeithing Renton as the left back when they won the Fife Cup in 1910-11. He then moved to Inverkeithing Thistle (United), winning the Scottish Junior Cup in 1912-13 and was the club captain. In 1913-15, the left back moved to Hull City for two seasons, making 64 appearances and scoring one goal, before settling back in Inverkeithing.

After enlisting with the 168th Siege Battery, Royal Garrison Artillery, Doug served in Belgium. He was killed on 31st December 1916 during shelling in West Flanders, whilst celebrating Hogmanay with his comrades. A German shell exploded next to him, and he died from his wounds later that day in hospital. He was buried in Vlamertinghe Military Cemetery (V.B. 14); he was 26 years old and married to Agnes Morgan.

John 'Jackie' Smith was born on 15th September 1886 in the Tyneside pit village of Wardley. From an early age he was displaying his rare talent as a prolific goal-scoring forward at Hebburn Argyle. Signed by Hull in 1905 and was

Hull City, 1913.

an instant favourite with the fans after he scored seven goals in one game for the reserve side. By the end of the year he was a regular in the first team and top goal scorer, continuing this for most of his career at Hull. In 1908 he had the clubs individual record of 31 goals in 37 games, later bettering this with 32 in 35 games. His overall record was 168 games with 102 goals. He was described as a born comedian with a big heart standing at 5ft 7in who loved the chance of charging at a 6ft plus defender.

During the 1910-11 season, Tommy Bromwell replaced him, so Smith signed for Sheffield United for £500, scoring seven goals in 12 games in the First Division. After four months, he moved to Nottingham Forest. Smith ended his professional career assisting Nelson and York City. In 1915 he was still playing, though now at full back for Heckmondwike. In the space of just over three years he had gone from Europe's top scorer to playing non-league football.

Smith enlisted in the York and Lancaster Regiment stationed in France and was listed as killed/missing in action between 4th September 1916 and 7th September 1916. This regiment lost over 72% of its men during the war, which was one of the highest death rates. They were also the most decorated. Jackie Smith was 29 years old and left behind a wife Annie and six children, two of which went on to play professional rugby league. He is commemorated on the Thiepval Memorial (Pier and Face 14A. 14B).

Leeds City FC, Division Two
(League position: 15th)

(Expelled and dissolved in 1919 for a number of irregularities. Leeds United formed the following year.)

Joseph Frederick 'Fred' Hargrave was born in 1877 in Atherstone, near Tamworth. A forward from a footballing family, he played for a number of clubs. He was on the books of Aston Villa, Walsall, Stafford, Stoke City and Burton United. Leeds signed him from Burton in 1903, after he scored 14 goals in 56 games.

Elected to the football league in 1905, Hargrave was a main part of the Leeds set up, he even captained the side on a number of occasions. In the opening season he scored 19 goals in 34 games. He then switched position to half back and was just as popular with the club in this role. In all he played over 60 games for them.

In 1908 he transferred to Stoke, scoring 11 goals in 15 games. This was his last known professional club.

Hargrave enlisted as a Gunner with the 346th Royal Garrison Artillery. He was killed in action in Belgium on 19th October 1917, and buried in the Steenkerke Military Cemetery, Belgium (A.1). His mother received his medals after his death. Fred was 40 years old.

John Anderson Harkins was born on 10th April 1881 in Musselburgh, Midlothian, Scotland. John, who was a centre half, was already a soldier in the Black Watch Regiment. A Middlesbrough scout spotted him in 1906 playing in a cup-tie for the army against Celtic. They bought him out of the forces and he played all but one game that season. He was switched to right half the following season and after nine games was for some unknown reason sold to non-league side Broxburn Athletic, followed in 1909 by a move to Bathgate FC.

In 1910 he signed for Leeds and had two good seasons there with over 63 games. He then moved to Darlington FC after Herbert Chapman became manager.

In 1914 he joined his former Leeds manager Frank Scott-Walford at Coventry City, playing 18 games and scoring one goal.

Harkins then re-enlisted with his regiment for the war, serving in the Middle East. He was killed in action at the attack on Kut Al Amara, Iraq, on 22nd April 1916. He was buried in the Amara War Cemetery (XVII.F.17); John was 35 years old and married to Lily Harkins.

Thomas Henry Morris was born on 14th September 1884 in Grimsby. He began his playing career with Haycroft Rovers in the Grimsby League and then moved on to Grimsby Rovers. Morris secured a deal with Second Division Grimsby Town in February 1906. He played 22 games before joining Brighton and Hove Albion in May 1907. Brighton manager Frank Scott-Walford then took over at Leeds and he was determined to sign Morris; he finally got him in 1909. Morris was a solid centre half and became the stalwart of the Leeds defence, a ferocious tackler and excellent header of the ball. He did lack pace but was rated as one of the best defenders in the Second Division; he read the game with ease.

Having played 109 games and by now a veteran, he joined Scunthorpe & Lindsey United as player-coach in 1913. In 1914 he re-joined Mr Scott-Walford at Coventry City, playing 19 games and scoring two goals.

Thomas enlisted with the 2nd Battalion Lincolnshire Regiment, attaining the rank of Sergeant. He was killed at the Somme on 24th March 1918 aged 33 years. He is commemorated at the Pozieres Memorial, Somme (Panel 23 and 24).

David Bruce Murray was born on 4th December 1882 in Cathcart, Glasgow, Scotland, and then adopted by a Mrs SE Sleight. A left back, he began his football career with Leven Victoria, before Glasgow Rangers

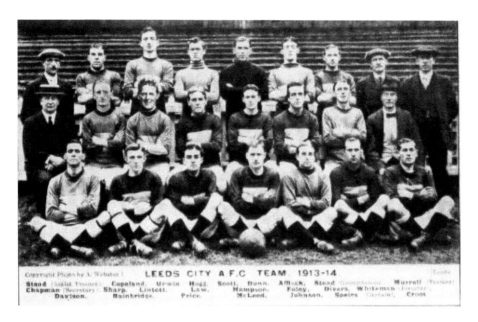

LEEDS CITY A F.C TEAM 1913-14

D B MURRAY,
LEEDS CITY.

picked him up. He struggled to break through and moved to Everton in 1903, where he again struggled and moved across the park to Liverpool, making 15 appearances for them.

A brief journey to Hull City in 1905 was followed by his best spell in football with Leeds City from 1905-09. He played 85 games and scored seven goals, and he was given the role as penalty taker, also captaining the side on a number of occasions.

A spell at Mexborough FC followed, before he finished his career at Burslem Port Vale.

David enlisted with the Argyll and Sutherland Highlanders. He was killed in action fighting in the quarries at Hulluch, Loos, France on 10the December 1915; he was 32 years old. He is commemorated at the Loos Memorial (Panel 125 to 127).

Leicester Fosse FC
(Leicester City after 1919), Division Two
(League position: 19th)

Thomas Charlesworth 'Tommy' Allsop was born on 18th December 1880 in Leicester. A good all-round sportsman who played at first-

class level as a cricketer as well as a professional footballer, Leicester signed him in 1899 as a winger. He had a brief spell at Luton Town, and then returned to Leicester, playing over 70 games in total for the club. During his time as Leicester he also played cricket in the summer, playing over 36 matches for Leicestershire Cricket Club and one for the M.C.C.

He then moved to Brighton and Hove Albion in 1905, followed by Norwich City in 1907. He continued his cricket in Norwich with over 27 games for the Minor Counties.

On retirement, Allsop ran the Hero of Redan Public House in Norwich with his wife Edith Rose, who continued to run the pub after Tommy joined the forces during the war. He signed up with the Queen's Royal West Surrey Regiment, which was a Labour Unit, attaining the rank of Sergeant. One of the duties they had was exhuming bodies after the war for reinterring, in itself an horrific task.

Although Tommy survived the war, he died on 7th March 1919 of Spanish Flu, which was widespread during this period. Buried in Norwich Cemetery (Ref 53.420.), he was 38 years old.

Thomas Charles Benfield was born in 1889 in Leicester. He was a player who could fill any role as a forward or a half back.

T. BENFIELD (Inside Right).

He began his football with Leicester Boys before joining the army with the Leicester Regiment, playing regularly for them. Fosse signed him in 1910 and he spent four years at the club playing 111 games with 39 goals. He scored a memorable goal against Arsenal, the first one ever scored at the new Highbury ground, in front of 20,000 people. The news report stated, *'without wasting time he took deliberate aim and crashed the ball against the rigging, a brilliant shot that left Caldwell helpless'.*

He signed for Derby County in 1914 and played over 38 games for them, before re-joining the Leicester Regiment for the war. Living in Leicester with his wife Elsie, he played over 36 war games for Leicester, scoring nine goals. His last game was in 1918.

Benfield served in the 6th Battalion as a Sergeant and they were engaged in fighting at Heudicourt, Somme, on 11th September 1918, when a sniper shot him. Thomas died in hospital eight days later on 19th September 1918, aged 29 years. He was buried in the Varennes Military Cemetery (I.V.A.6.).

Robert Messer was born on 18th July 1887 in Edinburgh. An outside forward with good skills, he began his career at Broxburn then Kings Park and Bo'ness. He moved to Leicester in the 1910 season, playing two games for the club.

He then moves back to Scotland with Broxburn, then East Fife. He was a printer's apprentice by trade and for the war effort enlisted with the 6th Battalion Queen's Own Scottish Borderers. They had been on the western front since 1915 and were part of the 9th Scottish Division.

In 1918, as part of the final advance into Belgium, Messer was involved in the Battle of Lys, near Ypres. Killed in fighting on 16th October 1918 at the Battle of Courtrai, he was aged 31 years. Ten days after Robert's death, his battalion were relieved from front-line duties. (He was posthumously awarded the British War and Victory medals, usually awarded to all serving soldiers.) He is commemorated at the Tyne Cot Memorial (Panel 66 to 68).

Ernest Albert Nuttall was born on 1st February 1871 in Leicester, playing locally before signing for Leicester in 1889 as a wing half. He played in their first-ever cup game in 1890 and also scored their first-ever FA Cup goal in 1891. He was eventually the club captain, playing over 35 games.

In 1892 he left to become a solicitor in Crouch End, London. In 1916 he joined the 25th Middlesex Garrison for the war, and by then he was in his forties. Assigned due to his age to a low-grade unit, Nuttall served in Russia and Siberia and was still there in 1919, after the conflict had finished. It was only through a campaign back home that the unit were able to return later in the same year. The Siberian winter had taken its toll and he was unwell on his return, having contracted tuberculosis. Nuttall died on 12th February 1920, less than five months after his return; he was 49 years old. Ernest was married with one son. His grave is in the East Sheen Cemetery, Surrey (C 264).

William George Pepper was born in 1895 in Faversham, Kent. He played for Sheppey United in the Kent league as a goalkeeper, before turning out for Leicester in 1913 in a 5-1 defeat at Leeds City. It was his only appearance for the club before moving back to Kent. He also played one game for Gillingham.

He enlisted in Sittingbourne with the Queen's Own, Royal West Kent Regiment, serving in India then Iraq as a Lance Corporal. Pepper was part of the offensive in 1917 in Bagdad. Then during 1918 at Mosul the British were protecting the oil fields against the Ottoman Army before the war ended (The Battle of Sharqat). He was killed on 25th October 1918 during this campaign at Mesopotamia, aged 23 years. Bill was one of 1,800 casualties. He is commemorated at the Basra Memorial (Panel 29).

William Albert Sharpley D.C.M. was born in 1892 in Bow, London. A left back recruited by Leicester in 1912 as a trialist, he made only one first-team appearance.

He became disillusioned with professional football and joined the army, namely the 2nd Battalion Essex Regiment. He continued to enjoy his football with them and he also excelled at boxing.

By 1914 he was on the western front, involved in fighting at the first battle of Marne.

A Sergeant by rank, he had been mentioned in dispatches and in 1916 won the Distinguished Conduct Medal, second only to the Victoria Cross. He was also awarded the Russian Medal of St George.

The Intelligence Report stated, *'At about 6am on 6th February 1916, Lance Corporal Rogers, was severely wounded at an isolated post in front of one of our trenches south east of Hebuterne. It was impossible to reach him except over the open and Sergeant Sharpley, accompanied by a Lance Corporal went out at 7.30am under hostile fire and succeeded in getting*

Lance Corporal Rogers back to our trenches. Owing to the exposed nature of the ground and the deep mud, it was not until 1.15 pm that this was safely accomplished.'

Four months later Sharpley was involved in fighting at the Somme and was killed on 1st July 1916, his body lost in the mayhem of the first day of battle. He is commemorated at the Thiepval Memorial (Pier and Face 10 D.); William was 24 years old. A sad end to this particular story is that when his sister Kate went to receive his medal from Queen Mary she was so overcome by grief and anger that she threw it back towards the Queen. She was arrested by the police, but thankfully released later that day without charge. She continued to campaign thereafter as an anti-war activist until her death in 1978, aged 82 years.

John 'Jack' Davenport Sheffield was born 1879 in Coalville, Leicester. He initially played his football locally for numerous teams, before enlisting as a soldier serving with the Leicester Volunteers during the Boer War in South Africa, from 1901-02.

On his return, he played initially for Burton United as a left back in 1902-03, making 12 appearances. He moved to the Fosse in 1904-05, but only managed two games in the first team, though he was a regular in the reserves. He then continued playing locally with his last recorded club being Coalville Wednesday. He also played rugby for Coalville, making headlines for over aggressive play, the referee reporting him for his conduct.

Sheffield enlisted for the war with the Leicester Regiment and was a Corporal by rank. They were soon on the western front in 1915 at Neuve Chapelle, Artois, France, after taking it from the Germans. Due to inadequate resources, they suffered heavy losses when the Germans made a counter offensive and had to withdraw. H is recorded as being killed on 13th March 1915 during this assault; Jack was 35 years old. He is commemorated at the Le Touret Memorial (Panel 11). Over 13,400 other British force personnel lost their lives during fighting in this area on the western front.

Bertie Waterfield was born in 1893 in Birstall, Leicester. A full back, he played locally for Belgrave St Peters then Leicester Imperial. He enlisted with the 2nd Royal Army Medical Corps Service Battalion

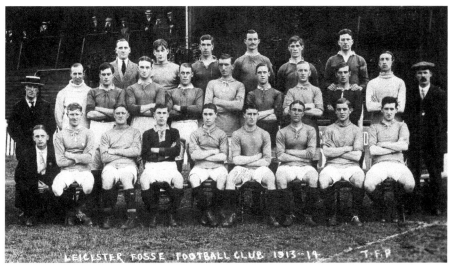

London Regiment. During training at Salisbury Plain in April 1916, he was used by Leicester Fosse on two occasions in the Wartime Midlands League. By June he was in France, ranked a Lance Corporal and involved in fierce fighting for a number of weeks in the Vimy Ridge area, near Pas de Calais.

Killed in action on 27th July 1916, he was buried in the Ecoivres Military Cemetery, Mont-St Eloi (III.C.10); Bertie was 23 years old. He is also remembered at Belgrave St Peters Church, Leicester.

Lincoln City FC, Division Two
(League position: 16th)

Thomas Asnip was born on 18th February 1883 in Sheffield and played his football as an amateur with St Catherines as an outside left, after he moved to the Lincoln area. He made one appearance for Lincoln City in 1904, in a 2-0 home defeat against Manchester United. He was then with local side Adelaide FC, who were a prominent amateur side during the early 1900s. His elder brother John also played one game for Lincoln in 1902.

Asnip served as a Lance Corporal with the Lincolnshire then North Staffordshire Regiments in

Flanders. He was killed in action on 24th July 1918; Thomas was 35 years old. He was buried in the Locre No 10 Cemetery, Belgium (A.13).

Peter Mackin was born in 1878 in Gateshead. He was a shipyard apprentice playing amateur football for Hebburn Argyle as an inside forward. Sunderland signed him from 1899-1903, though he usually played in the 'A' team. He then played for local side Wallsend Villa until Lincoln signed him in 1905-07, where he played 59 games and scored 21 goals. After badly injuring his knee, he moved to Blyth Spartans in 1907. Mackin was so popular there he became club captain, staying until 1911. They won the Tynemouth Cup twice during this period and Mackin became somewhat of a celebrity in the area.

Mackin enlisted with the Royal Northumberland Fusiliers (Tyneside Scottish and Irish Units). He was killed in action at the Battle of Vimy Ridge, part of the Battle of Arras, on Easter Monday – 9th April 1917. He was buried in the Roclincourt Military Cemetery (II.A.40); Peter was 38 years old. His brother Thomas, who had enlisted with the 3rd Tyneside Irish, lost his life in 1916, aged 24 years. He is commemorated on the Thiepval Memorial. Both are remembered on Blyth War Memorials.

In September 1917 a benefit match took place in Blyth for Peter played by local women's teams Wallsend Slipway and Blyth Munitions in aid of his widow and family.

William Morris was born on 13th February 1890 in Arnold, Nottinghamshire, one of four children. A centre forward, he playing

Lincoln City, 1913–14.

amateur football for a number of local sides, then Stanton Hill Victoria before Lincoln secured his signature in 1908-09. He played 18 games for them in total scoring 13 goals in the Midland and Northern league. One of his goals was in an FA Cup tie against Liverpool in a 5-1 defeat. He impressed Liverpool that much they signed him the following season in 1909. He was a regular for them mainly in the reserve team. Released in 1910, he returned to his home town and played for the Stanton Hill side. He worked as a Greengrocer before the conflict.

Morris enlisted with the Royal Navy Volunteer Reserve serving on HMS *Polesley*, a defensively armed Merchant Ship. On 21st September 1918 a U-Boat torpedoed the ship off the Cornish coast. It was on passage from Cardiff to France, with the loss of forty-three men including Morris. He is commemorated on the Plymouth Naval Memorial (Ref 30). William was 28 years old, married to Maud and had one son.

Thomas Philips Strong was born in 1890 in Newcastle-Upon-Tyne. A left or half back, he played eight games for Lincoln in the 1913-14 season.

Strong enlisted with the South Staffordshire Regiment, and after training he served in France. He was killed in action in the Pas-De-Calais area on 15th July 1917.

He is buried in Croisilles Railway Cemetery, Nord-Pas-De-Calais, France (II.A.8); Thomas was 27 years old.

Liverpool FC, Division One
(League position: 13th)

Arnold Dargie was born in Bangor, North Wales, in 1891. He was educated at Grove Park School, Wrexham, and St Deiniols School in Bangor. He is described as, *'An excellent all round thoroughly honest sportsman. An exceptionally talented striker of superb stature, he put fear into both defenders and goalkeepers alike. With a thunderbolt of a shot that could take both ball and keeper flying into the back of the goal.'*

A. DARGIE, Liverpool F.C.

He played for Bangor FC, scoring over 100 goals for them, and was a cult hero in the area. He always retained his amateur status and gained three amateur caps for the Welsh international side from 1909-11. He was with Chester City during 1910-11 scoring 13 goals in 13 games. Dargie then attracted the attention of Liverpool FC and assisted the club after signing forms in 1911, though this was mainly with the reserve team. (Image 1911.)

Prior to the war, he had already received a commission with the Welsh Royal Garrison Artillery. In 1916 he served in France, initially as a Lieutenant then promoted to Captain. He was described by fellow officers and men, *'as braver soldier as ever seen, liked and respected by all'*. His actions leading his battery resulted in his promotion again to Acting Major with the 137th. He was killed on 18th September 1917 during fighting when a bomb exploded at his feet; he was 26 years old. Arnold's funeral had a large attendance due to his popularity. He was buried in Bully-Grenay Communal Cemetery, France (IV.F.7.). (In 1936 his father funded the building of a stand at Bangor's ground in his memory.)

Joseph Oscar Dines was born on 12th April 1886 in Kings Lynn, Norfolk. An outstanding amateur who resisted the temptation on many occasions to turn professional, his main club was Kings Lynn and he played in the Great Britain football team that won the gold medal in the 1912 Olympics in Stockholm, beating Denmark 4-2 in the final. He gained 27 England amateur caps. He represented Norfolk County and guested for a number of clubs including Queens Park Rangers and Millwall, as well as Arsenal and Norwich reserves.

Dines played one game for Liverpool in 1912, after he had signed a one-year contract with them.

A teacher by trade in Kings Lynn before he married, he then accepted a similar role in Ilford, East London. He also played for the Ilford team who at that time were a good amateur outfit. He was described as, *'The Smiling Footballer, a thoughtful young man and outstanding half back who was a master in the art of dribbling'*.

Dines joined the Middlesex Regiment then the Royal Liverpool

Regiment for the war effort, attaining the rank of Second Lieutenant. Originally, he had joined the Ordnance Corps before his commission. He was killed in action at Pas de Calais on 27th September 1918 by machine gun fire during an offensive. Joseph was 32 years old and married to Ethel Henriette Eugenie Dines. He was buried in the Grand Ravine British Cemetery, Havrincourt, France (A.42). (Pictured are the 1912 British Olympic side; Dines is back right.)

Wilfred Watson was born on 15th August 1892 in Atherton, Lancashire. An outside left, he had played for Wigan schools and was on Liverpool's books in 1914. He played in the reserves though and was only registered for one first-team game in the same year in an FA Cup match.

Watson enlisted with the 237th Siege Battery Royal Garrison Artillery, serving in France and Flanders. He was killed in Belgium on 24th July 1917, age 24 years, and is commemorated at the Lijssenthoek Military Cemetery (XVI.H.6A).

Liverpool reserve players:

William Henry Aldcroft was born on 23rd August 1887 in Liverpool. He was a reserve player in season 1909-10 and was killed on 17th May 1918 in Greece, serving with the 1st/10th Scottish and Royal Navy Reserve. He was buried in East Mudros Military Cemetery (III.H.237). William was 30 years old.

Joseph Barker was born on 23rd December 1884 in Liverpool. He was a reserve player in season 1907-08 and was killed on 13th January 1916, serving with the 18th King's Liverpool Regiment, 2nd City Battalion, in the Somme area, France. He was buried in Bronfray Farm Military Cemetery, Bray-Sur-Somme (I.B.29). Joe was 31 years old.

George Bradley was born on 6th April 1882 in Aughton, Ormskirk, Lancashire. On the books in 1913-14, he played for the Ormskirk team. He was killed on 25th September 1915, serving as a Lance/Corporal with the 1st/9th Battalion King's Liverpool Regiment near Loos, France. He is commemorated at the Loos Memorial (Panel 27 to 30). George was 23 years old.

Alfred Honess was born on 23rd November 1886 in West Derby, Liverpool. He was a reserve player in 1909-10 and killed on 22nd October 1917, serving with the 8th Black Watch Royal Highlanders near Etaples, France. He was buried in the Etaples Military Cemetery (XXX.F.17). Alfred was 30 years old.

Robert Randles was born on 1st May 1888 in Birkenhead. He was a reserve player, mainly with Tranmere, Chesterfield and Liverpool, and was killed on 8th October 1916 in France, serving with the 16th Canadian Infantry Expeditionary Force, He had emigrated to Canada before getting a first-team game. He was buried in the Anadac Military Cemetery, Miraumont (III.D.36).

Luton Town FC, Southern League Division One
(League position: 14th)

Ernest John Dodd was born in 1892, an only child, in East Common, Harpenden. A Chartered Surveyor by trade working for the Inland Revenue in St Albans, he was a good all-round sportsman and a renowned amateur footballer. He also played cricket for Hertfordshire.

He was in the England International amateur football team squad in 1912-13 and was on Luton's books prior to enlisting for the war effort in 1913-14 with one game as an outside right.

Dodd served in the Royal Field Artillery as a Lieutenant after a commission. He was killed on 17th July 1917 during fighting in Belgium, when a bomb exploded in his dugout. He was buried in the Brandoer Military Cemetery (I.M.30). Ernest was 25 years old.

Walter Robert Fairgrieve was born on 30th August 1874 in Edinburgh. Playing locally as a centre forward until 1897, he moved to Liverpool then Everton in the same year with no success at either club. Another brief spell with Southampton prior to 1899 followed before he signed for Luton in this same year.

This seemed to be his best spell, playing 19 games and scoring six goals. He then moved back to Scotland the following season, and was linked to Partick Thistle, Hibernian, Hearts and Dunfermline.

He joined the Royal Scots for the war effort, though he died unexpectedly near the end of initial training, on 2nd June 1915 with no cause specified. He was buried in the Edinburgh (North Merchistan) Cemetery (C.321). Walter was 40 years old.

Frank William Gilder was born in Luton in 1896, one of three brothers. He played football for Luton Amateurs as a forward and was then signed by Luton Town, playing mainly in the reserve team, though he managed one game in the first team before he was sent to France with the 1st/24th London Regiment as a private.

He was involved in fighting from February 1915 and on 30th December 1915 he was killed in action at Loos. A shell had apparently exploded over the top of him and others in a dugout. Later evidence via a letter from a colleague revealed that the reason for the explosion was more likely to be the fact the enemy had previously mined the area, and this was the probable cause of his death.

He is commemorated at the Loos Memorial (Panel 130 to 135). Frank was 19 years old.

John 'Jock' Jarvie was born in Dumbarton, Scotland, in 1889. He played for Maryhill before signing for Tottenham in 1912. He moved to Luton the following year and was the favoured left back for over a season with 27 games, helping them gain promotion to the Southern League First Division. Due to personal circumstances, he had to return to Scotland at the end of the season. Jarvie then enlisted in the 2nd Argyll and Sutherland Highlanders.

He was killed on 2nd January 1916 at Flanders with 13 colleagues when a mine exploded, killing them all instantly. An officer wrote to one of his friends, whose name was amongst his personal effects. This was in order to bypass the official delay with notifications and not delay the family's false hopes.

One of John's battalion had witnessed the explosion, which was so severe that the bodies were unrecoverable. The War Graves Commission report states he was buried in the Cambrin Churchyard Extension (E.7.). John was 29 years old.

Arthur Harold 'Nippy' Wileman M.M. was born in 1886 in Newhall, Derbyshire. He had initially worked as a miner in the Derby area. He began his football at Newhall Swifts before signing for Burton Swifts in 1906 with his brother Heneage. In 1909 they both signed for Chelsea, where Arthur played over 14 games for them, scoring five goals. He was described as a talented skilful winger, playing mainly on the right hand side.

A. WILEMAN

His brother then moved to Southend United, with Arthur initially signing for Millwall then Luton in 1912, playing as a winger or inside forward. In almost three seasons, he played over 81 games with 47 goals.

Four months into the war, he joined the Duke of Cambridge Middlesex Regiment and then transferred to the 11th Royal Sussex Regiment. He married Blanche Turner in 1915 before leaving for the front and France. Wileman soon gained the rank of Sergeant. He was awarded the Military Medal for bravery in the field in January 1918, 'when he helped repel a German attack resulting in the capture of prisoners and two machine guns'. He was offered a commission, which he turned down and was killed in action on 28th April 1918 in West Flanders near Ypres. Arthur was 36 years old. He is commemorated at the Tyne Cot Memorial, Ypres (Panel 86-88).

Manchester City FC, Division One
(League position: fifth)

Frank Booth was born in Hyde, Manchester, in 1882. A popular winger, he began his career at Glossop then Stockport County in 1901. He signed for City in 1902 and went on to play over 107 games for them, scoring 28 goals. They won the Second Division title and the 1904 FA Cup during this spell at the club. City were also runners-up in the First Division in 1903-04. As a result, he gained his only England cap in 1905 against Ireland.

Booth then moved to Bury FC in 1906, playing 61 games and scoring four goals, followed by a move to Clyde FC in 1910. He returned to City in 1911-12 for his final league season.

He enlisted under the Derby scheme in 1915 and was called to service in 1917 with the Royal Garrison Artillery as a Gunner, serving in France. He survived the conflict and returned home in 1919 but was still on paper as serving should the need arise, transferring to what was termed as Z- Reserve. He fell ill and on examination doctors found he had an inoperable tumour in the heart, and he was admitted to Manchester Royal Infirmary. Frank died on 22nd June 1919, leaving a wife Mary and two young children; he was 37 years old. He was buried in Denton Cemetery, Tameside, Manchester (B.63).

James Conlin was born on 6th July 1881 in Consett, County Durham, England. He began his football career playing for lower league clubs before signing for Hibernian and then Falkirk FC in 1900. He was an exceptionally talented winger, very head strong, with an unfortunate reputation for discipline. In 1901 he signed for Albion Rovers and this is where he made his initial impact playing in the Lanarkshire and Scottish Qualifying Cup finals, playing on the losing side in both, though Albion did secure a place in the Second Division.

He then signed for Bradford City in 1904 for a set fee of £60 after a dispute and appeal with the Scottish FA. He played over 67 games for them with 10 goals. He made his only England appearance whilst at Bradford in 1906, in a 2-1 defeat against Scotland in Glasgow before a world-record crowd of over 102,000. He was the first Bradford player to gain international honours. He also represented the Football League on two occasions.

In 1906 Manchester City paid over £1,000 for his services, a huge fee for the day. He played over 175 games and scored 30 goals for the sky blues, helping them to the Second Division title in 1909-10.

After 1911, he moved to Birmingham City, though he suffered a number of injuries, hampering his appearances to only 23 games and he scored only two goals, before moving on again to Airdrie FC in 1912 for £150. Conlin helped them secure the Lanarkshire Cup. However, his disciplinary problems increased and he developed a drink problem, making matters worse. He was eventually suspended and placed on the transfer list; the asking price was £200 as he had only played 26 games for them and scored seven goals. With no interest from the bigger clubs, he eventually ended up at Broxburn Athletic FC where he finished his career.

On outbreak of war, he was living in Coatbridge with his wife Elizabeth and young son. Conlin enlisted with the Highland Light Infantry in Glasgow. After spending time training in Shropshire and Salisbury and now part of the 32nd Division, he was in Boulogne and before long was involved in heavy fighting on the Somme. In 1917 the regiment served in Belgium. He was registered as killed in fighting near Nieuport during the third battle of Ypres on 23rd June 1917 and is commemorated at the Nieuport Memorial. James was 35 years old.

Patrick 'Paddy' McGuire was born in 1888 in Manchester. He went to Corpus Christie and Woodhouse schools in the area. A solid and reliable full back, he began at amateur level with Hurst FC, later Ashton United, though he had a spell with Manchester United in the reserve side. In 1912 he signed for Manchester City from Hurst. He made 15 first-team appearances.

In 1915 he joined the war effort and enlisted with the Manchester Regiment, training at Cleethorpes. Given permission to guest for Grimsby Town during this period, he made 31 wartime appearances. During his training he attained the rank of Lance Corporal.

By 1916 he was in France with the 17th Manchester Pals and involved in fierce battles at Montauban, Trones Wood and Guillemont. Thereafter he was stationed in the Bethune sector before returning to the Somme for the battle assault on trenches near the village of Flers on 12th October 1916. They suffered heavy losses, during which McGuire was missing, presumed dead. There were a number of unfortunate reports that he may still be alive, though these were to sadly all result in false hopes for his wife. Another soldier managed to speak to her with information that he was officially missing in action. The news of Patrick's death prompted a statement from Grimsby Town stating, *'they regarded the brilliant young full back as the best to have worn their livery for over a decade'.*

He is commemorated at the Thiepval Memorial to the missing (Pier and Face 13 A and 14C) and St Chads Church, Cheetham Hill, Manchester. He was 28 years old and married to Maria McGuire.

William Wallace was born in 1893 in Blaydon-on-Tyne, County Durham. He initially played for Newburn FC, before signing for City in 1912-14 as an outside left. He made 46 appearances, scoring nine goals before moving to Bolton Wanderers in 1914. He only played two games for Bolton and scored one goal before he signed up.

Wallace enlisted as a Sapper with the 151st Field Company, Royal Engineers, serving in France and Flanders. He was killed on 8th November 1917 and commemorated at the Ploegsteert Memorial, Belgium (Panel 1). William was 24 years old.

John George 'Jack' Yuill was born in 1885 in Hendon, London. After moving with his family to Manchester, he went to school at Manchester Grammar. As an amateur player, he worked for print firm Henry Blacklock & Co and played for Northern Nomads as a winger initially and then Sale Holmfield.

Yuill played at Manchester City as a back-up and reserve player in 1905 and 1908, playing three first-team games scoring one goal. He also made one appearance for Stockport County in 1908. A number of other clubs including Oldham, Wigan, Chester, Wrexham and Port Vale used Jack. He did, however, always return to his favourite club, the Nomads.

He enlisted in September 1914 with the 19th Battalion Manchester Regiment, stationed at

Manchester City, 1914.

Salisbury Plain and ranked as a Lance Corporal. He served in France from November and by December they were in the trenches.

In June 1916, now a Corporal with the regiment, part of the 30th Division, they secured Glatz Redoubt, Montauban. Thereafter, he became Lance Sergeant. On 7th July they supported the attack on Trones Wood and Maltzhorn Farm, France, where they were under constant bombardment for two days. They suffered many casualties, which included Yuill on 9th July 1916, aged 31 years. He is commemorated at the Thiepval Memorial to the Missing, Somme (Pier and Face 13A and 14C).

Manchester United FC, Division One
(League position: 18th)

Hugh Stewart Kerr was born in 1882 in Ayr, Scotland. He initially played for amateur side Westerlea FC before signing for Ayr FC as a forward. He moved to Manchester United in January 1904, but only after an enquiry as Ayr claimed United had made an illegal approach for him. After all this controversy and only playing two first-team games, he was released at the end of the season. Kerr does not appear on any other cub records after this. He worked as a tailor in Plumstead, London, prior to enlisting.

He served with the 14th London Scottish Regiment and fought in France. He was killed on 10th April 1918 and commemorated at the Etaples Military Memorial, Pas de Calais, France (XXXIII.F.4.). Hugh was 36 years old and married to Mary Agnes Kerr.

Harry Levis was born in 1889 in Eccles, Salford, one of eight brothers. A good all-round sportsman and athlete, he was an excellent cricketer who played for Eccles. He was a keen member of Eccles Wesleyan Church and Sunday school. On Manchester United's books in the reserve side, he could not break into the first team. Levis was in the Manchester Territorial Reserve Battalion, then drafted into the main Manchester Regiment in 1915, serving abroad for over two years.

He was killed at the Somme on 14th March 1917, though initially he was just reported as missing. He is commemorated at the Thiepval Memorial (Pier and Face 13A and 14C) and at Peel Cemetery, Salford. Harry was 28 years old.

Oscar Horace Stanley Linkson was born on 16th March 1888 in New Barnet, Hertfordshire. A full back or half back, he began his career at Barnet FC, helping them to win their local league in 1907-08. He signed for Manchester United in 1908 and was a member of their FA Cup-winning squad of 1909 and the First Division Championship in 1910-11. He made 59 appearances before transferring to Shelbourne FC in Ireland in 1913-15, prior to the war, playing 29 games and scoring one goal, winning the Leinster and Gold Cup trophies with them.

Linkson enlisted with the 1ˢᵗ Footballer's Middlesex 'Pals' Regiment. After training, he fought in France. At Guillemont during the Somme offensive, on 8ᵗʰ August 1916 he was reported missing presumed dead. A report read, *'Such was the withering fire and continual bombardment, that it is no surprise that his and many other bodies were never found'.*

He is commemorated at the Thiepval Memorial (Pier and Face 12D and 13 B). He left a wife Olive, who he married in 1912, and two children, Eric and Olive. Oscar was 28 years old.

Stephen Preston was born in Manchester in 1879. Mainly playing as a centre forward, he signed for Newton Heath in 1901, though the club renamed to its current one in 1902 after financial difficulties. In total, he played 33 matches for both, scoring an impressive 34 goals, before transferring to Stockport County.

For the war effort, he enlisted with the 12ᵗʰ Lancashire Fusiliers, thereafter serving in the Mediterranean. He was killed at the Battle of Machukova near the port of Salonica, Greece, on 14ᵗʰ September 1916.

He is commemorated at the Doiran Memorial and left a wife Catherine, who resided in Ancoats, Manchester. Stephen was 42 years old.

James Semple was born in Perth, Scotland, circa 1881. Initially playing amateur football in Scotland, he was a baker by trade. In 1908-09 he was on United's books, playing in the reserve side. He returned to Perth at the end of the season. In 1911, he was trading as a baker in the Liverpool area.

He enlisted for the war in Oldham with the 10ᵗʰ Lancashire Fusiliers, known as the Bury Pals. After training, James served in France, and was killed at the Somme on 7ᵗʰ July 1916, aged 35-36 years. He is commemorated at the Thiepval Memorial (Pier and Face 3C and 3D).

Alexander 'Sandy' Turnbull was born on 30ᵗʰ July 1884 in Hurlford, Scotland. He started his career at local club Hurlford Thistle as an inside forward. He worked for Portland Pit Company before he moved to Manchester City in 1902-05, helping then gain promotion back into the First Division. He played over 110 games for them, scoring 53 goals, during which time they won their first major honour, the FA Cup, in 1904, beating Bolton Wanderers 1-0 at The Crystal Palace.

He was then caught up in a match fixing controversy along with the famous Billy Meredith, which saw the whole team and its manager suspended from playing for the club again.

During 1906 he moved across to Manchester United. In 1907-08 he scored 25 goals in 30 games and was the mainstay in United gaining the First Division title for the first time, immortalising him as a club legend. He gained a second league-winner's medal in 1910-11 and an FA Cup winner's medal in 1908-09. Adding to his legacy, he scored the first-ever goal at Old Trafford when they moved there in 1910.

More controversy was to follow in 1914-15 when he was part of another match rigging scandal in a game against Liverpool and this was the end of his eventful career both on and off the pitch as the war now took priority, overshadowing his recent lifetime ban. He played 245 games for United, scoring 100 goals. (He did, however, guest for Rochdale and Clapton Orient.)

Turnbull enlisted with the 23rd Battalion Middlesex Regiment, fighting in France, but was transferred to the 8th Battalion Surrey Regiment in 1916 due to their heavy losses. By 1917 he was involved in offensives at Arras and in May 1917, and now a Lance Sergeant, the regiment was preparing to take part in the British spring offensive east of Arras, which had begun in April. The 8th East Surreys were to assault the northern approaches to the village of Cherisy as part of a series of attacks, which became known as the Third Battle of the Scarpe.

The attack itself initially provided some success, with the village reportedly falling into British hands during the first hours of the assault. Thereafter, fierce fighting followed and Cherisy itself would soon be back under German control. It remained there until regained by the Canadian Army in August 1918.

It was during the confusion of this early morning fight that Sgt Turnbull went go missing. While it is unclear what happened to

Turnbull, a letter was sent to his wife by a fellow soldier soon after the battle, which was subsequently published by the *Liverpool Echo* on 14th May 1917: *'After Alex had been wounded he carried on and led his men for a mile, playing the game until the last we saw of him. We all loved him, as he was a father to us all, the most popular man in the regiment. All here send our deepest sympathy.'*

There was some initial hope that Turnbull was a prisoner, with early reports suggesting he was in a German field hospital behind enemy lines. Hope soon faded with confirmation that he was missing, presumed killed. He left a widow and five children. In August 1918, Captain Lonergan, who had been wounded and taken prisoner during the attack, wrote to Turnbull's wife, Florence, in an effort to provide further details about the circumstances surrounding her husband's death.

'It was a great shock to me to hear that my best NCO was still missing. Of course, I knew there was no hope of him turning up after such a long period. He was one of the finest fellows I have ever met. A great sportsman and as keen a soldier as he was a footballer. He had been hit through the leg early on in the fight. When I saw him, his leg was very swollen, so I ordered him back to the dressing station. He pleaded so hard, however, to stay on until we had gained our objectives that I gave way. Sandy was in command of a platoon. The men would simply go anywhere with him. Well, the end of it was that, although we gained all our objectives, the division on the left did not. Consequently, the enemy got round our flanks and we had to get back the best we could. We came under very heavy machine-gun fire during the withdrawal. This was when I was hit. As I fell, I saw your husband pass me a few yards away. I saw him get to the village we had taken that morning. There was some shelter here from the bullets so I heaved a sigh of relief when I saw him disappear among the houses. I knew he could get back to our lines with comparative safety from there. I never heard anything more of him. Those who were wounded all thought that Sandy got back. It was a bitter disappointment to me to hear that he had not been heard of. The explanation I can give is that he must have been 'sniped' by a German who was lying low in one of the houses. It was a rotten bit of luck. I would have recommended him from Germany, but I had my doubts whether the German censor would allow it to come through. However, I put his case strongly when I wrote from Holland and I do hope that he will get the highest distinction possible. He certainly deserves it.'

A further report stated: *'There is the story of 'Sandy' Turnbull, the Scottish International professional footballer, who played inside left for the Manchester United team when they became champions of the Football League. Turnbull had become a sergeant in the 8th East Surreys. He was a good soldier, earnest, extremely wide-awake, and a man of good influence. He had gone through towards Cherisy with Captain Lonergan and his company; wounded, but went on. Early in the advance, he spotted some enemy machine guns and turned a Lewis gun on them. He got hit again when trying to rush an enemy gun; then a third bullet smashed his knee and brought him down. He waved his companions forward, shouting instructions from the map he carried. He directed other men who came up, and refused to be taken back. Afterwards he was missed and it was hoped that he had been taken prisoner, with a chance of recovery of his wounds. Nothing has ever been heard of him. He was a gallant man, and met a soldier's end with calm fearlessness.'*

He is commemorated at the Arras Memorial, Faubourg d 'Amiens (Bay 6). He was 32 years old and married to Florence Amy Turnbull. His official death date record is 3rd May 1917. He did not receive any posthumous awards.

Thomas Hornby Wall was born in 1888 in Boldon Colliery, County Durham. He was the younger brother of the famous United player George Wall, who also fought in the war, though he survived and resumed his career.

At the club from 1908-10, he was an outside left, like his brother. He could not break through and played mainly with the reserve side.

Wall enlisted with the 2nd/10th Manchester Battalion and fought in Belgium. He was killed in fierce fighting at Passchendaele on 9th October 1917, aged 29 years. He is commemorated at the Tyne Cot Memorial (Panel 120 to 124). Thomas was married to Dorothy Ann Wall.

Alfred Griffiths was born circa 1877-79 in the Manchester area. Initially, he was a goalkeeper with the Newton Heath side from 1899-1900. He then served in the Boer War during 1901. He went back to the newly renamed United and information shows that although mainly a reserve-squad player, he was still at the club around 1902. (William

Griffiths, his brother, also signed for Newton Heath/Manchester United in 1899-1905; he was a centre half.)

Alfred was enlisted into the 1st Battalion Manchester Regiment for the conflict, serving in Iraq. He was killed on 8th March 1916 at Mesopotamia and is commemorated at the Basra Memorial (Panel 31-64).

Harry Reynolds was born in Blakeley, Manchester, in 1884. A noted athlete, he was on the club's books in 1907-08 and played in the reserves.

He served with the 20th Battalion Manchester Regiment and lost his life on the first day at the Somme on 1st July 1916. He was buried in the Dantzig Alley Cemetery (V.C.6); he was 32 years old.

John Thornley was born in 1886 in Hayfield, Glossop, Derbyshire. He was the younger brother of Irvine Thornley who played for Manchester City and Glossop, and was also capped by England in 1907. (He served as a Gunner with the Royal Artillery.)

John was on the club's books in 1905 appearing in one game in the reserves. He served with the 5th and 10th Cheshire Regiment. He was killed on 31st March 1918 near Boulogne and was buried in the Wimereux Communal Cemetery (IX.B.5). John was 32 years old and married to Lily Thornley.

Supplementary Information:

Robert Pollock Bonthron was born in 1884 in Burntisland, near Dundee, Fife. A right back, he played for a number of clubs including Sunderland, Northampton, Birmingham and Raith Rovers. His main club was Manchester United from 1903-07, where he played 134 games and scored three goals. His last known club is believed to have been Leith Athletic. A 1911 census has him living in Aston, Birmingham.

He enlisted with the Gordon Highlanders in 1915, attached to the Labour Corps as a Lance Corporal. Some sites state, he was killed during the conflict, but there are no records of a death. (His medical card dates state 1915-1920.) He did survive the conflict.

Additionally **Eversley Mansfield** from Barrow-in-Furness was a reserve player with United and made one appearance for Manchester City in 1908. He is stated as a victim of the conflict on some sites.

E. MANSFIELD. Manchester United.

MANCHESTER UNITED FOOTBALL CLUB, 1914-15.
Back row : J. McGough (*Asst. Trainer*), J. W. Mew, Jas. Hodge, W. Wright, L. Moores, A. Allman, E. K. Hudson (*Linesman*).
Second row : H. Dale (*referee*), W. Meredith, T. Gipps, G. Wall, T. Ashworth, G. Anderson, S. Cubberley, r. O. Conner,
G. Stacey, R. Davies (*Trainer*).
Front row : Mr. J. Taylor, J. Norton, G. E. Travers, E. J. West, G. Hunter, A. Potts, A. Woodcock, W. H. Eaves, F. Knowles.
Photo, Chambers, Clayton.

He was a Major in the King's Own Lancaster Regiment and ancestry records show he survived the war. His medical records are available to view until 1921. Prior to enlisting, he resided in the Preston area. He survived the conflict.

Middlesbrough FC, Division One
(League position: 12th)

Henry 'Harry' Cook was born in 1893 in Middlesbrough. A wing half, he began his career locally at South Bank FC before signing for Boro in 1912-15. A teacher at Marton Road and North Ormesby Junior Boys School, he was married with two children.

Cook played over 25 games for the club prior to the outbreak of war. He guested for Brentford in 1915-16 playing 10 games before going overseas.

After enlisting with the 12th Service Battalion Yorkshire Regiment, he served as a Sergeant in France. Wounded at Maurepas, Somme, he died from his wounds on 9th

January 1917 in a field hospital, aged 23 years. He was buried in Grove Town Cemetery, Bray-Sur-Somme (IIL.6). Just prior to his death, Henry was in line for a commission and was due to return home for the respective training.

Andrew Jackson was born in Cambuslang, Lanarkshire, Scotland in 1891. He played for Ardrossan Rovers before signing for Boro from 1909-15 as a centre half.

He played over 137 games and scored three goals and was an ever-present of the defence, eventually becoming club captain. This was one of Boro's best performing league sides ever before the war intervened, with their highest known top-tier finishing position of third in 1913-14.

Jackson enlisted with the Queen's Own 5th Cameron Highlanders, attaining the rank of Sergeant. Whilst stationed in the South he guested for Chelsea before going abroad. He then saw action on the Somme, the Battle of the Lys and then the final advance in West Flanders, Belgium. Badly wounded and removed to the 36th casualty clearing station, he died from his wounds on 30th September 1918.

He was buried in the Haringhe (Bandaghem) Military Cemetery (III.C.55.) to the west of Ypres. Andrew was 27 years old.

Archibald 'Archie' Wilson was born in Newmilns, Scotland, in 1890. A forward, he won a Scottish Inter League cap aged just 17 before moving to the Nottingham area. The following year he signed for Spurs but struggled there, though he did impress in the reserves. In 1911 Southend signed him for £50 and stated it was probably the best money they had ever parted with. Although they lost their place in the league, he was popular with both management and the fans.

He formed a striking partnership with Heneage Wileman, the brother of Arthur Wileman from Luton Town, who was killed in 1918. Southend gained promotion back to the Southern League Division One in 1913, due to their goal scoring. After doing well in the cup with games against Brentford and Birmingham City, he came to the notice of Middlesbrough. The Boro manager was actually watching a Coventry player, though knew about Wilson, and after impressing in the game signed him for £400.

Wilson played 21 games for them scoring four goals in 1914-15, before the war intervened. He made 10 appearances for Spurs during the war period.

Initially working in a munitions factory, he then returned south and joined up with the London Scottish Battalion. After training, he made a return home to see family and friends before he left for France, stating that he had a feeling he may never return. Once abroad he was involved in the infamous Battles at the Somme.

His battalion the 1st/14th were now at trenches east of Hebuterne after moving up from Bayencourt. Their objective was to move defences from the German front line at Gommecourt. After early encounters, the Germans had the situation under control and bombarded the British with heavy shelling and machine gun fire, causing many casualties. The attack was so fierce that reinforcements could not be engaged or get through, the regiment eventually making it to trenches known as Fall, Farmer and Fair near an area known as The Farmyard.

It was 1st July 1916 and amidst the carnage and chaos of the events Wilson was one of the casualties. There were 871 men in his battalion, 616 were casualties with 220 killed. Casualties for this offensive in the Somme area during the next year were even more appalling. On the first day, the British suffered more casualties than their campaigns in the Crimean, Boer and Korean wars put together.

He is commemorated at the Thiepval Memorial (Panel 9.C to13.C). Archie was 25 years old.

Richard 'Dick' Cross Wynn was born in 1892 in Ashton-in Makerfield near Wigan. Initially with Chester FC from 1912-14, joining them from Liverpool amateur side Stirling FC, he signed for Boro in 1914-15. He was a striker, though he was capable of playing as a defender as well. During his time with Chester he played 47 games with 11 goals. He had played seven games and scored one goal for Boro before the war. He guested for Brentford from 1915-18, playing 22 war games.

OUR PORTRAIT GALLERY.

No. 249

W. Duguid S. Davidson. J. Howarth. A. Jackson. R. G. Williamson. J. Walker. G. Malcolm. F. Eyre

J. Stirling. J. Carr. W. Tinsley. J. Windridge. J. Cook.

MIDDLESBROUGH F.C.

He enlisted with the Yorkshire Regiment and worked with the Labour Corps as a Sergeant, then Acting Company Colour Sergeant Major.

Wynn was still in France after the end of the war. Unfortunately, he died near Boulogne on 9th August 1919 following an operation on wounds, aged 27 years.

He was buried in the Etaples Military Cemetery, France (LXXII.F.28). Richard was married to Mary Maud Wynn.

Millwall Athletic FC, Southern League Division One

(League position: eighth)

Charles Green was born around 1888 in the Deptford area of London. Occupied as a Carman and believed to be with Millwall, he was used as a reserve with the club in about 1915-16 as a full back.

He enlisted with the 2nd Battalion Royal Fusiliers serving in Belgium and was killed

MILLWALL FOOTBALL CLUB, 1913-14.

W. Barber

J. Kirkwood. P. Warren. H. Taylor. A. Pratt. W. Woodley. R. Jones. A. Gillies.
W. Dickinson (Director) R. Hunter (Trainer) F. G. Weedon (Director) W. Voisey, J. Hawkins. A. Garrett, A. Taylor, E. Moor (Groundsman)
J. B. Skeggs (Director) H. B. Lipsham (Manager)
G. A. Saunders (Director) W. Sullivan. H. Butterworth, J. Borthwick, J. Jeffrey. J. Wilson. S. Wayment. R. Liddell. J. Beveridge (Sec.)
G. Dodd. R, Dilley. R. Noble, W. Davis. H. Moody, F. Vincent, S. Lamb, G. Porter. T. Thorne (Director)

on 1st November 1917 in the Ypres area. He was buried in the Minty Farm Cemetery (II.B.6.). Charles was 29 years old and married to Eleanor.

George King was born in Dunblane, Scotland, in 1870. He began his football career with Sunderland Albion before signing for Burnley in 1892-94 as a wing half, making 33 appearances and scoring two goals. He then transferred to Millwall Athletic in 1894 where he played out the best part of his career. He was at the club until after 1898 with in excess of 74 appearances.

He enlisted with the 20th Tyneside Irish and Northumberland Fusiliers for the conflict. He was living in Sunderland with his wife Jane at this time.

He was killed in action on 1st July 1916 at the Somme and is commemorated at the Thiepval Memorial (Pier and Face 10B 11B and 12 B). George was 46 years old.

(Note: Regarding the plaque pictured from the Millwall FC Memorial: see the following club for players named thereon: Dines, Liverpool. Porter, Norwich City. Williams, Crystal Palace.)

Newcastle United FC, Division One

(League position: 15th)

Thomas 'Tom' Cairns was born in 1896 in the Chopwell area of Tyne and Wear. He played as an inside forward for Chopwell Villa then Newcastle City. He was on Newcastle's books in 1914-15 after earning praise from the Northern Combination League, playing his only game for the first team in  the final match of the season in a 3-0 defeat of Aston Villa, before suspension of the league.

He was one of the first to enlist, joining the Royal Field Artillery, Trench Mortar Battery, attaining the rank of Corporal. He was killed at Arras in fighting during the Cambria offensive on 13th October 1917. Tom was aged 22 years and has no known grave. He is commemorated at the Arras Memorial (Bay 1).

Dan Dunglinson was born in 1890 in Hexham, Northumberland. He worked for the Northern Railways in the Audit office. A talented amateur full back, he initially played for Brighton West End winning the Northern League in 1909-10. He then played for Blyth Spartans and was club captain, helping them to win the Aged Miners Cup in 1911-12.

On Newcastle's books, though still an amateur he was used in the reserves. In 1914 he was captain of the Northern team in an international trial match played at Oxford. He was also in the amateur international squad that played Germany in Berlin.

In 1914 he joined the Commercial Battalion, Northumberland Fusiliers, with his brothers Victor and William. He continued his football in service and was captain of the 16th Battalion football team, with a notable 3-0 victory over Bath City. Dan and his brother William were then moved to the 4th Platoon 'A' Company. Dan was now a Corporal. By the first day of the Somme offensive on 1st July 1916, Dan was with 1st Platoon. Reports say he was one of the first over the top and killed almost straight away.

Dunglinson left everything to his father in his will, who had also worked for Northern Railways. Dan's brother William also died from wounds in France on 21st August 1918, aged 33 years. his other brother Victor, although wounded, survived.

He is commemorated at the Thiepval Memorial (Pier and Face 10B.11B.12B) and the York Railway Memorial; he was 26 years old. (On 27th June 2015 in Authuile, Ancre Valley, where many Northumberland Fusiliers fell, a plaque was unveiled in honour of the battalions, as well as a bench next to the church. A box gifted to the Mayor of the town opened every Remembrance Day contains sporting memorabilia for the 16th Battalion and football shirts. One of the shirts bears the name of Dunglinson. The family headstone is in St Johns Church, Westgate and Elswick, Newcastle.)

Thomas 'Tommy' Goodwill was born in 1894 at Bates Cottages, Seaton Delaval, Northumberland. A coal miner playing for his local side until 1913, he was then signed by Newcastle as an outside left, and until 1915 he was a regular in the side, described as lethal with the ball at his feet and a big crowd favourite. He played over 52 games and scored four goals before the war.

After enlisting with the Northumberland Fusiliers and training, he served in France. He was killed on the first day of the Somme on 1st July 1916 along with two of his Newcastle teammates Hughes and Dunglinson. He is commemorated at the Thiepval Memorial (Pier and Face 10B.11B.12B). Thomas was 22 years old.

Nicholas Higgins was born in 1880 in Pendleton, Salford. He was on Newcastle books in 1911-12 and is in the squad photograph of the same season, though he was a reserve-team player. He did not break into the first team, but Newcastle had won the league title in 1905, 1907 and 1909 also winning the FA Cup in 1910, making opportunities difficult.

Higgins worked for Salford Corporation in the electricity department before signing up. He enlisted with the 7th Kings Royal Rifle Corps, serving in Flanders. He was killed in action on 8th December 1915 and commemorated at the La Brique Military Cemetery, Ypres (I.E.21. Cemetery 2). Nicholas was 35 years old.

Thomas 'Tom' Hughes was born in 1893 in South Hetton, Durham. He played for the local side before signing for Newcastle in 1912 as an inside left, making two appearances before 1914.

He enlisted with the 27[tte] Northumberland Fusiliers, 4th Tyneside Irish serving in France and Flanders. Thomas was killed in action on the first day of the Somme on 1st July 1916. He is commemorated at the Thiepval Memorial (Pier and Face 10B.11B.12B). Thomas was 22 years old.

Richard McGough was born in 1892 in Carlisle, Cumbria. He was initially with Carlisle FC then at Newcastle in 1914 as a centre half, making two appearances. He was also linked with Portsmouth FC prior to enlisting.

He enlisted as a Bombardier with the Royal Garrison Artillery, 102nd Siege Battery, stationed in France. McGough died of wounds at the 51st Field Ambulance Station on 18th April 1917. He was buried in the Feuchy British Cemetery, Nord, Pas de Calais (I.A.11) and commemorated at Our Lady and St Joseph's Church, Memorial, Carlisle. Richard was

NEWCASTLE UNITED A FC
1913 – 1914.

24 years old. (The Memorial was funded and erected by his family in 1921.)

George Stephenson Rivers was born in 1890 in Tudhoe, Durham. He lived in Thornley with his parents. A school teacher by trade in Birtley, he also played football for the local team. He was signed by Newcastle in 1914 for £50 as an outside left for the reserves, although he was rated as a good future prospect for the first team.

In memory of
George Stephenson Rivers
who died on Sunday, 13th August 1916

However, the war was to intervene and he joined the forces, enlisting with the Durham Light Infantry. He was then involved in fighting at the Somme, losing his life on 13th August 1916, He was buried in the Englebelmer Communal Cemetery, France (I.C.3). George was 26 years old.

Northampton Town FC, Southern League Division One
(League position: fifth)

Edward John 'Fred' Didymus was born on 13th April 1885 in Portsmouth, one of four children. He was a centre forward initially at Portsmouth and known in some circles as Fred. He was listed at Huddersfield Town in 1908 before a move to Northampton in the same 1907-08 season, where he played nine games and scored two goals. Blackpool signed him in 1909 where he played three games. Other clubs recorded for him are Plymouth and Port Vale after 1910. He later returned to his home town and his occupation was recorded as a tram driver.

Didymus enlisted with the 8th Battalion Middlesex Regiment, serving in France. He was killed on 12th April 1918, the day before his birthday, and he was buried in the Tilloy British Cemetery, Tilloy-Les-Mofflaines (I.AA.12). Edward was 32 years old, married to Mary Ellen and had two children. He is also remembered on the Portsmouth Corporation Transport Memorial Plaque.

George Fredrick 'Fred' Lessons was born on 30th August 1883 in Stockport and was brought up in an orphanage with his sister, as their parents had died from tuberculosis.

Living in the Nottingham area, he initially played for amateur side Nottingham Jardines Athletic. Nottingham Forest signed him 1904-07 as a centre forward, describing him as of great strength and stature. He played over 31 games for them and scored eight goals. He was part of the squad that toured Argentina in 1905, scoring four goals in one game in a 13-1 drubbing of local side Britanicos.

The famous Herbert Chapman then obtained his signature in 1907 for Northampton Town, serving them well until 1915, making over 249 appearances and scoring 79 goals. Lessons then went on to become player-manager, though his playing role was then at centre half due to injuries limiting his physical capabilities, then he became manager until 1918.

He enlisted with the Northamptonshire Regiment, serving as a Lance Corporal in France. Killed in Northern France on 7th September 1918, he died two months before Armistice. He was buried in the Eterpigny British Cemetery, Pas-de-Calais (A.I). Fred was 35 years old, married to Ethel Lessons and had one daughter. *The Times* reported his passing on 23rd September, confirming that one of his former colleagues at Nottingham Forest had witnessed his death.

Harold Arthur Redhead was from Northampton and was born in 1891. He was on Northampton's books from 1910-13 as an inside forward and is listed as playing in three games.

He served with the Northamptonshire Regiment as a 2nd Lieutenant and then as Captain in France. He was killed in action during an offensive in the Somme area on 7th August 1918, and is commemorated at the Dive Copse British Cemetery, Sailly-Le-Sac, Somme. (III.A.16). Harold was 27 years old.

Harold Thomas 'Harry' Springthorpe was born on 28th April 1886 in Stamford, Rutlandshire. He played amateur football initially for Stamford Town and Wolverton before signing for Northampton in 1904-08 as an inside forward, making 53 appearances and scoring 12 goals. Between 1908 and 1912 he had two spells at Grimsby Town, playing 25 games and scoring six goals, with a brief spell at Grimsby Rangers in between. In 1910 he represented England at amateur international level with a 6-0 defeat of Wales, scoring the opening goal.

He served with the Lincolnshire Yeomanry as a Lance Corporal and was killed at sea on 3rd November 1915 when a U-Boat torpedoed SS *Mercian* during the assault on Gallipoli. He is commemorated at the Helles Memorial (Panel 331) and the Stamford School Memorial; he was 29 years old.

Walter Daniel John Tull was born on 28the April 1888 in Folkestone, Kent, one of five children. His father was a carpenter from Barbados who married a local English girl named Alice. Both his mother and father died and from the age of nine he resided in a Methodist Children's Home in Bethnal Green, London, with his brother Edward. The Warnock family from Glasgow adopted Edward, leaving Walter alone in London.

He began his career at Clapton FC in 1908, one of the top amateur sides in the country. They won the London County and Senior Cups as well as the FA Amateur Cup, before he signed for Tottenham in 1909-11. He was the fourth recorded player of mixed heritage to play in top-tier football after Andrew Watson of Queens Park and Scotland, Arthur Wharton notably of Preston NE, Sheffield United and Stockport County and Billy Clarke of Aston Villa and Bradford City. An athletically built half back or inside forward, Tull made 10 appearances for Spurs scoring two goals. He suffered some racial abuse but did not rise to it and overcame that through his talent on the field. A news report stated, *'He was the brainiest and most talented player they had'*. He also toured South

America with the club. Nevertheless, the management and directors left him in the reserves, as they were not willing or brave enough to put the difference of ethnicity aside. This obviously affected his number of appearances in the first eleven.

In 1911 he transferred to Northampton Town where he became a stalwart of the first team, an instant hit with the fans. He played over 110 games for the club scoring nine goals up to 1914 before enlisting for the forces.

Tull joined the 17th Service First Footballers' Battalion and against the odds became the first commissioned black officer in the British Army as a 2nd Lieutenant, being highly respected by fellow officers and his men. This was against the norm, principles and regulations of the armed forces, with racism again rearing its ugly head. He also served with the 5th Reserve and 23rd Footballers' Battalion.

He was initially sent to France in 1914, although after attaining the rank of Sergeant he had to return home with shellshock (PTSD). After recuperating, he was back in France and involved in heavy fighting during the Somme offensives. There was then another spell in hospital with trench fever before travelling to Glasgow for officer training after his promotion in 1917. Whilst on this initial training in Glasgow he reconciled with his brother, a respected dentist, and spent a considerable amount of time with him and his family, who grew to adore Walter. He signed forms for Glasgow Rangers, as his brother Edward was friends with the Rangers chairman and had recommended Walter to him. He was supposed to have played for them after the war.

In August 1917 he was with the 23rd Battalion in Belgium, involved in the third Battle of Ypres before serving in Italy. It was here he led 26 men in a trench raid on 1st January 1918. He was mentioned in dispatches for '*showing gallantry and coolness*', although a recommendation for the Military Cross was not granted. In March 1918 he was back in France with the 23rd for offensives at Beugny, to counteract the German spring offensive. On 25th March 1918 they came under intense fire west of the Arras-Bapaume road. Walter lost his life here, felled by heavy machine gun fire attempting to rally his men. The ferocious assault continued and they could not retrieve him, as they had to withdraw. It showed the respect his men had for him as they risked their own lives trying to recover his body.

He is commemorated at the Arras Memorial to the Missing, Faubourg d'Amiens Cemetery (Bay 7). Walter was 29 years old. (There have been calls as recently as 2016 for Walter to be posthumously awarded the Military Cross (Not granted to date).) Walter Tull led his life with great dignity, standing as a testament to his ability to overcome the boundaries of ignorance in a time of inequality. The reward for his bravery is long overdue.

Arthur Harrison Allard Vann was born on 1st May 1884 in Bugbrooke, Northamptonshire. He was the elder brother of Bernard Vann V.C. and a student entry into Chichele College at Higham Ferrers, Northamptonshire, then aged 25 years in 1909 he went to Jesus College, Cambridge. His brother had been there since 1907.

He made an immediate impression as an all-round sportsman, excelling at hockey, sculling, cricket and football. He had a peculiar speech impediment for which he was nicknamed 'Baby'. Known for his academic abilities, undergraduates would often seek his advice prior to his departure in 1913. Vann was also an excellent bridge player; he apparently never lost a game.

Regarding his football, he had spent time at Burton FC before signing for Northampton in 1905-07 as an outside forward, playing 17 games and scoring two goals. He was also on Derby County's books.

He enlisted with the 1st/28th London Own Regiment, then the Prince of Wales Own West Yorkshire Regiment attaining the rank of Captain. He served in France and Flanders and was involved in the Battle of Loos. He was killed in action on 25th September 1915. Arthur was one of a number of men shelled, gassed and listed as missing in action. He is commemorated at the Loos Memorial (Panel 39 and 40); he was 31 years old.

Bernard William Vann V.C. M.C. and Bar, Croix de Guerre, was born on 9th July 1887 in Rushden, Northamptonshire. He was one of five boys to parents who were both teachers. His father died in 1906, so his mother went to live with her unmarried brother Reverend Thomas Simpson at Coates Rectory, Gloucestershire. Bernard lived here with them and was very fond of Simpson.

He followed his father into teaching in Ashby de la Zouch, Leicestershire, and was highly popular with his students. It was during his time here that he ventured into football, as an amateur footballer with Hugglecote United and Irthlingborough.

In 1905-06 he was on Northampton Town's books with his brother Arthur, making eight appearances and scoring five goals as a powerful centre forward. He played for Burton United in 1906, playing four games and scoring one goal, and Derby County in 1907, playing three games. He was on Leicester Fosse's books in 1907-08, but decided to go to Jesus College, Cambridge, at this time to further his academic career after 1909.

Described as '*a good student, but not the cleverest*', he excelled at oratory speechmaking. He was President of 'The Farragoes' debating society and founder President of the 'Roosters Society'. His sporting prowess also caught the eye, and he was captain of the football team, described as '*dashing…possessing both pace and weight…a good shot with either foot, he is always very dangerous in front of goal*'. He was most successful though on the hockey pitch, earning a blue in 1910 for the university.

Vann then decided to follow in his uncle's footsteps and was ordained in 1910 as Curate of St Barnabas New Humberstone, Leicestershire, then assistant master and Chaplin at Wellingborough School in 1912, teaching history and theology.

In 1914 he enlisted as a Private in the 28th Battalion London Regiment (Artist Rifles), though he had initially volunteered as a Chaplin. On 1st September 1914 he gained a commission as 2nd Lieutenant in the 1st/8th Sherwood Foresters. By February 1915 he was in France.

He took part in heavy fighting at Kemmel, during which he organised a defence rescue of a number of wounded men. He was promoted thereafter to the rank of Lieutenant on 26th April 1915 and then temporary Captain in June. Soon after this, he was awarded the Military Cross. The *London Gazette* reported the citation on 15th September 1915:

'*At Kemmel on 24 April 1915, when a small advance trench which he occupied was blown in, and he himself wounded and half buried, he showed the greatest determination in organising the defence and rescuing buried men under heavy fire, although wounded and severely bruised he refused to leave his post until directly ordered to do so. At Ypres on 31 July 1915, and subsequent days, he ably assisted another officer to*  hold the left trench of the line, setting a fine example to those around him. On various occasions, he has led patrols up to the enemy's trenches and obtained valuable information.'

Vann would then take part in the Battle of Loos, during which his brother Arthur lost his life. He himself received an injury to the left arm during fighting at the area known as Hollenzollern Redoubt on 15th October 1915. After treatment he returned to his unit in France with promotion to the rank of Captain on 1st June 1916. In September he was awarded a bar to his M.C., followed by the French Croix de Guerre five months later. In September 1917 Vann assumed command of the 1st/6th Sherwood Foresters as Acting Lieutenant Colonel. By 29th September 1918 he was with his Regiment near the St Quentin Canal, leading an attack under fire against an enemy machine gun position and then single-handedly rushing a German field gun.

Vann lost his life on 3rd October 1918 near Ramicourt when a sniper shot him. His actions four days earlier led to the award of the Victoria Cross. The *London Gazette* published the following citation on 14*th* December 1918. (Medals pictured.)

For most conspicuous bravery, devotion to Duty and fine leadership during the attack at Bellenglise and Lehaucourt on 29 September 1918. He led with great skill across the Canal du Nord through a very thick fog and heavy fire from field and machine guns. On reaching the high ground above Bellenglise, the whole attack held up by fire of all descriptions from the front and right flank. Realising that everything depended on the advance going forward with the barrage, Lt. Col. Vann rushed up to the firing line, and with the greatest gallantry led the line forward. By his prompt action and contempt for danger the whole situation was changed, the men were encouraged and the line swept forward. Later he rushed a field gun single handed, and knocked

NORTHAMPTON TOWN FOOTBALL CLUB.
SEASON 1912-1913.

out three of the detachment. The success of the day was in no small degree due to the splendid gallantry and fine leadership displayed by this officer.'

Prior to his death, he was wounded five times and mentioned in despatches twice. The Reverend Bernard William Vann rests in Bellicourt British Cemetery, Aisne (II.O.1). Bernard was 31 years old and married to a Canadian, Doris Victoria Vann, nee Beck. She was a nurse, and they had married during a period of home leave in December 1916. She gave birth to their son Geoffrey on 2nd June 1919.

A colleague wrote in *The Times* following his death: *'I can think of him only as a fighter, not merely against the enemy in the field, but a fighter against everything and everybody that was not an influence for good to his men. His many friends will rejoice that the constant gallantry and magnificent example of this fine Christian gentleman has been recognised by the highest award the country can bestow.'*

(Vann's Victoria Cross is part of the Lord Ashcroft private collection and currently on display in the Imperial War Museum.)

Norwich City FC, Southern League Division One
(League position: 13th)

Ernest Edgar Ellis was born on 30th November 1885 in Sprowston, Norfolk. He was one of seven children, his father being a renowned bootmaker into which trade Ernest followed as a boot operator.

PRIVATE ERNEST ELLIS.

Described as a big powerful full back, he played the game with complete fairness and honesty. Signed by Norwich in 1907, he made 85 appearances for them. He then moved on to Doncaster Rovers and by 1910 he was at Barnsley. By 1912 he was at Hartlepool United, playing over 74 games for them before moving to Hearts in 1914.

The war then seemed to take precedence, as he did not play any league games for Hearts, though he did go on their successful summer tour of Denmark in 1914. He later enlisted with the 16th Royal Scots and was part of the renowned McCrae's Battalion and the Hearts team that signed en-masse for the war effort. He was killed in action on the first day of the Battle of the Somme on 1st July 1916, dying alongside his Hearts colleges Currie and Wattie. Unfortunately, his grave was lost during further territorial fighting.

Ernest was married to Isobel; she gave birth to his daughter after he went to France. He is commemorated at the Thiepval Memorial (Pier and Face 6D and 7D). He was 30 years old.

George Oscar Porter was born in 1892 in Peckham, London, and is listed as the son of a Mr M.A. Witham. He was an outside right at Norwich City in 1908-09, playing nine games, though he was possibly on the books as an amateur as well. He moved from here to Luton Town in 1909-10, with only one listed game and one goal, in an away match at Southampton. It is not until 1913-15 that he is mentioned playing at Millwall FC, where he made two appearances.

George enlisted with the Duke of Cambridge Middlesex Regiment 16th and 18th Battalions, stationed in France as a Lance Corporal. He

died from wounds on 14th July 1918, and is buried in the Esquelbecq Military Cemetery, Nord France (III.C.31). He was 26 years old. He is also listed on the Lewisham War Memorial.

Robert McIntyre was listed as an outside left and is mentioned as playing one game for Norwich City in the 1904-05 season against Yarmouth Town in a 1-1 draw. He does not appear in other football records. Further information states he may have died in the war, but we cannot find any records due to insufficient personal career information about him to check against war deaths.

Notts County FC, Division One
(League position: 16th)

Arthur Clamp was born on 1st May 1884 in Sneinton, Nottingham, one of four children. A bricklayer by trade, he was a centre half described as having great stamina and strength. Signed by County in 1906, he was a regular at the club until 1914-15 before the war. A great servant, he made 289 appearances, scoring three goals.

Retired from top-flight football, he enlisted in April 1918 and was with the Sherwood Foresters

Notts County, 1914-15.

and then the 7th Queen's Royal West Surrey Regiment. After training he served in France, though within weeks he was seriously wounded and repatriated back home. He died on 19th September 1918 and was buried in St Paul's Church Cemetery, Nottingham (Ref 9887), with full military honours. Arthur was 34 years old and married to a local girl Annie Clamp.

Nottingham Forest FC Division Two
(League position: 18th)

Nottingham Forest FC, 1914.

George Alfred Hazard was born in 1892 in Radford, Nottingham. He was spotted playing for local side St Paul's Vicarage and signed up by Forest but he was used mainly as a reserve-team player.

He enlisted with the Special Reserve on 31st August 1911 and was mobilised on 6th August 1914 into the 2nd/4th Battalion Sherwood Foresters, Nottingham and Derby Regiment, serving in France.

He was killed in action on 28th February 1915 near Nord and buried in the Houplines Communal Cemetery Extension, Nord (III.B.26). George was 23 years old.

Oldham Athletic FC, Division One
(League runners-up)

Frank Hesham: see Croydon Common.
Sandy McAllister: see Sunderland.

Oldham Athletic, 1914-15.

Plymouth Argyle FC,
Southern League Division One

(League position: 17th)

William James Baker M.M. was born in Plymouth in 1882. A wing half, he initially played local football for Green Waves FC, also representing Devon and Cornwall in their county side before moving to America to continue his football. He then moved to South Africa playing for the De Beers club. After returning to Devon to re-join Green Waves, he signed for Plymouth in 1909, making over 202 appearances and scoring one goal. He is described as '*a player of great spirit and energy*'.

Baker played until 1915 before enlisting with the 17th Battalion Middlesex Regiment and again made his mark with army football teams. Ranked as a Sergeant, he was stationed in France, and later awarded the Military Medal. He was killed at Serre during the Battle of the Somme on 22nd October 1916. He is commemorated at the Sucrerie Military Cemetery, Colincamps, Northern France (I.I.26). He was 34 years old and married to Olive Blanche Baker.

His brother **Alfred Stanley Baker** was born on 22nd August 1884 and was a reserve player with the club. He enlisted with the Royal Navy and was a Petty Officer on HMS *Tornado*. He was killed on 23rd December 1917 when the ship hit a mine near 'The Mass' light buoy in the North Sea, off the coast of Holland. Ironically, it was on its way to assist others in trouble. He is commemorated at Tyne Cot Memorial and the Plymouth Navy Memorial (Panel 22). He was 33 years old and married to Rosina Ann.

Stanley Oscar Reed was born on 23rd January 1895 in Torquay, Devon. He played for Torquay Town, helping them win the Devon Senior Cup, and caught the eye of Argyle as a speedy left-winger. He made three appearances for them in 1913 before playing for Merthyr Town.

It was as a cricketer though that he made a real impact, playing for Torquay and the Devon County side. He came from a humble background

so making his way into the side was in itself a feat, as it was somewhat of an elitist sport at this time. He was a talented batsman and played 18 times for the County, and he is recorded as the youngest player to hit a century in April 1913, the record standing until 2010. He had a batting average of 40.88 for the County.

Reed enlisted on the first day of the war, serving with the 11th Devonshire Regiment, quickly impressing and appointed as a Lance Corporal.

On 25th April 1916, the day after he was awarded his stripe, he was involved in training at a camp in Dorset when a grenade he was given exploded in his hand as he was about to throw it, causing severe head injuries, and he died almost instantly. A tragedy that affected the whole community, his funeral was held in Torquay with full military honours, with most of the town in attendance. His colleagues transported the coffin to the railway station from Wareham Barracks on a gun carriage with a guard of honour, prior to transportation to Torquay. He was buried in Torquay Cemetery. Stanley was 21 years old.

Plymouth Argyle Football Club - Southern League Champions, 1912-13

(back row): J. Kirkpatrick, J. Butler, W. Horne, S. Atterbury, W. Dixon.

(2nd row): J. Bell, H. Raymond, F. Burch, H. Wilcox, W. Baker, B. Bowler, T. Haynes.

(3rd row): B. S. Barrett, L. Crabb (above), E. Harvey, A. Rogers, W. Sage, J. McCormick, A. Ham, A. Manico, E. Kelland, R. Jack.

(front row): W. Olden, S. Quigley, J. D. Spooner, S. Spooner, A. Gard, B. Edmonds, A.J. Maunder.

Portsmouth FC, Southern League Division One

(League position: seventh)

William 'Bill' 'Sunny' Kirby was born on 21st January 1882 in Preston, Lancashire. An inside left, his first club was Emmanuel Rovers, but he was spotted and signed by Preston North End in November 1900, though they were not impressed with him at this stage. He then went out on loan to Oswaldtwistle Rovers. Preston North End retained his registration between 1901 and 1911, therefore making his time with four Southern League clubs during these periods loan spells.

PROMINENT FOOTBALLERS.

W. KIRBY,
PORTSMOUTH.

In 1902 he signed for Swindon Town where he played 33 games, scoring 11 goals. The next club to sign him was West Ham United, where he scored on his debut and once again proved to be a useful asset, scoring 11 goals in 36 appearances. However, at the end of the 1903-04 season he returned to Swindon Town, scoring four goals in 21 games.

In 1905 he made his best career move, heading to the south coast and signing for Portsmouth, where he finally managed a settled period in his life as a footballer. He was a regular for Pompey for seven seasons, where he was a first-choice pick and scored 107 goals in 277 appearances. His best campaign was 1906-07, when he hit 28 goals to be the club's top scorer in that campaign. Kirby received a benefit of £220.00 in October 1910 after reaching 100 goals for Portsmouth. He had scored five hat-tricks and 14 braces for them.

In 1911 Preston North End decided to recall him, hoping to reignite his career with them. Over two seasons he scored 22 goals in 56 appearances for the North End side. (He was top scorer in the 1911-12 season, winning the Division Two championship.) He was on the move again in 1913, this time to Devon, signing for Exeter City where he played five games but it was the only club he never scored for. His final club before the conflict was Merthyr Town, playing 29 games and scoring six goals.

Kirby enlisted with the Royal Engineers, but due to injury he was invalided out. Woolwich Arsenal engaged his services, though he

reportedly never enjoyed his work for them. He did, however, continue playing football, appearing for both Croydon Common and Brentford. In 1917 he was allowed to re-enlist with his old regiment, but he died on 3rd October 1917 during fighting near Ypres, Belgium, aged 35 years. William was serving as a Private with the 6th Battalion of the Royal Engineers, attached to the East Yorkshire Regiment. He was buried in the Bard Cottage Cemetery (I.V.I.46). He was married with five children, all under the age of 11 years.

Preston North End FC, Division Two
(League runners-up)

John Ford was born in 1893 in Wishaw, Lanarkshire, Scotland, one of eight children. He began his career at Bellshill Athletic as a right-winger. Signed by Preston North End in 1913-15 and well thought of, he played 43 games and scored four goals, as they finished runners-up in the league. He was highly though of with much potential.

Ford enlisted in Scotland with the Cameronian Scottish Rifles 9th Service Battalion and was living with his parents at the time of joining in Wishaw.

After training, he served in France and was killed in action near Pas de Calais on 3rd May 1917. He is commemorated at the Arras Memorial (Bay 6). John was 24 years old. A memorial to the men from Wishaw who fell in the two wars 1914-18 and 1939-1945 was erected in the town in 1986; it does not contain individual names.

Thomas Pemberton Saul was born in 1889 in Preston, one of four brothers. He worked at Lancashire County Hall and played for Fleetwood, who won the Lancashire Junior Cup in 1913 but he was by then on Preston's books. He did not break into the first team, playing for the reserves.

In November 1914 he enlisted in the 20th Battalion King's Liverpool Regiment with his brother Frank; another brother, Harold, later joined him. (Frank and Thomas are pictured.) After training, they served in France, seeing action at the Somme. On 30th July 1916 Thomas and Frank were involved in fighting at Guillemont. He was seriously wounded in the neck, and his brother pulled him into a shell hole and then took him to a field hospital at 10 Rouen. The medical record states he was comfortable. His wife Amy, who was a nurse, and his father managed to get permission to go to France.

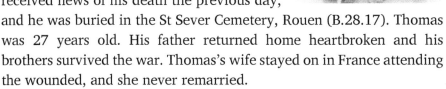

On Thursday 10th August 1916 they received news of his death the previous day, and he was buried in the St Sever Cemetery, Rouen (B.28.17). Thomas was 27 years old. His father returned home heartbroken and his brothers survived the war. Thomas's wife stayed on in France attending the wounded, and she never remarried.

Frank Shanley was born in 1889 in the Brierfield area of Nelson, Lancashire, one of four brothers. He played as a goalkeeper and his main club was Nelson FC, though he made one appearance for Preston on 13th December 1913. He was also renowned as a fine pianist.

Shanley enlisted with the 9th Gordon Highlanders, serving in France and Belgium. Frank died of wounds

Unnamed Preston North End FC team 1914-15.

received in action near Poperinge, Belgium, on the 4th July 1917 and was buried in the Lijssenthoek Military Cemetery (XV.C.11A). He was 28 years old.

Note: P.N.E. records mention a reserve player Michael Swarbrick as killed in the war. No other personal information is known and there is no trace on the C.W.G.C. site.

Queens Park Rangers FC, Southern League Division One
(League position: 12th)

Frank Cannon was born on 8th November 1885 in Hitchin, Hertfordshire. He worked for leading solicitors Shillitoe's in the town. He played football for Hitchin in 1903-06 as an inside forward and was capped for the district County. He was with Hitchin when they defeated Chelsea in 1905-06, before he moved to

Rangers in 1907. He was described as a dashing player, good dribbler and possessing a good shot.

He played 29 games and scored 10 goals, helping them win the league in 1907-08. He also played in the very first Charity Shield at Stamford Bridge in 1908 against Manchester United, scoring the equaliser after Billy Meredith had scored for United. They lost the replay 4-0.

He moved to West Ham in 1909, playing three games and scoring one goal before a brief spell at New Brompton in 1910. He then finished his career at Port Vale from 1911-13, playing 48 games and scoring 17 goals, top scoring in 1911-12. He helped them to win the Staffordshire and Birmingham Senior Cups in 1912 and 1913 respectively.

Cannon enlisted in 1914 with the Bedfordshire Regiment before transferring to the 11th Essex Regiment, attaining the rank of Sergeant Major. After training he served in Belgium. He was killed whilst involved in fighting at Ypres on 15th February 1916. The report stated, *'He was just about to leave the trench when several shells exploded above him and others, shrapnel wounding him in the back. It was thought he was going to be alright, but unfortunately he died on his way to the dressing station about an hour later.'*

He was buried in the Potijze burial ground (H.10), Ypres, and his headstone reads, *'Always Remembered by those at Home'.* Frank was 30 years old and left a wife Violet and three children. His name is also on memorials in Hitchin and Pirton.

Robert McLaren Law was born on 15th June 1891 in Glasgow, Scotland. He was listed with Queens Park Rangers in 1910-11 as an outside right, though he is only credited with one first-team game.

> Private R. M'L. Law, 4th Camerons, has died from wounds. In civil life he was employed with the British Legal Insurance Company, and was transferred to London about six years ago. He joined the Army in London. Private Law, who was only 24 years of age, was a well-known member of Bellahouston Harriers, and while in London played football for Queen's Park Rangers. His father resides at 19 Allison Street, Glasgow.

Robert enlisted with the Queen's Own Cameron Highlanders, 1st/4th Battalion, and was killed in action near Pas-de Calais at the Battle of Festubert on 18th May 1915, aged 24 years. He is commemorated at the Le Touret Memorial, France (Panel 41 and 42).

Henry John Pennifer was born in 1894 in Staffordshire. He joined Rangers in 1913-14 and was listed as a centre forward, playing three

games. His total for the club was nine appearances, the others coming in 1916-17 during the conflict, and one goal.

He enlisted with the Middlesex Regiment and was a Lance Corporal. He was involved in a number of battles on the Somme and was killed in action on 24th March 1918 at Pozieres. He is commemorated at the Pozieres Memorial, Ovillers-la-Boisselle, France (Panel 60 and 61). Henry was 24 years old.

Albert Victor Rogers was born in 1886 in Birmingham and listed with a number of clubs up to 1912. Initially with Aston Waverley, he then signed for Aston Villa in 1907, then again in 1909, though played mainly as a reserve player. He had signed for Rangers in 1907 as an inside right, making 37 appearances and scoring 10 goals up to the end of 1909. He then moved on to Bristol Rovers with 28 games from 1910-11.

He returned to the Midlands when he signed for Villa the second time then Walsall, before ending up at Shrewsbury Town in 1912. He then seemingly drifted out of football.

Rogers enlisted initially with the Middlesex Regiment in Aldershot and then transferred to the East Surrey Regiment. He was killed in action on 4th April 1918 in the Somme area. He is commemorated at

the Crucifix Corner Cemetery; Albert was 31-32 years old (IX.C.1).

Harold Victor Thornton was born in 1890 in the Leytonstone area of London. An inside forward, he joined the club 1911 until 1913 from Shepherds Bush FC. He made 35 appearances, scoring 10 goals.

After 1914 he initially enlisted with the Essex Regiment, Army Cycle Corps, before transferring to the Royal Air Force 28th then 34th Squadron, attaining the rank of Lieutenant as an air observer.

The report states he was 'killed in action on a flying mission on the 10/5/1918 over Italy, in Austrian held territory with his Canadian flying companion and pilot, Lieutenant John Blair Guthrie'.

He is commemorated at the Tezze British Cemetery, Italy (Plot 5. Row B. Grave 17.). Harold was 28 years old and married to Lillian Maud Margaret Thornton.

Albert Edwards see Newport County FC.

Reading FC, Southern League Division One
(League runners-up)

Albert Victor 'Ben' Butler was born in 1887 in Reading. He was known as a tough-tackling centre half or half back and began his career at Arsenal, although not in the first team. He was signed by Reading in 1908 until 1911, playing 24 first-team games and helping them to the Southern League Second Division title in 1911 before transferring to Queens Park Rangers in 1912, where he was used in their reserves. He supplemented his football career as an engine cleaner with the South East Railway Company.

Butler enlisted with the Footballers' Battalion 17th Middlesex Regiment. He was stationed in France and attained the rank of Corporal. He was involved in fierce fighting and on 3rd May 1916, in the small town of Calonne, where intense street-to-street combat was taking place, he was wounded by a shell that shattered his leg. In tremendous pain, they took him to the 22 Casualty Clearing Station, Bruay. Butler fought gallantly for 10 days before succumbing to his wounds on 13th May 1916.

Reverend Green, the army chaplain, wrote in his account: *'The great big chap in bed 5, his wounds bulged up by a rolled up blanket, a shattered leg, always dangerous these wounds. "Well how are you Corporal?" "Bad, this leg is done, no more football for me". He fought for dear life for ten days then goes out. He played the game. I doubt not, that he has won. A fine fellow, may he rest in peace.'*

Buried in Bruay Communal Cemetery (A.23), Ben was 29 years old and left a wife, Kate, and two sons.

James 'Jock' Comrie was born on 31st March 1881 in Denny, Stirlingshire, Scotland. A centre half who was highly thought of, he signed initially for Third Lanark in 1903 until 1906. A top Scottish side in this era, they had won the First Division in 1904, and he was part of the side that won the Scottish Cup in a replay against Glasgow Rangers in 1905. He was also playing when they were runners-up  the following year, losing to Hearts 1-0. He played 78 games with 18 goals for the club. Although signed as a centre half, he was used as a centre forward, scoring four goals in one game and a hat trick in another during the 1905-06 season.

Reading came in for him in the 1906-07 season, in which he made 37 appearances, before moving again to Glossop FC in 1907 where he played 38 games and scored three goals. This was followed by spells at Bradford City in 1908 (43 games and eight goals), Lincoln City in 1910 (12 games and four goals), Grantham, where he played one game, and a very brief spell at Stenhousemuir before returning to Reading from 1911-15.

He played a further 95 games for the club, scoring two goals.

Comrie enlisted with the 1st/7th Northumberland Fusiliers, landing in France in April 1915, and later seeing action at Ypres.

In August 1916 they were at Dranoutre, Belgium, assisting the 1st/6th Northumberland and came under heavy bombardment from the German front line, before eventually being relieved by the Royal Irish Rifles.

Three days later, on 9th August 1916, they were in Meteren, Gelderland, Holland. The report simply states: 'Comrie killed out on the front line, unable to recover the body'. There is confusion over the exact time and place, but this is the official recorded data.

He is commemorated at the Menin Gate Memorial, Ypres (Panel 8 and 12). James was 35 years old.

Joseph 'Joe' Dickenson was born in 1888 in Tamworth, Staffordshire, one of six children. He was already a serving soldier with the Household Division when Reading scouts saw him playing for the army. He was signed by the club in 1913 when he was playing for Two Gates Wanderers in Tamworth. The fee was £5.

He was a sturdy, well-built player who could play in a number of positions, and he made 10 appearances and scored one goal for Reading. He was also in the squad that toured Italy in 1913, receiving good reviews, which included a 5-0 victory against AC Milan. He was well-liked by supporters and settled at the club, and he kept in touch with them when he was in France. He wrote frequently, expressing his desire to return home and play for them again, as he was recalled to the forces on the outbreak of war. He served in France as a Lance Sergeant with the Grenadier Guards. In May 1915 he was involved in heavy fighting at Festubert, in which the total numbers involved were over 50,000. On 19th May 1915 he was part of a group responsible for burying the dead, but there was heavy shelling on their position. Dickenson was the only fatality in this incident.

He is commemorated at the La Touret Memorial (Panel 2). He was 26 years old and left a wife, Winifred, a son and a baby daughter. He was one of the first professional footballers killed in the conflict.

Allen Foster was born in Rawmarsh in the Rotherham borough of Yorkshire in 1887. A solid strong forward, who had an eye for goal, he began his career at Rotherham Town before signing for Bristol City from 1909-11, playing 13 games and scoring one goal. He then moved to Reading in 1911 and made his mark as a finisher in front of goal.

In 158 games he scored 71 goals and was an established fixture in the side, loved by both the club and fans alike. He made another name for himself on the team tour of Italy in 1913, scoring a hat trick in the 5-0 thrashing of AC Milan.

Foster enlisted with the 17th Middlesex Regiment, serving in France and Flanders. He died from wounds at No. 5 Corbie Clearing Station on 8th August 1916, after being involved in fighting at Delville Wood, Somme.

He was buried in Corbie Communal Cemetery Extension (Plot 2. Row A. Grave 70.). Allen was 29 years old and married to Beatrice.

Leonard Martin Hawes was born in Reading on 26th July 1890, the second son of former soldier Harry Hawes. The family had moved to Twyford, Hampshire, after he was born and they ran the Station Hotel there.

He was a promising forward signed by Reading prior to the war, but he decided to enlist with the Berkshire Yeomanry in 1912, and by 1914 he was ranked as a Lance Corporal then later a Sergeant. In 1915, after sailing from Avonmouth, the division landed in Cairo, Egypt.

Hostile fighting at Gallipoli followed, and he was seriously wounded in the neck and spine by heavy machine gun fire and taken to the hospital ship *Salta*.

Sergeant Hawes died from his wounds on 25th August 1915, aged 25 years. He is commemorated at the Helles Memorial (Panel 18 and 19) and on a memorial stone mounted on his father's grave at St Mary's Church, Twyford.

His father offered his services to the Berkshire Yeomanry after Leonard's death and served as an Instructor with them, though he had to retire through ill health the following year. He died in 1918, aged 54 years. His other son, Lieutenant Harry Victor Sutherland Hawes, served with the Bengal Lancers in India; he survived the war and left the forces in 1922.

John Warwick 'Jack' Huggins was born on 2nd June 1886 in Crosby Ravensworth, Westmorland (now Cumbria). The youngest of four children, his father at one time kept the Crown Inn in Eamont Bridge, Westmorland. His father died in 1893, but his mother continued to run a number of establishments in the area.

He was a student at St Bede's College, Durham, and was part of the college 'B' Company, linked to the Durham Light Infantry. A good athlete and footballer, he played mainly as a winger, usually on the left.

He was signed by First Division Sunderland FC from 1906-08, making 14 appearances and scoring two goals, then transferred to Reading in 1908-09, playing 34 games and scoring six goals. He was by occupation a teacher and is on the staff at Swansea Road Council School in Reading. He could not settle and moved back to Sunderland in 1909. It appears he was out of first-class football after this year and is listed playing for Durham City and Wingate. He also played cricket for Sunderland, Wheatley Hill and Castle Eden.

Huggins was a teacher at Wheatley Hill Boys Secondary School, Durham, though he was still playing football and attracted some criticism from the head teacher. On a number of occasions, he was absent from his teaching duties either playing football or through injury. He did, however, form a school team, which was apparently very successful, sweeping all before them in the area.

He enlisted with the Durham Light Infantry in 1914 and fought in Belgium. He was reported as missing/killed in action in April 1915, but further reports suggested that he could in fact be a prisoner of war. However, further information came to light from the Red Cross that he had been killed in action on 26th April 1915 at Gravenstafel Ridge, east of Ypres. He was buried by German soldiers at Wallemolen Cemetery and reinterred at Perth Cemetery (China Wall), Ypres (XII.B.29) after the war. Jack was 28 years old.

Edward Thomas 'Ginger' Mitchell was born in 1887 in Middlesbrough. He was signed as a forward by Reading in the 1912-13 season, playing eight league games before transferring to Swansea in 1913. He was eventually used by them as a left back and quickly became a popular character at the club. An army reservist, he was called up to the Royal Field Artillery 117th Battery at the outbreak of the war. A large crowd of supporters turned up at the railway station to cheer him off on 5th August 1914. He was in France by September, and was shot during fighting and taken to a French hospital. After recovering, he returned to his unit and was promoted to Sergeant. He was allowed home in 1915 for four days to marry his sweetheart, Dolly. He apparently attended the ceremony in a uniform covered with mud from the trenches. He returned to France soon after and was killed in action the following year, on 6th January 1916 near Pas de Calais. He is commemorated at the Bethune Town Cemetery (IV.G.89); Edward was 29 years old.

Herber Percy 'HP' Slatter was born in July 1886 in Wokingham, Berkshire, one of three children. He was a rate collector by trade and had married Kate before moving into a house at 77 Norfolk Road, right next to the Reading ground, Elm Park.

Signed by the club in the 1909-10 season, he was a small but stocky tough-tackling half back, standing at 5ft 5in tall, and he was nicknamed HP. He was a great asset to the Reading club, and he played four seasons making 38 appearances. He is then linked with Oxford City FC.

In November 1915 Slatter enlisted with the 156th Royal Garrison Artillery as a gunner, serving in France. They were constantly on the

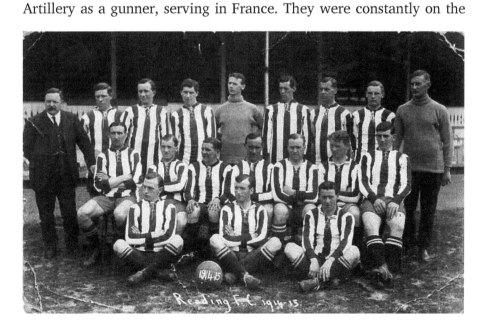

receiving end of shelling, though surprisingly had few injuries. There was only one casualty in his section, which was Slatter himself, on 3rd May 1918. He died from his wounds four days later.

His wife tried for 10 months to get his belongings returned to her, and when she eventually got them all he had was some English, French and German coins, photographs and a pack of playing cards. They had two small children so the club arranged a benefit game and collected one hundred and ninety six pounds, nine shillings and six pence for them. He was buried in the Couin New British Cemetery, Pas de Calais (D42). Heber was 31 years old and married to Kate Slatter.

Sheffield United FC, Division One

(FA Cup winners, League position: sixth)

James 'Jimmy' William Revill was born in 1891 in Sutton-in-Ashfield, Nottingham, one of six children. He was playing as an outside left for Tibshelf FC when Sheffield United signed him from 1910-15. He was described as a player of exceptional speed and for some reason gained the nickname 'old aeroplane legs'. He struggled to make himself a regular in the strong First Division outfit, playing mainly in the reserves, though he made 71 first-team appearances and scored four goals. He was part of the team that reached the FA Cup semi-final in 1913-14 and the winning squad from the 1914-15 FA Cup final, with a 3-0 win at Crystal Palace against Chelsea. He did not play in the final, but still got a winners' medal with an additional presentation of a pocket watch and chain.

The down side of this cup win was the open criticism received for allowing the competition and league football to continue during the war, which did overshadow the club's success. (This is the only English Cup final ever played during a conflict of war; the league suspension was authorised after it.) A book entitled *Red, White and Khaki* details the 1915 final and Revill's part in it.

His career with the club seems to end in 1915, when he was living in his home town after marrying Olive, and they had one son. He was

SHEFFIELD UNITED ENGLISH CUP WINNERS 1915

a bricklayer by trade. The other clubs he played for were Chesterfield Town and Sutton Town.

Revill enlisted with the Royal Engineers in 1915, stationed in Chatham, Kent, before serving in France. A Lance Corporal, he was involved in fighting with the 104th Field Company during the Battle of Arras on 9th April 1917 and he was seriously injured by a gunshot to the back and spine, which perforated his chest. He was removed to the 33rd clearing station and died a short time later.

Buried in the Bethune Town Cemetery (VI.C.80), he was 25 years old. Jimmy's name also appears on the war memorial in Sutton-in-Ashfield. The Sheffield football club held a benefit match for his family in 1918.

Southampton FC, Southern League Division One
(League position: sixth)

Edward Inkerman Jordan Bell M.C. and Bar was born in Gibraltar in 1886, the son of an army Major famous for his bravery at the Battle of Alma in the Crimean War in 1854, when he took over his regiment after all the officers had been killed, bringing them back to safety after capturing enemy positions and guns. He was awarded the Victoria Cross.

Although from a military background and brought up in Ireland, he was initially a post office clerk in Farnborough, Hampshire. He played as an amateur for Farnborough, Portsmouth and Crystal Palace. He then signed for the Saints in 1907 as an outside forward, making eight first-team appearances and scoring one goal, but he was mainly used in the reserves after turning down a professional contract.

PROMINENT FOOTBALLERS.

E. BELL,
SOUTHAMPTON.

In 1908 he left the club and took up the role of a Government Contractors' Inspector in Farnborough. Bell enlisted with the Duke of Cambridge Middlesex Regiment during the war, serving as an adjutant to Major Frank Buckley as a Captain.

With Major Buckley wounded in 1916 at Delville Wood, Bell took command, and soon after he was awarded the Military Cross for 'conspicuous gallantry'.

'He repelled an enemy counter offensive rescuing several men from a blown-in dug out. He then supervised the holding of positions in daylight close to enemy lines, often under heavy fire and shelling.'

On 24th March 1918, Bell took charge of the 99th Infantry Brigade. During fighting at Albert on the Somme he was killed by an enemy shell. A few months after his death, in July 1918 citations he appeared in the *London Gazette* for 'conspicuous gallantry and devotion to duty'. A Posthumous Bar was added to his Military Cross.

Edward is buried in the Albert Communal Cemetery (SP.MEM.5). He was 32 years old and left a wife Edith and a son born six months after his death, who was given the same distinctive name. His son went on to fight in the Second World War as a Squadron Leader in the RAF. He was captured and held prisoner in Stalag Luft 111 and later awarded the DFC (Distinguished Flying Cross). Before he left the forces, he also served as a Major in the Korean War.

Edwin Cecil Russell Christmas was born on 13th January 1886 in Southampton, one of eight children, and he lived at the Edinburgh Commercial Hotel and public house. He joined Southampton in the 1908-09 season, but left the following year to concentrate on business interests. He was persuaded to sign forms and return in 1912 by reserve-team manager George Carter, who was impressed with his speed and ball control as a forward. Having made two appearances, he was then injured and although retained he was forced to retire in 1913.

He enlisted with the 28th London Regiment and commissioned as a Second Lieutenant in the 18th King's Royal Rifles. He was killed on 7th October 1916 in action during offensives on the Somme. He is commemorated at the Thiepval Memorial (Pier and Face 13A and 13B). Edwin was 30 years old.

Arthur Herbert Coleman was born 1885 in Cannonore, Madras, India. He was from a military background and in the army when Southampton gave him a trial in April,1904, but he got a bad review in a 5-1 defeat.

Coleman, therefore, continued his army career with the Royal Fusiliers. He was killed in action in Northern France on 25th January 1915, and was buried in the Chapelle-D'Armentieres (B18). Arthur was 29 years old.

Frederick 'Frank' G. Costello was born in 1882 in Birmingham. He began his football locally then was at West Brom as an amateur in 1904 as a forward, but he did not impress so he moved to Halesowen. He was signed by Southampton from 1907-09, making 62 appearances and scoring 19 goals. He usually played as an inside left and scored on his debut. Costello also took part in a good run to the FA Cup semi-final in 1908, losing to the eventual winners Wolves 3-2. Thereafter he was plagued by injury, and on his return

PROMINENT FOOTBALLERS.

G. COSTELLO,
SOUTHAMPTON.

he played at centre forward without success. In 1909 he transferred to West Ham, then Bolton in 1910.

His talent began to wane and, unable to get into their first team, he moved on to Nelson then had trial at Burnley, before ending up at Merthyr Town in 1910-11.

After 1911 he returned to the Southampton area, playing the occasional game for Salisbury City.

Costello enlisted with the 2nd Battalion Warwickshire Regiment in his home county at the outbreak of war, and after training he was stationed on the western front. He was killed in Belgium on 19th December 1914, the battalion suffering heavy losses.

He was buried in the Ploegsteert Memorial Cemetery, Hainaut, Belgium (Panel 2 and 3). Frank was 31 years old.

William Edward Crabb was born on 19th June 1878 in Southampton. He worked for the local parks department as a fitter. He was offered a place at Southampton in 1899-1900 in the reserves, though he made three first-team appearances as a right back. He was released at the end of the season. He was described as plucky, standing at only 5ft 2in tall.

Crabb is listed in war records as, 'died of Cerebral Malaria' after operating complications on 23rd May 1917, serving with the 618th Motor Transport Army Service Corps in East Africa. He was buried in the Morogoro Cemetery, Tanzania. (II.E.3). William was 39 years old, married to Alice Beatrice Crabb and had four children.

William Durham of the 14th Hampshire Regiment made one first-team appearance for Southampton in the 1915-16 season. He is listed as dying from wounds in France on the 12th September 1916, serving with the 14th Hampshire Regiment. He is commemorated

at the Doullens Communal Cemetery (I.V.F.1), Extension 1, Somme.

Harrison 'Harry' Eke was born in February 1888 in Kent. An amateur trialist from St Mary Cray, he had also represented Kent County at junior level. He played for the Southampton reserves in 1913, scoring seven goals in four games. He managed one game for the first team in 1913 as an inside right, but did not impress. He returned to Kent in 1914, working as a milk hand. Eke served in the war as a Private with the 13th Royal Fusiliers in France. After contracting tuberculosis, he was discharged and repatriated home in 1916. Harry died

the following year on 30th April 1917. He was buried in Bexleyheath Cemetery (501) and is commemorated on their War Memorial. He was 29 years old.

William George was born in Southwick, Sussex, on 11th July 1878. An amateur winger with Bitterne Guild, he was reported as a good local find and signed by the Saints in 1902. He was at the Dell for three seasons and played three first-team games.  George left the club in 1904, enlisting with the 7th Royal Sussex Regiment on a five-year engagement. Thereafter, he worked in Bognor as a bricklayer's labourer. He re-enlisted with the regiment for the war, serving in Northern France. He was officially reported missing presumed dead on 3rd May 1917. He is commemorated at the Arras Memorial (Bay 6) and the family headstone at St Mary the Virgin Churchyard, Felpham. William was 39 years old and married to Elizabeth George.

Tom Hargreaves was born in Haslingden, Lancashire, in 1891. He was a winger who played for Oswaldtwistle Rovers then Accrington Stanley in the Lancashire Combination, before eventually moving to Southampton in 1910 with teammate Martin Dunne.

Dunne played for the first team, but Tom was mainly a reserve and only managed one game in the Southern Cup competition. He then moved back to Accrington. Prior to enlisting, he was living in Padiham with his wife Alice.

He enlisted with the Machine Gun Corps (Infantry 87th Coy) and attained the rank of Sergeant, serving in France. He was killed in action on 20th November 1917 near Louverval, Northern France.

He is commemorated at the Cambrai Memorial. Tom was 26 years old.

John 'Harry' Hunter was born in Clapham, London, in 1887, one of five children. He was a police officer working in the London area as a plain-clothes detective.

Playing as an amateur goalkeeper, he was recommended to the Saints by a fellow policeman and brother of the famous Southampton favourite Sid Kimpton.

Being a policeman made it difficult for him to play
for a professional club as he wanted to continue his
career. He only made one appearance in 1913 against
Brentford, near to where he worked. He impressed but
could not be tempted away from his day job.

Hunter enlisted with the Royal Flying Corps for the
war effort and was a 2nd Lieutenant serving in France.
He was fatally wounded and died on 5th November
1917.

He is commemorated at the Wimereux Communal Cemetery near
Boulogne (IV.K.4) and the Stockwell Memorial, London. John was 30
years old.

Charles George Ireland was born in 1888 in
Southampton. He played amateur football for local
parks side Crow's Nest, be signed for the Saints in
1907, although he was a reserve player. He played as
an inside forward, but he was given a first-team outing
for Southampton in 1909 against Brentford at outside
left.

He left in 1909 and played in the Hampshire league
for Winchester, then Boscombe and Bournemouth.

Ireland enlisted in the 5th Battalion Hampshire Regiment and was
a Lance Corporal. He was seriously wounded in action in 1915 and
brought back home.

Charles died in Netley Hospital, Southampton, on 7th December
1915, and was buried in Netley Military Cemetery, Southampton; he
was 27 years old.

John Robert Sibley was born in 1888 in Southampton, one of seven
children. He was on Saints' books in the 1912-13 season but as a reserve
player. He was an inside left and made one appearance
in a cup match in 1912, resulting in a draw. He seems
to disappear from football after this season.

Sibley was a firefighter during the war with the
Mercantile Marines, and he died on board hospital
ship S.S. *Liberty IV* on 24th November 1918 of disease,
thought to be Spanish Flu. It was a fortnight after the
armistice.

He was buried in Southampton Old Cemetery (Ref 155). John was 30 years old and left a wife and three children.

Owen Richard Thomas was born in Southampton in 1880, the son of a doctor. He signed in the 1898-99 season from Banister Court, when Southampton had won the Southern League Shield for the third time.

A full back scoring on his debut against Kettering, he made five appearances, but was thereafter in the reserves where he began playing half back. He only stayed for one season.

During the war he enlisted with the Welsh Horse Yeomanry, then in the Assistant Provost-Marshal 54th Division. Serving in the Middle East, he attained the rank of Captain.

Owen died on active service in Palestine on 21st August 1917 and is buried in the Deir El Belah War Cemetery (Ref: A234) near the Egyptian border. He was 37 years old. He is also listed in the South Africa war graves project and Roll of Honour.

Frederick William Wheeler was born in Swallowfield, Berkshire, in 1887. Although from the Reading area, he began playing football in Lancashire with Colne FC as an inside forward. He was signed by Southampton in 1910 and was soon offered professional terms. He managed three first-team games, though he struggled to get out of the

SOUTHAMPTON 1913/14
Top Row: Mr.Arnfield (Sec), J.Smith, J.Denby, E.Stevenson, J.McAlpine, R.Brooks, J.Small, J.McIntyre (Trn.)
Middle Row: Mr.W.Hammock, Mr.H.Ashton, W.Bradley, G.Kimpton, E.Lee, S.Ireland, G.Handley, E.Burt, Mr.A.Wood, Mr.W.Helpitt.
Front Row: T.Binder, A.Dominy, W.Smith, F.Prince, T.Dominy.

reserve side. He was released in 1911, playing locally for Eastleigh Athletic then Woolston in the Hampshire leagues.

Wheeler was working as an insurance agent before enlisting with the 233rd Field Company Royal Engineers as a Sapper. He was killed in action serving in Italy on 2nd January 1918 in the Montello sector.

H was buried in the British Cemetery, Giavera del Montello (Plot 2.Row C. Grave 2). Frederick was 31 years old.

Southend United FC,
Southern League Division One
(League position: 18th)

Edward Ernest 'Dits' Anderson was born in Prittlewell, Southend, in 1890, one of five children. Known to many as Dits, he was a student at Leigh Road High School. They had a good footballing pedigree, winning two championships during his time there.

He joined Southend and was there for two seasons as a reserve-team player. He did, however, play a number of games in the team's tour of Germany in 1910. Prior to 1913, he is believed to have been at Woolwich Arsenal again in the lower tier sides, before moving to live in the Tottenham area of London, where his football career with local league sides continued. He was by this time working as a carpenter by trade.

Anderson enlisted in Shoreditch in January 1915 for the 56th Company Royal Engineers, serving in the Ypres area. Mortally wounded at Voormezele in the head and back, he died from his injuries at the clearing station near Dixmude on 11th December 1915.

He was buried in the Lijssenthoek Communal Cemetery, Belgium (IV.C.24A). Edward was 24 years old.

Dudley Lacey was born in 1891 in Southchurch, Southend. Known as 'Tom', he was a postman by trade, used by Southend in their reserve

side. A centre forward who also played for Southend Amateurs, he later played as a centre half.

Lacey enlisted with the Royal Field Artillery in 1915 as a driver. He served overseas until 1918 and then unfortunately contracted pneumonia, dying on 28th November 1918, 17 days after hostilities ceased. He is commemorated at the Etaples Military Cemetery (L.1.D.1.). Dudley was 27 years old.

Harry Owen was born in 1882 in Sulgrave, Northampton. In 1905 he was living in Southend with his twin sister, playing football for Southend Athletic as a centre half in the South Essex League. After helping them to the championship, United signed him, with the famous Bob Jack securing his signature in 1906.

He was a regular until 1909, helping Southend to the Southern League Two title twice. He was also part of the team that beat Clapton Orient in the FA Cup 3-1 in 1907, the press lauding him for his display.

In a sad twist of fate, a serious injury in 1909 in a game against Northampton Town, his home town, forced his retirement. They lost the game 11-1, the club's worst-ever defeat. A good sportsman, he still played cricket locally after he retired. He kept in regular contact and became a frequent visitor at the Southend club.

Owen enlisted with the 23rd Royal Fusiliers, Sportsman's Battalion, in Hornchurch, Essex, in May 1915. After training, he was in France by November 1915. Regularly in the thick of it, he had a number of narrow escapes. However, on 13th March 1916 he was on guard duty at Noulette, an area in Northern France. At 3.55am, five minutes before he was due to be relieved, there was a mortar attack on the camp. A college stated, 'Owen saw it coming and gave warning, probably saving three parts of the section'. The shell landed in front of him, causing some 40 to 50 wounds. He lived for an hour, though he was unconscious, before dying peacefully from his injuries.

News was received back home and a local sports writer who knew Owen penned the following: *'Whatever he took up he believed in doing thoroughly and he was a gentleman on and off the field. It was a rare thing to see a free kick given against Owen for a foul, when it did happen it was because of his over-keenness or accidentally. The war had not been long in progress before Owen felt the Call for King and Country. I remember meeting him in the High Street about twelve months ago one Saturday night, when he said, "I am going to join the Sportsman's Battalion tomorrow. I have no ties and I feel all of us single men ought to go." He went and I remember seeing him at a meeting one Wednesday evening just before his departure for the front. When I gripped his hand and wished him luck, I had little thought it would be the last time we should ever meet. The cruel lottery of war has, however claimed him, but the memory of Harry Owen will remain a treasured recollection to the end, as it must do with all who had the pleasure of his acquaintance. What better epitaph could he have than; "He died for his country".'*

Buried near to where he fell, after the war he was reinterred at the Lievin Communal Cemetery, Pas de Calais (IV.F.14.). Harry was 34 years old.

William Urquhart Sutherland was born in Falkirk in 1884. A career soldier, he joined the Argyll and Sutherland Highlanders, serving in the South Africa Campaign from 1899-1902. A keen footballer, he was also a physical training instructor with his regiment.

In 1908 Bob Jack spotted him playing for the army in a game at Gillingham. He therefore left the army and signed for Southend as an inside forward, spending three seasons with a reported good game to goal ratio. He was also on the team tour of Germany in 1910.

He met his wife Enid during his time at United, living in the area with her and their two children. In 1911 he re-joined Jack at Plymouth Argyle for £100. Only managing one first-team game, he stayed until 1913, though he was described as an essential asset to the reserve team. He then played for Chatham before retiring and returning to Southend, working as a groundsman and caretaker at the Jones Memorial Ground for children.

A reservist, he re-joined his regiment and was in France by August 1914. As part of the 19th Infantry, they made assaults on the enemy at Solesmes and retreated to Le Cateau. The Battle of Le Cateau then ensued and they suffered many casualties. This was early days in the

Southend United, 1913-14.

war, and the tactics used were criticised as outdated and inhumane. Machine gun fire used against them was effective and deadly, and this unfortunately was a recurring theme during the conflict. The whole of the unit, under the leadership of Major Alexander McLean, died – 44 men in total, including Sutherland, and only seven were identified. His date of death is recorded as 26th August 1914, when he was reported missing/killed in action.

He is commemorated at the La Ferte Sous-Juoarre Memorial to the Missing, east of Paris. William was 30 years old. (He was the first professional footballer killed in the Great War.)

Stalybridge Celtic FC, Southern League Division Two

(League runners-up)

Philip Smith. See Burnley FC
Norman Arthur Wood. See Stockport County

After turning professional the club only spent one season in the league in 1914-15, finishing second after election in 1913-14 via the

Stalybridge Celtic, 1921.

Lancashire Combination and Central League. This would have meant them being promoted to the Southern First Division. The war then took precedence. In 1919 they decided to return to the Lancashire league, mainly for financial reasons.

Stockport County FC, Division Two
(League position: 14th)

Edwin 'Ted' Bardsley was born in Denton, Manchester, in 1883. An outside left, he began his career at Glossop in 1903 before signing for Stockport in 1905. He played 86 games and scored 11 goals. His career ended in October 1906 during a game against Sheffield United. He broke his leg after colliding with their renowned goalkeeper William 'Fatty' Foulke, who weighed 23 stone.

Stationed in France after enlisting with the 3rd/9th Second Battalion Manchester Regiment, he was involved in the fighting at the Somme. He was killed in action on 18th November 1916, aged 33 years.

He is commemorated at the Thiepval Memorial (Pier and Face 13A and 14C).

Richard 'Dick' Hegarty was born in 1884 in Stockton on Tees. He was a right back who initially played locally for Belle Vue Athletic then West Hartlepool, with whom he won the FA Amateur Cup in 1905. A move to County followed in the same year, where his brother Tom joined him, until 1906. He is listed as having played one official first-team game.

They both returned north and played together for a number of teams. Dick had his best spell from 1908-10 with Hartlepool United, playing 29 games and scoring one goal.

Hegarty enlisted for the war with the Royal Field Artillery and attained the rank of Sergeant. He was wounded and gassed in France in 1917 then shipped home.

Richard died in Gosforth Military War Hospital from his injuries on 3rd October 1917, aged 33 years, leaving his wife, Emily Hegarty. He was buried in the Hartlepool Stranton Cemetery (II.C.117.R.C.).

John Chapman Hodgkinson was born in December 1883 in Stockport and had the nickname 'Cobbler'. Also known as James, he played semi-professionally for Edgeley then Stockport as an inside forward. He made 49 appearances and scored nine goals in two spells at the club between 1905 and 1909. He was also on the books of Grimsby Town and finally Nelson FC.

He enlisted within days of the outbreak of war in Burnley, with the East Lancashire Regiment. Hodgkinson had been a pre-war Territorial.

By September 1914 he was in Alexandria, Egypt. For the next few months they had to undergo intense physical training. In June 1915 the 1st/4th were involved in fierce fighting at the Battle of Krithia against Turkish troops. The machine gun fire against them was ferocious, yet they managed to capture three enemy lines.

However, the enemy returned with intense heavy shelling and a retreat was hastily ordered. When they were relieved they had lost another 33 men in the shelling, including John. Officially reported missing/killed in action on 5th June 1915, he was just 31 years old. He is commemorated at the Helles Memorial (Panel 113 to 117).

Frederick Houghton was born in Stockport in 1890. Playing as a left back, he was signed by County from 1911-15 from local side Park Albion. Although not a first-team regular, he played 29 games. He worked in the area at Portwood Spinning Company.

After enlisting with the Cheshire Regiment, he was stationed with the 8th Service Battalion in Mesopotamia as a Lance Corporal. They lived and fought in terrible conditions, plagued by disease and intense heat. Houghton fell gravely ill; his death is listed as from fever on 15th November 1918, four days after the armistice in Europe.

He is commemorated at the Basra War Memorial (III.F.18). Fred was 28 years old and married to Emily. After the war she moved to New South Wales, Australia, where she started a new life and remarried.

Thomas Christopher Porter was born on 25th October 1885 in Stockport. An inside forward or half back, he initially played for Northern Nomads then signed for Stockport from 1906-09, making 68 appearances and scoring 23 goals before moving to Glossop until 1911, where he played 44 games and scored 11 goals. He finished his time as a player back at Nomads.

Highly thought of, he was picked for the England amateur side from 1908-10, playing eight games and scoring 13 goals. Porter made the squad for the 1908 Olympic team, though he did not get a game.

After enlisting with the 1st/6th Manchester Regiment, Thomas fought at Gallipoli. He was killed in action on 4th June 1915, aged 29 years. He is commemorated at the Helles Memorial (Panel 158 to 170).

Robert 'Bob' Suart was born in October 1888. A centre half, he started out at local side Edgeley before signing for County from 1903-08. Described as 'a sterling player', Suart was an ever-present in the team, playing 174 games and scoring 14 goals.

No. 249—SUART

He then signed for Fulham for a fee of £550, playing 102 games for them and scoring one goal. In 1911-12 he moved to Port Vale. They played in the North Staffordshire League due to financial difficulties. He played over 175 games for them until the war in 1915, winning the Staffordshire and Birmingham Senior Cups. (He also guested for Stockport during the war on three occasions.)

Suart enlisted with the South Lancashire Regiment before transferring to the Royal Warwickshire Regiment after training. Once in France, he saw action at the Somme and then the Battles of Arras and Ypres. In 1917 he was in Italy before returning to France in 1918.

On 27th September 1918 they were involved in fighting at Gouzeaucourt, nicknamed the African Trench, near Arras. They were heavily bombed and Bob was one of 9,000 casualties from fighting in this area. Thereafter he was reported as missing presumed dead. He

Stockport County 1914-15

is commemorated at the Vis-En-Artois Memorial (Panel 3). He was 36 years old and left a wife, Beatrice Suart.

Norman Arthur Wood was born in Tooting, London, in 1889. Described as 'an artistic inside forward', he played for a number of clubs. He was initially at Bromley, then on Tottenham's books, before playing one game for Crystal Palace in the 1909-10 season. He moved to Plymouth the following season, playing two games there.

In the 1911-12 season he moved to Croydon Common, where he scored 18 goals in 38 games. On Chelsea's books in 1912, he then signed for County from 1913-15, playing 60 games and scoring 12 goals. Prior to enlisting, he was on the books of Stalybridge Celtic.

Wood then signed up for the war with the 17th Duke of Cambridge Middlesex Regiment, Footballers' Battalion, representing their football team. By 1916 he was a Sergeant. He was killed on 28th July 1916 at the Somme during the fierce Battle of Delville Wood, where many bodies were sadly lost. He is commemorated at the Thiepval Memorial (Pier and Face 12D and 13B). Norman was 26 years old.

Stoke City FC, Southern League Division Two
(League winners 1914-15 –
elected to Division Two proper 1919-20)

Henry Hargreaves was a right-winger from Wolstanton and was described as very fast. He started at Newcastle Town before signing for Stoke in 1912.

He played over 60 games in total up to and including 1916. Stoke City's only information states he was killed in France during 1916, aged 23 years. (No other personal information is known.)

Albert 'Arthur' Hartshorne was born in Darlaston, West Midlands, in 1880. He began his career at Moxley White Star and briefly at Wolves before joining Burslem Port Vale in 1902-03, playing 23 games and scoring three goals as a left back. By trade, he was a toolmaker.

He signed for Stoke from 1903-05, making 56 appearances. He then moved on to Southampton, staying there during 1906 where he played 25 games. He was at Northampton Town in the 1906-07 season and played 13 games.

Hartshorne enlisted with the South Staffordshire Regiment and served in France. He died from wounds received in action on 10th February 1915.

Buried in the Boulogne Eastern Cemetery, Pas-de Calais (III.B.88), Albert was 30 years old. He was married to Florence Baker and had two children.

Richard 'Dickie' Herron was born in Durham, Northumberland, in 1890. He started with local side West Stanley before signing for Stoke in 1910 as a goalkeeper.

His appearance record gradually increased, and by 1917 he had made 106 appearances with war games included. He was part of the 1914-15 team that won the Southern Division Two title and gained re-election.

Herron joined the 2nd Sherwood Foresters, Notts and Derby Regiment, in 1917 and after training he served in France.

He was killed in action on 19th September 1918, and was buried in the Trefcon British Cemetery, Caulaincourt, France (B.14). Richard was 27 years old.

Thomas 'Tom' Kinson was born in 1883 in Measham, Stoke on Trent. He is listed as playing two games as a midfielder in 1916-17.

He enlisted with the 7th Battalion Leicestershire Regiment in Atherstone and served in France and Belgium. He was killed in Belgium on 6th October 1917 and has no known grave. This was during the period of the battles at Ypres and Passchendaele.

He is commemorated at the Tyne Cot Memorial (Panel 50 to 51) and the Measham Memorial. He was 38 years old.

William John 'Bill' Nixon was born in 1886 in Stoke on Trent. There is not much personal information available. He played locally for

Trentham FC. He was an amateur player and is listed as playing two games for Stoke in 1911-12 as an outside right. Stoke City's information shows that William enlisted with the Staffordshire Regiment and died in France during 1916, aged 30 years.

William Stanley 'Stan' Ripley was born in 1893 in Seaham, County Durham. He played for Seaham Harbour and then signed for Stoke in 1914, playing one game against Brentford in a 3-0 win. His position was at half back.

Ripley then enlisted with the Duke of Cambridge 17th Middlesex Regiment and the 5th Reserve, serving in France. He was injured during fighting near Longeuval, Northern France, and repatriated back to his home town.

He died at home on 10th March 1917 and was buried in the Mere Knoll Cemetery, Sunderland (Ref: 12A. 1968), aged 24 years. He is commemorated on the Longeuval War Memorial.

Leigh Richmond Roose M.M. was born on 27th November 1877 in Holt, Wales. He was brought up by his father, who was a minister, after the death of his mother when he was just 2 years old. He was educated privately and at one point was taught by the famous H.G.

Wells. He attended Aberystwyth University, studying to become a doctor. Whilst there he kept goal for the town's football team.

In 1901, after attracting attention from Stoke City, he signed for them, though he remained an amateur and did so throughout his career. This suited his personal life and work with King's College Hospital, although he never officially finished his university studies. Described as 'a strappingly good-looking figure', he was known for not taking any heavy-handed tactics from opposition forwards. In fact, up to 1912, goalkeepers could bounce the ball from their area right the way to the half way line, which he used to his advantage. It was partly because of this that the rule changed to the eighteen-yard box rule we know today. He was reportedly an excellent shot and penalty stopper and a superbly agile athlete.

He moved to Everton in 1904, followed by a return to Stoke 1905-07. In total, he played over 159 games for Stoke. Between 1908 and 1912 he played for a number of other clubs, namely Sunderland, Celtic, Port Vale, Huddersfield Town, Aston Villa, Arsenal, Aberystwyth and Llandudno Town. In total he played in excess of 300 games. He also received international honours between 1900 and 1911, making 24 appearances for Wales.

A celebrity in more circles than just football, he was somewhat a ladies' man and a trendsetter. He had a highly publicised relationship with famous music hall star Marie Lloyd, though he never married.

At the outbreak of war he joined the Royal Medical Corps, serving in France and Gallipoli. He returned to London in 1916 and signed up straight away with the 9th Royal Fusiliers. He returned to France in the summer of the same year and won the Military Medal when he carried on fighting during a skirmish with the enemy even though he was unarmed.

Killed during fighting on enemy lines near Gueudecourt on 7th October 1916, it is though his body was either blown up or lost in the deep mud. Roose was 38 years old and is commemorated at the Thiepval Memorial (Pier and face 8C, 9A and 16 A). On enlistment, his surname was recorded as 'Rouse', which is what appears on the memorial. Despite numerous requests to have this rectified, which continue to this day, it remains unchanged.

John 'Jack' Shorthouse is listed as a reserve player for Stoke prior to the conflict. He has no recorded games for the first team. He enlisted with the 6th Leicestershire Regiment and was injured in action at the Somme. His death is recorded as 17th July 1916 and he is commemorated at the Thiepval Memorial.

William Mountford 'Bill' Williamson was born in 1884 in Longton, Staffordshire. His father was a china manufacturer. He played as an outside right and began his football with North Staff's Nomads before signing for Stoke from 1906-08, making eight first-team appearances.

He then moved to Crewe Alexandra from 1908-10 then to Leicester in 1910, making two appearances. He then returned to Stoke in 1911 and was a reserve player. Thereafter, he is listed with amateur side Wellington Town, later renamed Telford United.

In 1912 he enlisted in Stoke on Trent with the Gordon Highlanders on a long-term contract. He trained in Aberdeen before being sent to Colchester and eventually overseas to Egypt.

Williamson then returned home at the outbreak of war, though by October he was fighting at Ypres with the 20th Brigade, 7th Division. He was wounded in the knee at the end of the month and captured by the Germans. From records, he appears to have been in a Prison of War Camp in Krefeld, Germany, during 1916. In 1918 the Allied troops had placed a shipping embargo on Germany, and this had a serious effect on food and other supplies.

Reported to have died of unknown causes on 2nd August 1918, it is thought it may have been Spanish Flu. Bill is one of 25 names commemorated at the Cologne Memorial, Germany. He was 34 years old. His family received his war medals.

George Limer is listed in Stoke records as a midfielder, playing 17 games and scoring one goal in the 1916-17 season during the war.

Stoke City, 1914.

According to their records, he was killed in action during the conflict. The only Limer listed is a G.F. Limer with the Royal Air Force, though it appears he survived the conflict. George remains listed here should any other records emerge regarding him. (The spelling of his surname is not confirmed.)

Sunderland FC, Division One
(League position: eighth)

Samuel Hartnell was born in 1897 in Kirk Merrington, County Durham, one of seven children. From a mining family, he is listed on Sunderland's books as a promising up and coming centre forward in the reserve side.

The war then put an end to his hopes of first-team football. He enlisted in Middlesbrough as a Gunner with the Royal Garrison Artillery, 111th Northumberland, North Riding, and Heavy Battery. He was 17 years old.

Killed in action on 8th August 1918 in France, he was interred at the Warloy-Baillon Communal Cemetery Extension, near Arras (Grave VI H9). He is also remembered on the family headstone in St John's Churchyard, Kirk Merrington, and on three memorials in Chilton, County Durham. He was 21 years old.

Albert Milton was born on 18th October 1886 in High Green in the Sheffield district of Yorkshire, and he later moved to the Rotherham area. A left back starting out as an amateur with South Kirkby, he later signed for Barnsley in 1907. After 15 games, Sunderland signed him from 1908-13.

During his time there they won the league in 1912-13 and were runners-up in the FA Cup, but he sustained an injury for most of the season and was ineligible for medals. In total he made 140 appearances for the club. He then moved to Swindon Town, where he played 30 games in 1914-15.

Milton enlisted with the 64th Brigade Royal Field Artillery 'B' Battery serving in France and Belgium. He was killed in action at

Passchendaele on 11th October 1917. He is commemorated at the Tyne Cot Memorial, Belgium (Panel 4-6 and 162). Albert was 31 years old and married to Agnes Milton.

Alexander 'Sandy' McAllister was born in 1877 in Kilmarnock, Scotland. A census in 1911 shows him as being born in Durham, where he was living with his wife Isabella and four children at that time, aged 34 years.

He was a strong, tough centre half, listed initially from recorded information at Kilmarnock FC before signing for Sunderland in 1896. (There is no mention in records of game stats for Kilmarnock.)

A stalwart of the Roker Park team and popular with the fans, in all he made over 222 first-team games for the club and scored five goals. He was part of the team that won the First Division Championship in 1901-02. In 1904 he signed for Derby County, playing 24 games.

He enlisted with the Northumberland Fusiliers, serving with the 20th, 11th, 1st and 10th Battalions in Italy. Sandy contracted food poisoning and died on 31st January 1918, and he was listed as being 41 years old. He was buried in the Giavera British Cemetery, Arcade, Montebelluna (Plot 6, Row C, Grave 2).

Thomas Sowerby Rowlandson M.C. was born in June 1880 in Newton Morrell, Darlington. He was the son of an agricultural landowner who owned 1,030 acres and employed 23 workers with five house servants. He was well educated, attending Charterhouse School and Cambridge University. He was a Cambridge Blue, playing as a goalkeeper for the university.

Rowlandson then played for Corinthians before briefly being on Preston's books in 1902, then moved on to Sunderland in 1903-04, making 12 appearances. A season at Newcastle followed in 1905, with one first-team game.

He then moved back into amateur football with Corinthians again and Old Carthusians. Reported as 'the best amateur goalkeeper of all time with the best moustache in the world to match', he was part of the Corinthians squad that toured the world promoting the game

O.T.NORRIS. CAPT W.SIMPSON C.H.WILD. C.F.RYDER. A.R.HAIG-BROWN. T.S.ROWLANDSON.

O.E.WREFORD-BROWN. W.U.TIMMIS. W.F.H.STANBOROUGH. G.O.SMITH. C.WREFORD-BROWN. E.H.S...

of football, receiving wonderful reviews in 1910. He also made two England amateur team appearances in 1906-07. The Corinthian team were about to tour again in 1914, but he had to return home as war was declared. In his spare time Rowlandson was a Justice of the Peace.

He enlisted almost immediately with the Yorkshire Regiment in Northallerton as a Lieutenant and donated his farmhouse as a hospital. By April 1915 he was a Captain, and he was involved in fierce fighting near Ypres, Belgium. In October the same year he is mentioned in dispatches. On 1st January 1916 he was awarded the Military Cross, but eight months later he died.

His adjutant wrote, *'I have always thought of him the finest type of Englishman I have ever known, and his death was just as fine as his life.*

He died where of all places; I think he would have chosen if it had to be – on the parapet of a German trench at the head of his men, with his Officers stick in hand. A Boche bomb hit him on the shoulder. Death must have been instantaneous.'

His men followed him into the trench, which they captured – it was the 15th September 1916 at the Battle of Flers-Courcelette on the Somme. He was buried in the Becourt Military Cemetery (I.G.7), Becordel-Becourt, France. Thomas was 35 years old.

Charles Buchan, pictured in the above team photograph, served as a Lieutenant in the war and received the Military Medal. He survived the conflict. A prolific goal scorer, he also played six times for England before becoming a broadcaster and sports magazine producer.

(Teammates of Rowlandson from Corinthians who were also killed in the Great War include: Reg Rodgers, Frank Tuff, Lancelot Vidal, John Tetley and Cuthbert Everard Brisley. In total 22 Old Corinthians died during the conflict. An interesting fact is that Brisley, although a Corinthians player and highly rated England international amateur, was regarded the best player in Europe and some say the world prior to the war.)

Major Brisley lost his life on 30th November 1918, aged 28 years, in a flying accident. He was buried in Market Drayton Cemetery (54163573) and was married to Marjorie Beryl Brisley.

(Charles Buchan, pictured in the above team photograph, served as a Lieutenant in the war and received the Military Medal. He survived the conflict. A prolific goal scorer, he also played six times for England before becoming a broadcaster and sports magazine producer.)

Swindon Town FC,
Southern League Division One
(League position: ninth)

George Bathe was born in 1890 in Shrivenham, Oxfordshire. He is listed on the books at the club prior to the Great War, though he is not registered with any first-team games. He was living in the town when he enlisted with the 1st Battalion Wiltshire Regiment and fought in Belgium. He was shot and killed in action on the 20th February 1915. He is commemorated at the Kemmel Chateau Military Cemetery near Kemmelseweg (H.20). George was 25 years old.

Arthur Beadsworth was born in Leicester in 1876. He was an inside forward with a varied well-travelled career. He started at Hinckley Town before signing for Leicester Fosse in 1900, where he made four appearances. Brief spells at Coventry and Preston followed, before he signed for Manchester United in 1902-03, playing 12 games and scoring two goals.

Swindon signed him from 1903-05, where he played 54 games and scored 11 goals. Listed at Blackburn, followed by New Brompton, he finished his career back in the Midlands with Hinckley, where he resided with his wife Polly.

Beadsworth was working as a shoe operative before enlisting with the Leicestershire Regiment 7th Battalion, and by July 1915 he was in France. He was then with the 110th which became part of the 21st Division, and became a Colour Sergeant, seeing action at the Somme. He was badly wounded in the third battle of Ypres, Belgium, in October 1917 and gassed. He was removed to a military hospital near Wimereux, but he died on 9th October 1917. The exact cause was not specified.

He was buried in the Wimereux Communal Cemetery (VI.C.19). Arthur was 41 years old.

William Arthur 'Billy' Brewer was born in 1893 in Chippenham, Wiltshire. A centre forward, he was signed by Swindon from Chippenham Town and played in their Southern League winning side of 1913-14. A reserve player in the main, he was allowed to guest for Chippenham when necessary. He made two appearances for the first team before returning to Chippenham.

After enlisting with the Duke of Edinburgh's 1st Wiltshire Regiment, he was in Belgium by late 1914. He was listed as missing/killed in action at Hooge, Ypres, on 13th November 1914. He is commemorated at the Ypres Menin Gate Memorial (Panel 53). He was 21 years old. Brewer is on the club memorial with the other victims. William also has a roadway in the town named after him.

James Chalmers was born on 3rd December 1877 in Old Luce, Wigtownshire, Scotland. A man of many clubs, he started his career at Beith as an outside forward, with whom he won the Ayrshire Cup. He is then listed at numerous clubs, namely Morton, Sunderland, Preston, Notts County, Beith, Partick, Watford, Spurs, Norwich, Bristol City, Beith again, Clyde and finally back to Beith in 1911. In between all this, he signed for Swindon from 1904-06 where he played 78 games and scored 16 goals.

Swindon Town, 1914.

Chalmers enlisted with the 1st/4th Battalion Royal Scots Fusiliers, and his date of death is listed as 12th July 1915 in Turkey, during the Gallipoli campaign.

He is commemorated at the Helles Memorial (Panel 72 to 75). James was 38 years old.

Harold Victor Warren M.M. was born in 1893 in Highworth, Wiltshire. He is listed on the Swindon Town Memorial plaque as registered with the club. He did not play any first-team games. Records show he was with the XI Heavy Field Artillery and received the Military Medal. Unfortunately, he died of Influenza on 15th November 1918, four days after the armistice.

The Wednesday FC
(Sheffield Wednesday after 1929), Division One
(League position: seventh)

Walter Eaton was born in 1882 in Sheffield, Yorkshire. He was on the books of Wednesday in 1904, playing one first-team game. He also played for Rotherham County and Rotherham Town.

He enlisted with the York and Lancaster Regiment then Northumberland Fusiliers, 24th Battalion Tyneside Irish. After training he fought in France and died from wounds he received during action in Northern France on 15th May 1917. He is remembered at the Etaples Memorial (XVIII.N.12A). Walter was 35 years old and married to Jane Eaton.

Vivian Sumner Simpson M.C. was born in Sheffield on 5th February 1883, one of nine children. His father was a solicitor. He was educated at Wesley College, Sheffield, and after graduating he joined his father's firm.

Although an amateur, he was on the Wednesday books from 1901-07, making 38 appearances as a forward and scoring 11 goals, including a hat trick against Manchester United in a 6-0 win.

During his time there, the club was one of the country's best, winning the First Division in 1902-03 and 1903-04. They also won the FA Cup in 1907. He played two games in the cup campaign, injury forcing him out of the final. He also represented the Sheffield district during the same period. In 1904 they won the Amateur FA Cup, though an injury playing for Wednesday ruined his chances of playing in the final. He had scored two hat tricks for them on the way to the final, including one in the quarter final against Darlington-St-Augustine's. The team took the trophy to his home on their return to Sheffield, as he was recuperating there from his injury, to celebrate with him. He also played for Norwich City and Northern Nomads before the war.

Simpson enlisted with the newly formed 12th Service Battalion, Sheffield, York and Lancaster Regiment as a Captain as he was eager to assist the campaign, in 1914. By 1916 he was involved in fighting at the Somme and played a major part in the attack on Cordorna Trench. He was first there and involved in hand-to-hand combat, helping to consolidate the newly won position. He was awarded the pictured Military Cross and the citation read:

Second Lt /Acting Captain Simpson.

'For conspicuous gallantry and devotion to duty during and after an attack upon enemy trenches. He was first to reach the trench and engaged in hand to hand fighting with the enemy. Later, he displayed the greatest ability and energy in organising his company for the work of protection and consolidation. His work has been consistently excellent on previous occasions.' (The *London Gazette*, Supplement 13143, 19th September 1917)

On 13th April 1918 he was serving with the 13th York and Lancaster Regiment when he was shot and killed by a sniper in the village of Outtersteene. He was reportedly attempting to cheer up his men with 'his unquenchable optimism'. He was buried in the Outtersteene Communal Cemetery Extension, Bailleul (I.E.56). Vivian was 33 years old and married to Marion May Simpson.

Tottenham Hotspur FC, Division One
(League position: 20th – relegated)

Alexander Glen was born on 11th December 1878 in Kilsyth, Stirlingshire, one of three children. An inside forward who was much travelled in football terms, he studied medicine as a student at Glasgow Royal Infirmary. Glen then served as a medical dresser during the Boer War before beginning his football career around 1902 with Clyde initially, then Grimsby Town, Notts County and Tottenham, where he has his best spell, playing 66 games and scoring 24 goals. From 1906-07 he was at Southampton, playing 29 games and scoring 10 goals. From 1908-10 he turned out for Portsmouth and finally Brentford.

He re-enlisted with the Royal Army Medical Corps during the war, serving as a Lieutenant. During 1916 he was suffering from what was diagnosed as depression. Unfortunately, he took his own life on 21st September 1916 at the Ripon Army Camp, leaving a detailed suicide note. He was buried in Ripon Cemetery. Aged 37 years old, Alex left a wife, Gertrude, and daughter Elizabeth who resided in the Leigh area, Lancashire.

John Joseph Hebdon was born on 1st February 1895 in Portsmouth. After moving to London he played for local side Silver Street United.

He was, however, used by Spurs in 1915, mainly playing in the London League team during that year.

He then enlisted with the 1st/14th London Regiment (London Scottish) serving in France as a Lance Corporal. He was involved in heavy fighting during the Somme offensive and killed on 9th April 1917 in Northern France during an attack on the village of Neuville-Vitasse, at the Battle of Arras. John was 22 years old. He is commemorated at the London Cemetery Neuville-Vitasse, Wancourt Road (Cem 2. Panel 3), Pas de Calais.

Alfred Hobday was born on 12th December 1886 in Blackhill Consett, County Durham. He joined the Northumberland Fusiliers in 1905 after initially working at Consett Ironworks. After training in Newcastle, he served in India, working in the Punjab and the North West Frontier.

He quickly gained a reputation as a good all-round sportsman, excelling at football, cricket and athletics. Initially he represented the forces as a goalkeeper and then moved outfield to full back.

In 1910 he played at centre forward for the 5th Fusiliers, scoring five goals in one game as they won the Royal Hussars Cup. They retained the trophy the following year. After receiving the Indian General Service Medal, he returned to the North East and civilian life, but he remained on the reservist list.

Spurs spotted Hobday playing football whilst working for North Eastern Railways. He signed after a trial match at Tunbridge Wells in 1913. Hobday found it difficult to get into the first team and only managed one game against Arsenal. He returned to the North East as the war was gaining momentum and was recalled to the Fusiliers, and he was soon in the thick of the action at Mons, Le Cateau, The Marne, The Aisne, La Bassee and Messines.

After promotion to Sergeant, he received the French Croix de Guerre (Legion dHonneur) for saving an officer's life at Ypres under heavy fire. There is mention of a recommendation for the Victoria Cross (unconfirmed). On 16th May 1916, the Fusiliers were involved in the Battle of Bellewaarde, Belgium, suffering heavy losses from bombardment and hand-to-hand fighting. He was reported missing, presumed dead, during this assault, somewhere near Railway Wood.

Alf is one of 54,000 commemorated at the Menin Gate Memorial, Ypres (Panel 8 and 12). He was 29 years old. Posthumous awards were made to his family for the 1914 Star Medal, Victory Medal and British War Medal.

Edward John 'Teddy' Lightfoot was born in Litherland, Liverpool, on 13th November 1889. Starting his career at local side Horrowby, he then briefly signed for Southport Central in the Lancashire Combination in 1910. Tottenham signed him in 1911-12 as a half back. He made 83 appearances and scored two goals for the club up to the 1914-15 season. He then returned to Southport Central, scoring four of the five goals in a game against Preston. Called up to the Royal Garrison Artillery, he played for the army at Fulwood Barracks, Preston. He attained the rank of Sergeant and served in France from 1916 with the 1st Siege Battery.

On 20th July 1918 he died from wounds at the 1st Australian Casualty Clearing Station at Esquelbecq. He was buried in the Esquelbecq Military Cemetery (III.E.26), Nord-Pas de-Calais. Ed was 28 years old. A report in the *Lancashire Post* read: *'Edward Lightfoot was a splendid footballer but, more than that, he was a good sportsman, a player that respected both himself and his opponent. He has joined a noble company who will leave a big void in football.'*

William J. Henry Lloyd was born on 25th March 1888 in Wrexham, Wales. He played for Tufnell Park and was used by Spurs in 1908-09. He played eight games in the South East league. He was a regular with the reserve side.

Lloyd enlisted with the Grenadier Guards 2nd Battalion and was a Corporal. He was killed in action on 7th November 1914 near Ypres, by a shell. He is commemorated at the Ypres Menin Gate Memorial (Panel 9 and 11), Exton Memorial and at Whitwell Church, Rutland. William was 26 years old, was married to Ada Sophia Lloyd and had three children.

Alexander McGregor was born in 1893 in the Caithness area. He came to Spurs from Glasgow club Yoker Athletic in 1914 as a centre forward and played in the South Eastern League and the London League for the reserves. He was dismissed by the club for disciplinary offences relating to training and returned to Scotland in October the same year.

He enlisted straight away for the war with the Gordon Highlanders and was in France by December 1914. He was killed in action on his first day of fighting on 14th December 1914.

He is commemorated at the Ypres Menin Gate Memorial (Panel 38). Alexander was 21 years old. He is also listed on the Latheron Memorial, Caithness, Scotland.

PTE. ALEXANDER M'GREGOR
GORDON HIGH⁺⁵.

William Findlay Weir was born in Glasgow on 18th April 1889. A wing half, he began his career locally with Campville, Waverley then Maryhill before signing for The Wednesday from 1909-12. He played 72 games and scored one goal, before signing for Tottenham from 1912-15. Again, he became a regular feature in the side, making 101 appearances and scoring two goals. He played a further four wartime games.

Weir then enlisted with the Royal Engineers 3rd Reserve Battalion in 1915. He was posted to France and promoted to Sergeant. Wounded in 1916, he recovered sufficiently to return to his unit, and by 1918 he was serving in Newark, Nottinghamshire, at the R.E. Demolition Training Depot.

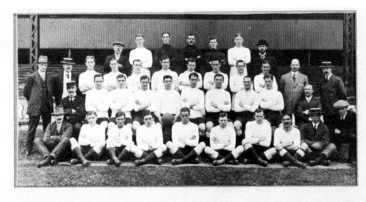

Jones Bros., **Tottenham Hotspur Football Team,** 708, HIGH ROAD, TOTTENHAM.
SEASON 1913-14.

On 2nd July 1918 Weir was admitted to the 2nd Eastern General Hospital, Brighton, where he died. (It is not known if his death was related to the wounds he received in 1916.) He was buried in the Glasgow Lambhill Cemetery (Grave Ref Q.205). William was 29 years old.

Watford FC, Southern League Division One
(League winners 1914-15)

George Huntley Badenoch was born in Castle Douglas, Scotland, one of eight children, on 9th April 1882. An outside forward, he began briefly at Hearts before signing for Glossop from 1901-03, playing 48 games and scoring four goals.

He then signed for Watford from 1903-06, where he played 80 games and scored nine goals. In 1903-04, they won the Southern League Second Division title (medal pictured). Tottenham signed him in 1906, although he only played one first-team game before moving to Northampton Town from 1907-09. He played 47 games and scored one goal. A bad knee injury prompted his decision to leave the game and emigrate with his wife Ellen Henrietta to Canada in 1910. Before the war he had recovered sufficiently to play for the Indian Head football team in Saskatchewan. He

enlisted with the Canadian Expeditionary Force, Canadian Infantry 9th Battalion, West Ontario Regiment, serving in France during 1915. He was killed on 15th June 1915 during fighting at the Second Offensive at Givenchy. He is commemorated at the Vimy Memorial. George was 33 years old.

Albert Ernest Farrow was born in Gainsborough, Lincolnshire, in 1886. He was a half back who could also play as a winger. He began his career with Gainsborough Working Men's Club and Institute before signing for Gainsborough Trinity from 1906-08, playing over

Watford - Southern League champions, 1914-15. From the left, back row: T. Coulson (Trainer), H. Bulling, V. Gregory, R. Williams, J. Kennedy, F. Gregory, A. Stewart. Front row: H. Kent (Manager), W. Hastings, P. Ronold, G. Edmonds, A. Green, T. Waterall, W. Swain (Secretary)

35 games and scoring one goal. He then signed for Watford in 1908-09, making nine appearances before moving on to Worksop Town.

Farrow enlisted for the war with the Lincolnshire Regiment, and then served with the 12th Labour Battalion South Staffordshire Regiment in France. After contracting Tuberculosis, they discharged him as he was no longer fit. Albert died at home on 28th September 1916. He was 29 years old and married to Pollie Sarah Farrow. He was buried in Gainsborough General Cemetery (A.CO. 2022).

West Bromwich Albion FC, Division One
(League position: 10th)

William Hickin Jackson was born in 1894 in the Oldbury area of West Bromwich, Birmingham. A centre forward known usually as Bill, he initially played local football for Langley St Michaels and Oldbury Town. He was on the books of West Brom from 1912-17, making three first-team appearances.

He enlisted with the 15th Battalion Prince of Wales own West Yorkshire Regiment. A 2nd Lieutenant, he fought in France, and is listed as being killed in action on 3rd May 1917.

He is remembered at the Arras Memorial (Bay 4). William was 22 years old.

Harold Godfrey Bache was born on 20th April 1889 in Churchill, Worcestershire. He was a pupil at King Edward Grammar School, Birmingham, in the same class as J.R.R Tolkien. He excelled at all sports but in particular cricket, football, rugby, hockey and tennis. He was captain of the rugby second team who went through a whole season undefeated. An exceptional student, graduating from Cambridge University, he represented them in many sports. He played cricket for them three times and for Worcestershire 17 times from 1907-10.

He was a member of the famous Corinthians football team, with a remarkable record of 95 goals in 43 games. He was part of their tours to Brazil and in 1911, scoring 34 goals in 18 games. He was recorded as an England amateur international on four occasions.

He was awarded a Cambridge Blue at football and tennis, but not cricket as he was not considered to be playing to the required standard, which was apparently very high. He was the first tennis player to use the double-backhand return when he won the University Lawn Tennis Championship in 1911. He was selected as a member of West Bromwich hockey club to represent his county, Staffordshire, on several occasions.

WEST BROMWICH ALBION F.C.

205

An amateur in status, he was on West Brom's books in 1914 as a centre forward, recorded as playing 14 games and scoring four goals. Judging by his previous sporting exploits, it seems he could have been on the verge of a great career with them, but the war intervened.

Bache enlisted initially with the Staffordshire Regiment as a Corporal and then transferred to the Lincolnshire's before the 10th Lancashire Fusiliers on commission as a 2nd Lieutenant. After training he served in France and Belgium as a Bombing Officer (grenade throwing platoon). In September 1915, whilst stationed near Ypres, a shell blasted through a billet killing 20 and wounding 27 men. Ordered to take cover as shells were still exploding, Bache ignored this and bravely went to the assistance of others.

On 16th February 1916 he was returning with his men after attempting to retake a trench when a sniper shot him; they were unable to recover his body. He is commemorated at the Ypres Menin Gate (Panel 33). He was 26 years old. His brother, who was the Mayor of West Bromwich, set up the Bache Memorial Fund after his death, which paid for a permanent Memorial at King Edward School and a Sports Cup award, thereafter presented every year to the school's best sportsman.

West Ham United FC, Southern League Division One

(League position: fourth – elected into Division Two proper in 1919-20)

Sydney Frederick Hammond was born in 1882 in Woolwich, London. He worked as a commercial clerk and lived in the Leytonstone area. Playing as an amateur, he was on West Ham's books from 1904-08 as a full back. He is registered with 34 games.

Hammond enlisted with the 242nd Brigade 'C' Battery, Royal Field Artillery, serving in France and Belgium. He was killed on 18th October 1917 in the Passchendaele offensive.

He was buried in the La Clytte Military Cemetery, Heuvelland, Belgium (III.E.10). Syd was 35 years old and married to Florence Emily Hammond.

William James Jones was born 1876 in Penrhiwceiber, Glamorgan, Wales. He was a half back who started his career at Aberdare Athletic in 1898 before moving to Kettering in 1901.

In the 1901-02 season he was at West Ham, making 15 appearances. From 1902 he was linked with Ameraman Athletic, helping the club reach the Welsh Cup final, which they unfortunately lost against Wrexham. He then moved to Rogerstone FC from 1904-06, finishing his career soon after this.

In 1901 he was capped by Wales, winning four caps in total before the end of 1902.

Jones was with the 11th Battalion Royal Welsh Fusiliers, seeing service in the Balkans. He was killed in action at Lake Doiran, Salonika, Greece on 6th May 1918 as part of his battalion was making an advance. The report from the war diary on 7th May 1918 stated: *'as the patrol advanced towards a pillbox they found two bodies (one believed to be Jones), but were unable to recover them due to bombs being thrown and rifle fire, which seriously wounded two other men. Lieutenant J. Tinniswood thereby ordering the retreat.'*

William has no known grave. He is commemorated at the Doiran Military Cemetery. He was 41 years old.

William Kennedy was born in 1890 in Grays, Essex, one of eight children. He was a centre forward, initially at Northfleet United, playing alongside the famous Charles Buchan of Sunderland and Arsenal fame. In 1909-10 they were part of the team that won their league and both regional area cups. He guested on several occasions for Southend United before West Ham signed him from 1910-12. He played 23 games for the Hammers, scoring 10 goals, but a serious knee injury forced his retirement from the first-class game. He was a schoolteacher by occupation.

Kennedy enlisted with the 1st/14th London Scottish Regiment and attained the rank of Lance Corporal. It was during the Battle of Loos on 13th October 1915

that he lost his life. He had volunteered to move forward into enemy territory to check on the situation during an ill-fated advance at Hohenzollern Ridge. It was foggy and heavy shelling was taking place, and a large amount of barbed wire was also in their way. This was the last heard of Kennedy. He was one of 3,643 casualties in the first 10 minutes of battle. He is commemorated at the Loos Memorial (Panel 132). William was 29 years old and described as 'a genial kindly soul'.

His brother, John, an engineer on troop ship HMS *Minnekonta* was an earlier casualty on 12th September 1915, aged 33 years. He was buried in the East Mudros Cemetery, Lemnos, Greece (II.N.246). Both are remembered on the Grays War Memorial.

Edward Arthur James Stallard was born in 1892 in Hackney, London. He signed from Chatham in 1913 as a forward, making 13 appearances and scoring eight goals for West Ham before suspension of the league. In all, with war games, he played 50 games and scored 33 goals up to 1917.

1913. **WEST HAM UNITED FOOTBALL CLUB.** 1914.

ALL WORKING PEOPLE. ALL KINDLY PEOPLE. ALL KEEN PEOPLE SHOULD READ "THE DAILY CITIZEN."

Stallard enlisted with the 1st/14th County of London Battalion, London Scottish, and after training he served in France. He is reported as being killed in action on 30th November 1917 during the Battle of Cambrai, when the Germans fired over 16,000 shells at the allied troops in the main exchange.

Edward has no known grave. He is commemorated on the Cambrai Memorial, Louverval (Panel 11 and 12). He was 25 years old and married to Patience Amelia Stallard.

Wolverhampton Wanderers FC, Division Two
(League position: fourth)

Walter Lovegrove Blunt was born in 1896 in Staffordshire. He is listed on the war gravesite as a former footballer killed in action in the Somme area, France, on 28th July 1916, serving with the 17th Middlesex Regiment. Information states that he was linked with Wolves and Bristol Rovers.

From research, there is only one player with this surname listed in football records. This is a William 'Billy' Blunt, born in 1886, who played for Wolverhampton Wanderers from 1908-12. He then transferred to Bristol Rovers. Injuries curtailed his career soon after. He was from the Bilston area of Birmingham and died in 1962. No other Blunt is listed in Wolverhampton Wanderers' record statistics.

The image above is of Walter Blunt from his time in the forces. Our research has also found an image of a player from the unnamed 1912-13 Wolves reserve/first combined team photo, also pictured. This could well be the same man from the forces image and therefore a reserve player.

Walter Blunt served with the 17th in France as stated. He is commemorated on the Thiepval Memorial Pier and Face 12D and 13B. He was 19 years old. His brother Percy was killed in France the following year, in August 1917.

John Edward 'Jack' Shelton was born in 1885 in Wolverhampton, Staffordshire. He signed for Wolves from 1907-11 as an inside right of half back. He played 94 games and scored 17 goals for the club. The highlight of his career was being part of the 1908 FA Cup final side that beat Newcastle 3-1 at the Crystal Palace. He scored a goal in an earlier round against Bradford City. From 1911-18 he was at Port Vale, where he again had a good career winning three local county trophies, playing 249 games and scoring 25 goals. His younger brother George also played for the club.

Conscripted into the North Staffordshire Regiment in 1918, Shelton eventually transferred to the 10th Service 2nd Battalion Lincolnshire Regiment, stationed in France. He was killed on 7th September 1918 during fighting at the Hindenburg Line, eastern France. He was buried in the Epehy Wood Farm Cemetery (V.I.14). Jack was 33 years old, married to Sarah and had two children. She later remarried his former Wolves teammate Jack Needham.

SCOTTISH LEAGUE TEAMS

Scottish football continued throughout the war. From season 1914-15 the divisions changed to A and B from One and Two (34 clubs), but stayed in the same format. From 1915-16 it became one division of 20 clubs. From 1917-19 the division was reduced again to 18 clubs after the withdrawal of Aberdeen, Dundee and Raith Rovers, with Clydebank coming in. Clubs were suffering financial difficulties or were understrength due to players signing up or being conscripted into the forces.

Abercorn FC, Division B

(League position: 12th)

Charles C. Jeffrey was born in 1891 in Dundonald, Irvine, Ayrshire, Scotland. He signed with Abercorn in 1913-14 as a forward, making three appearances and scoring one goal. The following season he played one game before enlisting in Kilmarnock with the 1st Battalion Black Watch.

Jeffrey served in France and attained the rank of Sergeant. He was killed during fighting in Northern France on 9th May 1915. He is commemorated at the Le Touret Memorial (Panel 24 to 26) and the Irvine Memorial. Charles was 23-24 years old.

Robert Gardner Houston was born in 1888 in Kilbarchan, Renfrewshire, Scotland. Playing as a goalkeeper, he started out with local club Kilbarchan Athletic, before signing for Partick Thistle in 1912, making eight appearances, though usually as a reserve player. He then moved to Abercorn, where he played 14 games in 1913-14. Prior to joining up, he was at Johnston FC, where he made three appearances.

Houston enlisted with the 1st Battalion Seaforth Highlanders, and was killed in France on 9th May

Abercorn FC, 1911-12.

1915. Sergeant Scott wrote to the club to inform them of the death, describing him as, *'a fine man, no better soldier had ever worn the British Uniform'.*

He is commemorated at the le Touret Memorial (Panel 38 and 39). Robert was 26 years old.

Aberdeen FC, Division A

(League position: 14th)

Alexander Laing Halkett was born on 9th October 1880 in Dundee. A right half from a footballing family, he began his career at Parkmore FC with his brother. Both were signed by Dundee, Alex signing in 1901 and making 16 league appearances. In 1904-05 he signed for Aberdeen and became a fixture of the side, at one time captaining the club. He played 129 games for them and scored two goals, and it was said that he never had a bad game.

Halkett moved south to Portsmouth in 1909 and had two unhappy seasons there in footballing terms, spending most time in the reserves. From 1911-13 he was at St Johnstone, where he played 50 games and three goals. He is shown as being a wheelwright by trade.

After 1914 he enlisted with the Royal Field Artillery 'C' Battery, 87th Brigade, as a Gunner, stationed at Rosyth Naval Base, and he was eventually posted to France in December 1916.

He was killed in action on 21st February 1917 near Pas-de-Calais, Northern France. He is commemorated at the Sailly-au-Bois Military Cemetery (II.A.6). Alex was 36 years old and had been married for 10 months. His son was born one month after his death.

Andrew Hamilton was born on 10th June 1882 in Aberdeen. A reserve player for the club and a regular scorer as a centre forward, he made one first-team appearance in 1905. He was injured in a scaffolding accident in 1906 and was unable to force his way back into the first team, so he was released. Hamilton enlisted with the 4th Gordon Highlanders and after training served in Belgium. He was killed in action on 20th July 1915 near Ypres, aged 33 years. His commanding officer wrote to his wife informing her of his death. Andrew had written in his diary eight days before his death that all his belongings should go to his wife, Jessie Hamilton. He is commemorated at the Ypres Menin Gate Memorial (Panel 38).

Allan Lawrie was born in Aberdeen. An inside forward, he joined Aberdeen in 1906-08 and was used in the reserve side. He gained a first-team appearance after only a few weeks against Hearts in a 3-3 draw, playing at centre forward without impressing and returning to the reserves. He was eventually loaned out to junior side Harps and after 1908 is believed to have returned to lower league football. After enlisting with the 2nd Battalion Queen's Own Cameron Highlanders, he was killed in Belgium on 10th May 1917. He is commemorated at the Ypres Menin Gate Memorial (Panel 38 and 40), and was listed as 29 years old (CWGC site). (Aberdeen FC have him recorded as being born on 24th May 1885.)

Angus Cameron McLeod was born on 11th January 1890 in Inverness, Scotland. He was a forward who signed for Aberdeen from 1913-16, where he made 22 first-team appearances and scored six goals.

McLeod enlisted with the 1st/5th (Buchan and Formartin) Battalion of the Gordon Highlanders. He is listed as a Lance Corporal, and was killed in action in

Northern France on 16th May 1917. He is commemorated at the Arras Memorial (Bay 8 and 9) and the Aberdeen War Memorial. Angus was 27 years old.

John Munro was born on 14th April 1893 in Invergordon, Scotland. Munro signed as a left back from 1914-16, making 14 appearances. He had played as an amateur for Aberdeen East End.

He was living with his parents when he enlisted with the 315th Battery 'C' Brigade Royal Field Artillery as a gunner in 1916. He was killed in action near Arras, France, on 8th May 1917. He is commemorated at the Anzin-Saint-Aubin British Cemetery (I.C.26). John was 24 years old.

Herbert Murray M.C. was born in Newhills, Aberdeen, on 11th December 1885. He graduated from Aberdeen University in 1908 with a degree in Arts before joining the teaching staff at Gordons College, Aberdeen. A credited sportsman, he began his football career at college in around 1906 with Arbroath FC, before playing for Clyde in 1906-07 as an outside right, playing 46 games and scoring five goals. He then moved to Aberdeen, playing over 40 games and scoring three goals from 1908-10.

In 1910-11 he played 11 games for Queens Park FC, followed by 16 games for St Johnstone, scoring four goals. In 1912 he returned to Aberdeen and before the end of 1914 had played 51 games, scoring six goals for the club.

In 1915 Murray enlisted with the 1st/4th Battalion Gordon Highlanders and after training was wounded during fierce fighting in France. He returned to England for treatment.

During August 1915 he was commissioned as Captain in the 3rd and 4th Gordon Highlanders. Whilst recuperating he was an instructor in his district at musketry, involving the use and conduct of weaponry. In April 1917, however, he was back at the front.

Again he was involved in fierce fighting and awarded the Military Cross for *'brilliant and courageous action during the spring offensive in 1918'*. He was killed in action on 20th July 1918 at Hois de Courton, north of Epernay. He was buried in the Marfaux British Cemetery (I.B.7). Herbert was 32 years old.

Charles Neilson was born on 27th November 1889 in Montrose, Scotland. He graduated from Aberdeen University in 1913 in Arts and took up a teaching role in Lossiemouth. From 1910-12 he was with Aberdeen as an outside left, making eight first-team appearances. He was also a talented cricketer.

In September 1914 Neilson enlisted with the 5th Battalion Gordon Highlanders as a Private. He served in France and attained the rank of Company Sergeant Major. He was killed in action on 1st June 1916 at Neuville-Saint-Vaast, Northern France.

He was buried in the Maroeuil British Cemetery, Pas de Calais (I.F.6). Charles was 26 years old.

James Hadden Neilson was born in 1888 in Montrose, the brother of Charles Neilson. He was also on the books of Aberdeen in 1911-12 as an outside left. He managed one first-team game. After enlisting with the Lovat Scouts, a mounted division, he transferred to the Queen's Own Cameron Highlanders Infantry Battalion. Stationed in Greece, he was killed in action near Thessaloniki on 28th October 1917. He was buried in the Kirechkoi-Hortakoi Military Cemetery (G.O.2. Grave 27). James was 29 years old.

Aberdeen FC, 1916.

A third brother, Rolland Miller Neilson, another victim, was killed in action on 13th April 1918 in Belgium, aged 26 years. He is remembered at the Ploegsteert Memorial (M.R.32. Panel 9). The tragic events for this family did not end here. The youngest brother William Neilson was too young to fight in the First World War. But, fighting in the Second World War, he lost his life, killed in action on 12th June 1940 in Northern France. He was buried in the Manneville-es-Plains Churchyard; he was 36 years old. (All the brothers are commemorated on the Aberdeen Memorial.)

Frederick Watson was born in Aberdeen on 30th November 1888. A half back, he was on the books in 1912-13, playing two registered games for the first team.

He served in the Royal Navy Reserve as a Trimmer on H.M. *Drifter* 'Petrel'. He was taken ill in June 1917 and he died at home on 29th June 1917. (The illness is not specified.)

He was buried in Aberdeen St Peters Cemetery (Cyt.O.12.). Fred was 28 years old and married to Georgina Watson.

Note: Captain Joseph Ellis Milne D.S.O. was the Aberdeen club doctor before enlisting with the 164th Brigade King's Own Liverpool Regiment, 55th Division. He was killed by a sniper at Gully Trench, near Railway Wood, Belgium, on the 22nd February 1917. He had received the D.S.O. on the Somme in October 1916 for, 'Bravery in the field, tending the wounded under continuous shellfire. He had shown utter disregard for his own safety'. He was buried in the Lijssenthoek Military Cemetery (X.A.8). He was 48 years old.

Airdrieonians FC, Division A
(League position: ninth)

Thomas 'Tommy' Farrell was born in Earlestown, Lancashire, in 1887. After playing as an inside forward locally, he was briefly on Arsenal's books in 1904, before signing for Manchester City from 1905-07, making three first-team appearances.

He then moved north to the Airdrie club from 1907-09, with 14 games and one goal to his credit. After 1909 he registered with Eccles Borough in the Manchester League.

Farrell enlisted with the Lancashire Fusiliers 3rd then 1st Battalion, ranked as a Corporal, initially in action in Gallipoli. He was killed in France on the first day of the Somme offensives on 1st July 1916 during an assault on Hawthorn Ridge Redoubt. The report stated, 'they stood no chance and were "cut to pieces" from three sides, 480 of the battalion losing their lives'. The bodies lay in situ for four months until British forces captured the area and recovered them. Tommy was 29 years old, and married with three children. He was buried in the Auchonvillers Military Cemetery (II.E.19).

John Findlay, also known as 'Jack or Jock', was born in 1881 in Kilmaurs, Ayrshire, Scotland. A right half, he started out at Knibshill United before signing for Newcastle in 1905, making two appearances.

From 1906-09 he was at Vale of Leven after finding it difficult at Newcastle, playing nine first-team games there. From 1909-10 he was at Airdrieonians, with 22 games to his name, before he returned to Leven in 1910-11, where he played a further eight games.

Airdrieonians, 1914.

He enlisted with the 2nd Battalion Scots Guards in Girvan and is listed as killed in Northern France on 25th September 1916. He is commemorated at the Bienvillers Military Cemetery, Pas de Calais (XV. III.J.1). John was 35 years old.

Robert Williams from Newmilns, Ayrshire, was born circa 1883. A centre or wing half, he joined Airdrie in 1910-11 making 123 appearances with 12 goals before the war. He was still at the club when he enlisted for the conflict.

Williams joined the Royal Scots Fusiliers and served in France. He was killed in the Somme area on 31st August 1916.

He is commemorated at the Thiepval Memorial. Robert was 32-33 years old.

Albion Rovers FC, Division B
(League position: ninth)

ALBION ROVERS QUALIFYING CUP WINNERS 1913/14

Back: R. Boag, W. Smith, E. McLaren, W. Johnstone, W. Gibb.
Centre: S. Trainor, W. Smith, A. Bell, R. Ewing, D. Harrigan, H. Thom, D. Ewing, J. Grant, T. Muir.
Front: S. Scott, R. Archibald, J. Weir, D. Galbraith, G. Watson, R. Ralston, R. Martin, C. Prentice, J. Chambers, D. Millar.

Archibald Campbell. See Ayr United
James Conlin. See Manchester City
Patrick Slavin. See Motherwell

Arthurlie FC, Division B

(League position: 13th)

ARTHURLIE FOOTBALL AND ATHLETIC CLUB
(WINNERS OF SCOTTISH CONSOLATION CUP 1909/10)

Thomas Gracie. See Hearts

Ayr United FC, Division A

(League position: fourth)

John Bellringer was born in 1892 in Port Glasgow, Inverclyde, one of six children to Captain Edward Bellringer.

A draughtsman by trade, he was also a keen and well thought of footballer locally. He was on Ayr United books as a reserve player, but he made one first-team appearance.

Bellringer enlisted with the Argyll and Sutherland Highlanders and was soon promoted to Corporal. As part of the 1st /5th Battalion he fought in Turkey. He was reported missing/killed in action at the Battle of Achi Baba Nullah on 12th July 1915 and is commemorated

at the Helles Memorial (Panel
183 and 184) and the Port
Glasgow Memorial. John was
23 years old. His brother George
Connell Bellringer of the Seaforth
Highlanders was a victim, killed
in action on 7th April 1917, aged

33 years. He was buried in the St Nicolas British Cemetery (I.A.4.), Pas
de Calais.

Archibald 'Archie' Campbell was born in 1880 in
Kirkintilloch, Dumbartonshire. He was an outside forward
who began playing at local side Rob Roy before signing
for Clyde in 1906 after a very brief spell at Carlisle.
After 10 games, he moved to Ayr FC in 1909, making 20
appearances and scoring two goals.

They then amalgamated with Ayr Parkhouse to become
Ayr United in 1910, Campbell playing a further 67 games
and scoring 12 goals. In 1914 he moved to Abercorn,
making 23 appearances and scoring one goal.

He enlisted with the Royal Field Artillery 'D' Battery 119th Brigade
as a driver. Seriously injured in the Nord area, France, he died from
his wounds on 14the September 1918. He was buried in the La Kreule
Military Cemetery, Nord (III.D.26). Archie was 38 years old and married
to Marion Campbell.

PTE. R. CAPPERAULD,
Ayr.

Robert Capperuald was from Ayr and was listed
as a reserve player and a regular in their side prior to
the war.

After enlisting with the Royal
Scots Fusiliers 1st/5th Battalion, he
served in Gallipoli, Turkey.

His was listed as having, 'died
from shrapnel wounds received to
the right shoulder' on 12th July 1915 at the Clearing
Hospital 'W' beach (149th Field Ambulance). His
death date is recorded as 14th July 1915.

He was buried in the Lancashire Landing Cemetery
(D.59). Pictured is a strikingly stark image of Robert's

and other comrades' graves after burial and it is a haunting reminder of the sacrifice they made many miles from home.

Samuel Herbertson was born in Irvine in 1889. He was a goalkeeper who began his career at Beith FC, before signing for Ayr in 1913. He made 10 appearances for the club before the war.

After enlisting with the Royal Scots Fusiliers 1st/4th Battalion, he served in the Balkans. He was killed at the Dardanelles, Turkey, on 12th July 1915.

He is commemorated at the Helles Memorial (Panel 72 to 75). Samuel was 26 years old.

Archibald McMillan was born in 1894 in Campbeltown, Argyll, Scotland. An outside left, Celtic signed him in 1913 but he failed to get into the side. In 1914 Ayr signed him and he made four first-team appearances.

McMillan joined the 1st/7th Argyll and Sutherland Highlanders for the war serving in France. He was reportedly shot/killed in action on 23rd November 1917 at the Battle of Cambrai, north of Arras, after two days of intense fighting.

He was buried in the Rocquigny-Equancort Road British Cemetery, Manancourt (II.C.6.). He was 23 years old.

Ayr United, 1915.

Celtic FC, Division A

(League and Scottish Cup winners 1914-15)

Peter Johnstone was born on 30th December 1887 in Cowdenbeath. He was also a coal miner and played for Glengraig Celtic FC, before signing for Celtic in 1908 as a forward or midfielder. He could play a number of roles but in the main excelled as a centre back for the club.

He quickly became a club legend and was idolised by both the club and fans alike. He was described as, *'having a lion's courage, he never let the club down'*.

In all he played 233 games and scored 19 goals, helping secure four league titles, two Scottish Cups, three Glasgow Cups and four Glasgow Charity Cups, playing into 1916, though by this time he had returned to work in mining. He assisted the club until he enlisted.

In 1916 Johnstone signed up with the 1st/6th Morayshire Battalion, Seaforth Highlanders, serving in France. He was involved in the Battle at Vimy Ridge and was reportedly killed in action on 16th May 1917. (Between 9th and 16th April the allies had over 158,000 casualties in this area.)

He is commemorated at the Arras Memorial (Bay 8). Peter was 29 years old and married to Mary Arnott Johnstone.

Donald 'Donnie' McLeod was born on 28th May 1882 in Laurieston,

the Falkirk district of Glasgow. He was a two-footed full back described as of tremendous speed and skill. McLeod began locally at Stenhousemuir before signing for Celtic in 1902. A regular from the off, he was a first choice as part of the highly successful side of that era.

In his four seasons there to 1908, Celtic won four championships in a row. They also won the Scottish Cup in 1907 and 1908. He made 176 appearances for the club and scored two goals.

He then moved to Middlesbrough in the 1909-10 season and had a good run there, playing over 138 games for them. He won four caps for Scotland from 1905-06 and represented the Scottish League on two occasions.

McLeod enlisted with the Royal Field Artillery 466th Battery, 65th Brigade. He was wounded during the bloody battles at Passchendaele, Belgium. He died from his injuries on 6th October 1917 and was buried in Dozinghem Military Cemetery (V.G.7). Donald was 35 years old, married and had three children.

William 'Wull' Strang was born on 16th September 1880 in Dumfermline, one of four brothers. He was a full back who played for Wallsend, Dunfermline Athletic Juniors and Orion FC, and he then signed for Celtic in 1903.

Mainly a reserve-team player he managed three first-team appearances from 1903-05, though he was also loaned out to Renton FC.

Bizarrely he and his twin Alexander 'Sandy', also a footballer, got into trouble with the Scottish FA in 1904. During a game, the referee sent one of them off, but neither accepted responsibility at the hearing. The FA imposed a suspension on both players.

In 1905 the family emigrated to Canada and the two brothers played for Calgary Caledonian, Sandy becoming the more successful player, captaining the side. William joined the Canadian Infantry for the war effort serving in France with the 56th and 31st Battalions, attaining the rank of Lance Corporal. He was killed in action on 7th October 1916 and is commemorated at the St Sever Cemetery, Rouen (B.18.12). William was 36 years old.

His other brother Norman (also pictured) was a victim, killed during the conflict on 3rd June 1917, aged 34 years, at Vimy Ridge, France, serving with the Canadian Infantry, Alberta Regiment. He is remembered on the Vimy Memorial.

PTE. NORMAN STRANG
Killed

John Young was born in 1887 in the Calton district of Glasgow. He was a winger or inside forward and joined Celtic from 1908-11, though he only played three first-team games in all competitions.

He went to Dundee Hibernian (United) on loan, playing three games for them including an appearance in the Consolidation Cup before returning to Celtic in 1913. They then released him at the end of the year.

Young returned to his job as a foundry labourer prior to the war.

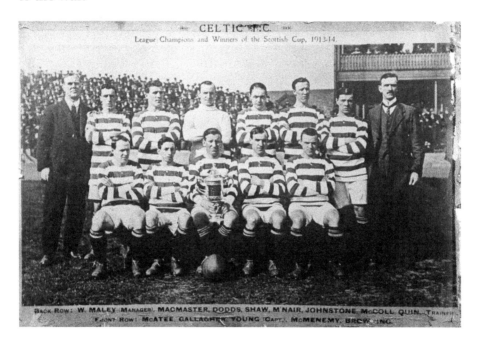

CELTIC F.C.

League Champions and Winners of the Scottish Cup, 1913-14.

BACK ROW: W. MALEY (MANAGER), MACMASTER, DODDS, SHAW, M'NAIR, JOHNSTONE, McCOLL, QUIN, TRAINER
FRONT ROW: McATEE, GALLACHER, YOUNG (CAPT.), McMENEMY, BROWNING

He enlisted with the 5th Battalion Queen's Own Cameron Highlanders serving in France. He was involved in the Battle of Little Willie Trench during the Battle of Loos and listed as missing believed killed in action on 25th September 1915. Out of the 820 men from his battalion who took part in the assault, only 70 returned. The battles at Loos grossed over 59,000 casualties in total during 1915.

He is commemorated at the Loos Memorial (Panel 119 to 124). John was 28 years old, married to Margaret Young and had one child.

John McLaughlin is listed as being on the books of Celtic prior to the war, but not as a first-team player. He enlisted with the 11th

Battalion Highland Light Infantry serving in France. Badly wounded at the Battle of Cavalry Farm, north of Arras on the 23/4/1917, he died on 10th May 1917. He was buried in the Etaples Military Cemetery, Pas de Calais (XVIII.L.18).

Sergt. ROBERT DOWNIE. V.C.

Note: Robert Downie V.C. M.M. was born on 12th January 1894 in Glasgow. He was a supporter and later employee at the club, although he did not play for them. Downie was a Sergeant with the 2nd Battalion Royal Dublin Fusiliers. He was awarded the Victoria Cross and Military Medal. He gained his Victoria Cross at the Somme. Although wounded, he led an attack on an enemy machine gun post, capturing it and eliminating the threat. He continued to work for the club after the war. He also played a prominent role in the Home Guard during the Second World War. Robert died on 18th April 1968, aged 74 years. He was buried in St Kentigern's Cemetery, Glasgow. He had donated his medals to Celtic prior to his death and they are on display at the Celtic Park ground.

Clyde FC, Division A
(League position: 16th)

Charles Clunas was born in 1894 in Johnstone, Renfrewshire. He attended Johnstone High School and played amateur football for Kilbarchan Athletic. He signed for Clyde from 1912-15, making 19 appearances and scoring three goals. It appears he was capable of playing in a number of positions.

He joined up with the 23rd Royal Fusiliers 1st Sportsman's Battalion, ranked as a Lance Corporal. Clunas was a regular player in the regiment football team.

He was killed in action on 8th February 1916 in Northern France, aged 22 years, and is commemorated at the Windy Corner Guards Cemetery, Cuinchy (II.K.6).

Robert Milligan was born in 1892 in Stoneykirk, Wigtonshire. He played amateur football for Newton

Villa and worked in the coal industry at Douglas Park Colliery. On Clyde's books, he made one first-team appearance in 1912-13. He enlisted with the 8th Seaforth Highlanders for the conflict.

He was killed in action at the Battle of Loos on 25th September 1915 and is commemorated at the Loos Memorial (Panel 112 to 115). Robert was 23 years old. He is also remembered on the memorial wall in the Parish of Kirkgunzeon, Dumfries and Galloway. His brother Alexander served in the same regiment.

William McAdam Sharp was born 1889 in Paisley. An inside left, he played for Kilbirnie and Ladeside amateur sides before signing for Clyde in 1910-11.

He played five first-team games during his time there. After that, he is listed as having spells at St Mirren then Johnstone FC, where he made one appearance.

Sharp enlisted with the 1st Battalion Scots Guards and after training served in France. He was killed in action near Loos on 8th June 1915 during heavy shelling. He is commemorated at the Dud Corner Cemetery (VII.D.12). William was 26 years old.

Back Row: W. Chambers *(Assist. Trainer)*, G. McTurk, H. McL. Thomson, A. S. Maley *(Sec. re Manager)*, A. Watson, J. Wylie, G. Robertson, Major R. L. Stevenson *(Director)*. R. Greer, P. Travers, T. McAteer, W. Mossman *(Chairman)*, W. Struth *(Trainer)*. Front Row: J. Kerr *(Director)*, J. Gilligan, W. McCartney, J. Chalmers, W. Walker *(Captain)*, J. Blair, J. Stirling, T. Booth, T. M. Colquhoun *(Director)*. Photo by Agnew & Son, Glasgow]

CLYDE F.C. SEASON 1909–10

Clydebank FC, Division B
(League position: fifth)

CLYDEBANK A.F.C. 1920-1921

No players listed. Clydebank formed in 1914 and were elected into Division B. From 1917 to 1919, as previously stated, it was part of the one division of 18 clubs. The club struggled thereafter for a number of years and dissolved in 1931.

Cowdenbeath FC Division B
(League winners 1914-15, after round robin play-off)

Charles Penman Scott was born in 1886 in Auchterderran, Fife, one of nine children. He was signed by Cowdenbeath from Hearts of Beath in 1905, and he played 17 games and scored one goal. By 1910 he was linked with East Fife, but no information shows he made a first-team appearances. By trade, he was a coal miner.

He enlisted with the 11th Battalion Argyll and Sutherland Highlanders. He was killed in action at

Cowdenbeath FC circa 1895.

the Somme on 10th August 1916, aged 29 years, and was married to Elizabeth and had two children. He was buried in the Gordon Dump Cemetery (III.M.1) near Albert, France, and is commemorated on the Cowdenbeath War Memorial that overlooks the town.

Dumbarton FC, Division A
(League position: 12th)

Henry 'Harry' Gildea was born in 1890 in Broxburn, West Lothian. He began with Lochgelly St Patricks, before signing for Hibernian in 1908-09 as a half back, playing six games and scoring three goals. He then moved to Grimsby Town in 1909, where he played three games.

From here, he was briefly involved with a number of clubs, namely Bristol City, Lochgelly United, East Fife and York City. From 1913-15 he played for Dumbarton and is listed as playing over 27 games and scoring four goals. In the 1915-16 season he was back at Lochgelly prior to enlisting. His two brothers also played as half backs: Peter at Bury and William at Bradford City, the latter playing in the FA Cup final of 1911, but not the replay.

Gildea joined the Black Watch Royal Highlanders, 8th and 1st Service Battalions serving in France. He was killed in Northern France on 9th April 1917 and is commemorated at the Mindel Trench British Cemetery (B.23), St Laurent-Blangy, Pas de Calais. Harry was 26-27 years old.

Dundee FC, Division A
(League position: 14th)

David Glen M.M. was born in Crosshill, Brechin, on 31st March 1881, one of five children. He was a centre or inside forward, starting his career with Brechin Hearts. He then signed for Brechin City in around 1906. He assisted the club in winning the Forfarshire Cup. Prior to the war he was briefly on the books of Dundee in 1906-07, playing four games, and then at Millwall in 1909-10, though he again returned to Brechin and was with them up to 1914.

Glen enlisted with the 13th Royal Scots Lothian Regiment and served in France, attaining the rank of Sergeant, being awarded the Military

Medal for bravery, and had also been recommended for the Distinguished Conduct Medal.

He was killed on 9th April 1917 during the first day of an offensive at Arras whilst assisting the French Troops, one of many Scottish casualties. His commanding officer wrote to his mother stating, *'that he had on more than one occasion recommended the gallant sergeant for his courage and bravery, he was held in high regard by the battalion'*. He is commemorated at the Cabaret-Rouge British Cemetery, Souchez (XVII.G.11). David was 36 years old.

James Hamilton was from Broxburn and was a Broxburn United FC

player. He was listed as being on the books of Dundee in 1913-14 as a centre forward. (No first-team appearances are listed.) A report in the Edinburgh News Roll of Honour on 13th May 1915 states that Sergeant Hamilton of the 2nd Battalion Seaforth Highlanders had been killed in action in France.

Dundee Hibernian FC, Division B
(League position: 11th)

(Formed in 1909, and after 1923 the name was changed to Dundee United.)

Robert 'Bobby' Craig was born in Beith on 2nd May 1888. A full back starting at Vale of Garnock Strollers, he signed for Celtic in 1906. He

failed to hold down a regular spot and moved to Brighton FC in 1909. He is listed at a number of other clubs, namely Morton, Carlisle, Darlington and Renton, before signing for Dundee Hibs in 1911-12, where he played 19 games and scored four goals.

Craig may well have moved south again after this, as he is not listed at any other clubs before joining the 5th Service Battalion South Wales Borderers during the war.

Wounded in fighting at Bolougne, France, on 11th April 1918, he died from his wounds 8 days later in hospital. He was buried in the hospital cemetery at Bolougne Eastern (Plot 9, Row A, Grave C). Robert was 29 years old.

David 'Collie' Martin was born in Brechin on 18th March 1890. A prolific striker, he began at Brechin Hearts then Brechin City. In 1911 he signed for Dundee, playing eight games and scoring three goals. From 1913-15 he moved the short distance to Dundee Hibs. Martin was the division's top scorer in his two seasons there, scoring five goals in one game. He made 59 appearances and scored 53 goals. His occupation is listed as a bleachfield worker.

In late 1915 he enlisted with the 3rd/5th Black Watch and attained the rank of Corporal. He was killed in action by a shell on 26th March 1917, prior to the third offensive at Ypres. He was buried in the Railway Dugouts Burial Grounds, near Ypres, Belgium (VII.J.27). David was 27 years old and married to Catherine Martin.

Henry 'Harry' Taylor was born in 1881 in Falkirk. He began playing as a right half in amateur football with Cowie Wanderers then Kings Park before signing for Dundee in 1911, making three appearances. In the same year he moved to Falkirk, where he played two games for them. The 1912-13 season saw him at Stenhousemuir FC prior to the war. He supplemented his football by working as a brakesman for the Callender Coal Company.

Dundee Hibernian, 1914.

Taylor joined the 8th Service Battalion Gordon Highlanders (1st/7th Deeside), serving in France. He was killed on 27th May 1917 near to Rouex and is commemorated at the Browns Copse Cemetery (I.G.37). Henry was 35-36 years old.

Dunfermline Athletic FC, Division B
(League position: sixth)

James Gray was born in Dunfermline circa 1893. He is listed as being with the club from 1913-14, making three appearances over almost two seasons, mainly used as a reserve. A good all-round sportsman, Gray represented Dumfermline Carnegie Cricket Club, regularly topping the season batting averages. In 1914 he was the overall champion at the Carnegie Trust Annual Sports Day event challenge.

Gray enlisted with the 14th Argyll and Sutherland Highlanders, attaining the rank of Sergeant. He was killed in action in the Somme, France, on 24th April 1917 and is commemorated on the Thiepval Memorial (Pier and Face 15A and 16C). James was 23-24 years old.

David Heron Izatt was born in 1892 in Dunfermline. Playing as a half back, he signed for the club from 1911-14. His occupation was a plumber.

Starting in the reserves, he progressed to the first eleven, and prior to enlisting he had made 62 appearances and scored seven goals.

Izatt joined the Royal Scots, Lothian Regiment 16th Service Battalion (2nd Edinburgh). He was

Dunfermline Athletic's team pictured with the Scottish Qualifying Cup which they won in 1913. Back row (l to r): T. Robertson (vice-president), Liddell, Crichton, R. Philp (secretary). Third row: E. Millar (treasurer), J. Philp (trainer), Donaldson, Pratt, Brown (captain), Wilkie, Thomson, Ballancine, J. Berwick (treasurer). Second row: G. Anderson (vice-president), Murray, Slavin, Gibson, Newlands-Robertson, J. Farrell (president). First row: J. McLaughlin (trainer), Duncan. The other trophies are the Loftus Cup and the Calder Shield.

killed in action on the first day of the Somme, on 1st July 1916. He is commemorated at the Thiepval Memorial (Pier and Face 6D and 7D). David was 24 years old.

East Stirlingshire FC, Division B
(League position: fourth)

James Higgins Laing. See Falkirk FC

Falkirk FC, Division A
(League position: fifth)

Robert Graham was born in 1884 in the Camelon area of Falkirk. He was a local amateur player with Camelon Juveniles, Laurieston Juniors, Falkirk Juniors then with Falkirk FC from 1904-06. He had represented Scotland at junior level in 1902-03. After this, it is believed he was at Leicester Fosse for a short time.

Around 1908 he joined the Royal Navy, serving initially on the H.M.S. *Roxburgh* as an engineer, his trade prior to enlisting.

Graham later served on HMS *Invincible*, seeing action in the Falklands.

A Chief Petty Officer, he was killed when the ship was torpedoed and sunk during the Battle of Jutland on 31st May 1916.

He was believed to have been living in the Leicester area after marrying Ethel Benn, the daughter of one of the directors at Leicester Fosse Football Club; they had one child. A naval representative for the area informed his wife of his death. He is commemorated at the Portsmouth Naval Memorial. Robert was 32 years old.

Alexander Johnson was born in 1880 in Falkirk. He also played for Camelon and Falkirk Amateurs. He was registered with Falkirk from 1899-1900 and from 1904-06. Johnson worked at the post office in

the town for 20 years before he enlisted in 1916. He served with the Royal Garrison Artillery in Flanders and is listed as being killed in action on 17th August 1917. He is commemorated at Leper Memorial, Menin Gate, Belgium. Alex was 37 years old and married with a family.

James Higgins Laing was born in 1897 in Falkirk and lived in the Carron area of the town with his parents. He was a reserve-list player and Falkirk FC held his league registration. He was a regular player for East Stirling as well. An engineer by trade, he had enlisted with the

Territorials then the Argyll and Sutherland Highlanders. He was reportedly killed on 23rd April 1917 in France, aged 19 years and is commemorated at the Roeux British War Cemetery (A1.), which is to the east of Arras.

John Bryce Ramsay was born in 1897 in Grangemouth, Stirlingshire. He was a forward at Denny Athletic before Falkirk FC put him on their books in 1914-15, and he played 28 games and scored 10 goals in total. A budding career was cut short when he enlisted with the Royal Navy 6th Howe Battalion. He fought in and survived the

Dardanelles campaign, Turkey, but is listed as being killed in action in northern France on 28th April 1917. He is commemorated at the Arras Memorial (Bay 1). John was 20 years old.

His brother Alexander, aged 18 years, also perished, reportedly killed on 14th November 1916, serving with the Drake Battalion, Royal Navy. The third and youngest brother had his enlistment rejected as he was too young. At the time of John's death, he was due to re-enlist with the forces. There is no record of him being a victim of the war.

James Sharp was born in 1894 in Denny, Stirlingshire. He was on the books of Falkirk in 1913-14 and had been playing for Grange Rovers. He was a left back and played five games with the first team.

He enlisted with the 1st/7th Argyll and Sutherland Highlanders, but was killed in action on 26th April 1915. James was 21 years old. He is commemorated at the Ypres Menin Gate Memorial (Panel 42 and 44) and the Denny Memorial, Falkirk.

William Mitchell Whytock was born on 17th August 1887 in Falkirk. Initially with Falkirk Thistle Amateurs, he is on the club's books from 1905-07 before returning to the Falkirk Amateurs. There is

Falkirk FC, 1914-15.

little information about his football career thereafter. He could possibly have been in Ireland.

After enlisting with the Leinster Irish Regiment for the war, he was killed in action on 6th November/ 1917 at Passchendaele. He is commemorated at the Roisel War Memorial, France. William was 30 years old and had attained the rank of Sergeant.

Hamilton Academicals FC, Division A
(League position: sixth)

Hamilton Academical, 1911.

Thomas Gracie. see Heart of Midlothian FC

Heart of Midlothian FC, Division A
(League runners-up)

John Allan was born on 2nd March 1887 in Greenlaw, Berwickshire, and was a joiner by trade. He was a centre half described as wholehearted, and was listed as playing for Hearts in 1914-15, where he played one game. Prior to this, he played for Wemyss Athletic and Tranent Juniors.

Allan enlisted with the 9th Royal Scots and was a Lance Corporal. He is listed as being shot and killed in action near Roeux, France, on 22nd April 1917. He is commemorated at the Arras Memorial (Bay 1 and 2). John was 30 years old.

James Boyd was born on 14th November 1894 in Seafield, Livingston, West Lothian. He was educated at West Calder School, passing through to the higher grade. He was a shale mine underground worker and listed with Hearts prior to the war, signing in 1914. His brother Archie was already with the club as a goalkeeper. James then made the decision to sign up as Archie was engaged to be married.

He enlisted with the 16th Royal Scots (McCrae's) Battalion and served in France as a Lance Corporal. He was wounded by shrapnel and died from his injuries on 3rd August 1916, after one of the Somme offensives near Bazentin. He was buried in the area, but his grave was later lost due to shelling.

He is commemorated at the Thiepval Memorial (Pier and Face 6D and 7D). James was 21 years old.

Duncan Currie was born on 13th August 1892 in Kilwinning, Ayrshire. He assisted one of his brothers as a hairdresser's assistant before signing for Hearts from 1912-15 as a full back, where he played 47 games. He was following in the family footsteps as his father was a goalkeeper of good repute and two of his brothers played for Bury and Leicester Fosse respectively.

Currie enlisted with the 16th Royal Scots and fought in France, ranked as a Sergeant. He was killed on the first day at the Somme, leading 'C' Company Platoon, when he was hit in the shoulder and upper body. He was buried near to where he fell, but the grave was lost after heavy shelling.

An officer wrote, *'He was a soldier with a most loveable nature, his death being a blow to the battalion. The grave is now a shell hole in no man's land.'*

He is commemorated at the Thiepval Memorial (Pier and Face 6D and 7D) and Kilwinning Memorial. Duncan was 23 years old.

Thomas Gracie was born on 12th June 1889 in Yorkhill, Glasgow. A meat salesperson and qualified bookkeeper, he played for a number of local clubs as a forward, before signing for Airdrie in 1907, then Hamilton and Morton. Everton signed him in 1910 where he played 13 games and one goal, and he then moved to Liverpool in 1912 playing a further 34 games and scoring five goals. In 1914-15 he signed for Hearts and his career took off immediately, scoring 28 goals in his first season and becoming the club's top scorer as they finished runners-up in the league. In total he made 46 appearances and scored 35 goals before he enlisted. He earned an international cap in 1915 against the Irish League.

Gracie joined the 16th Royals, stationed in Leeds as a Corporal. He had started to feel unwell, though still managed to assist the club and do his training. For some unexplained reason the illness was kept secret.

In October 1915 they admitted him to Stobhill War Hospital, Glasgow. Tom died on 23rd October 1915 from his illness, diagnosed as Leukemia. He was buried in Craigton Cemetery, Glasgow. He was 26 years old. He is the only Hearts player with a known grave. (His brother John was killed at Loos on 28th September 1915, and his brother in law also fell at Gallipoli.)

David Carswell Philip was born in 1880 in Dundee. He was a half back who began at Edinburgh Myrtle. Hearts signed him from 1902-10, where he made a total of over 140 appearances and scored six goals in all games. He was part of the team that secured the Scottish Cup in 1905-06 against Third Lanark and he again played in the final the following year on the losing side against Celtic. They also finished second in the First Division in 1903-04 and 1905-06.

He went on loan to Leith Athletic in 1910 before Raith Rovers secured his services. He was just as popular there, playing over 83 games for them and scoring 15 goals.

Philip enlisted with the Royal Scots 13th Service Battalion and was commissioned as a Second Lieutenant with the Northumberland Fusiliers 23rd Service, 4th Tyneside Scottish Battalion, in 1917. He was killed fighting in France and Flanders on 29th April 1917 near Arras, and he is commemorated at the Arras Memorial (Bay 2 and 3). He was 36-37 years old.

James Hodge Speedie was born on 17th November 1893 in Edinburgh. He was an insurance agent with the town's top firm and an amateur footballer. Hearts secured him on their books in 1913-14 as a forward from Tranent Amateurs. He played 12 games and scored seven goals. He also played on loan at St Mirren, playing 10 games and scoring three goals.

Described as a reliant and most likeable person, he readily enlisted for the cause with the Queen's Own Cameron Highlanders, 7th Service Battalion.

He was killed in action near Loos, France, on 25th Spetember 1915 and is commemorated at the Loos Memorial (Panel 119 to 124). He was 21 years old. His brother Lieutenant John Gibson Speedie, serving in Northern France, lost his life on 14th June 1917, aged 25 years. This left the family with just a surviving daughter.

Henry Benzie 'Harry' Wattie was born on 2nd June 1893 in Edinburgh. As is the norm with birth dates from this era, there are varying dates as well of 1891 and 1892.

1914

HARRY WATTIE

The first stated date is the C.W.G.C. listed date. The youngest of five brothers, he was signed by Hearts from Tranent Juniors and played for them from 1913-15. An instant hit, he was described as the probable natural successor to his teammate the famous Hearts forward Robert Walker, who had several international caps. He had a dry sense of humour and had the tendency to take the mickey out of opposing defenders. Known by his teammates as Harry, his career ended when he enlisted with the 16th Royal Scots, along with his colleagues, as he had been a pre-war territorial. Wattie made 74 appearances and scored 22 goals.

On the first day of the Somme on 1st July 1916, he was seen by a fellow comrade to fall during an assault against the enemy. Due to the heavy shelling and machine gun fire, they had to leave the area.

He is commemorated at the Thiepval Memorial (Pier and Face 6D and 7D), and he was 23 years old. His brother John was Chaplin of the Fleet.

As previously stated, 11 Hearts players initially enlisted after George McCrae formed the 16th Royal Scots, which was the catalyst for other club players and supporters following suit and enlisting as well the formation of other battalions. You will not be surprised to know that the Midlothian area holds this history close to its heart. There are numerous memorials in this region to those who gave their life. One such is the pictured Hearts Memorial. The Hearts team squad from 1914-15 are also pictured.

TEAM 1914 15

Hibernian FC, Division A

(League position: 11th)

John Aitken was born in 1894 in Perthshire. An inside left or left winger, he was initially at Perth Violet playing amateur football.

He played for Hibs from 1913-15 and made 18 appearances in total, scoring two goals. He was sold to Broxburn United in 1915.

Aitken enlisted with the Gordon Highlanders and after training was stationed in France and Belgium as a Lance Corporal. He was killed in action near Ypres on 13th July 1917. John was 23 years old, married to Christine Aitken and had a daughter, Edwina.

He is commemorated at the Vlamertighe New Military Cemetery, Ypres, Belgium (IV. H.4).

Robert William 'Bob' Atherton was born on 28th July 1876 in Bethesda, Wales. He was a highly regarded midfielder highly regarded initially signed by Hearts in 1897, but this was very brief as he moved to Hibs in the same year. He was part of a squad that won the Scottish Cup in 1901-02 and the League the following season, thereby holding both trophies at the same time. In total he played 97 games and scored 36 goals for the club. He was with Hibs when he gained

his first Welsh international cap in 1899, winning nine in total and scoring two goals up to 1903.

Atherton transferred to Middlesbrough and from 1903-06 he played 66 games and scored 14 goals, also becoming club captain. He was at Chelsea in 1906 for a short time before retiring from professional football.

He joined the Merchant Navy and served on S.S. *Britannia* (Leith), a defensively armed ship, as a steward. It was torpedoed in the English Channel and sank, causing 22 deaths, including Atherton, on 19th October 1917. He is commemorated at the Tower Hill Mercantile Marine Memorial, London. Robert was 41 years old and married to Margaret Jane Atherton.

Bernard 'Barney' Donaghy was born in Derry, Northern Ireland, on 23rd December 1882. An inside forward, he began in the Irish League with Derry Celtic, Belfast Celtic then Glentoran. He was signed by Hibernian in the 1904-05 season, making 17 appearances and scoring eight goals. He then returned to Derry Celtic before Manchester United signed him in 1905-06, where he made three appearances in their first team.

1907-08 saw him at Burnley, where he played five games and scored two goals before returning to Derry Celtic again to finish his career. He gained one international cap in 1902 against Scotland, and also represented the Irish League on two occasions.

Donaghy was a pre-war reservist and enlisted with the 1st Battalion Royal Inniskilling Fusiliers. He was killed in action on 1st July 1916 at the Somme and is commemorated at the Thiepval Memorial (Pier and Face 4D and 5B). He was 33 years old. Prior to his death Bernard had been living in Derry and was married to Sarah Donaghy.

James Hendren was born on 12th August 1887 in Annbank, Fife. Other information states he was born in 1885, but an ancestry birth certificate shows the year as 1887. A centre forward, he began at Nithsdale Wanderers, then had short spells at Kilmarnock and Cowdenbeath before signing for Hibs from 1912-15, making 135 appearances and scoring 56 goals. Hendren was in the side that lost to Celtic in the 1914 Scottish Cup final replay 4-1. The first game ended in a 0-0 draw.

He registered for enlistment, training with the Army Transport Corps in 1915, but was allowed to delay this as his wife had just given birth to their second child. A short time after this he fell seriously ill and died in Edinburgh Hospital on 17th June 1915 from acute pneumonia. He was 27 years old.

Adam Miller was born in Eyemouth, Berwickshire, in 1883. A centre forward, he signed for Berwick Rangers in 1905 before signing for Hibs in the 1905-06 season, making two appearances. He then moved to Raith Rovers in 1907, where he played one game for them in the first team. In 1912 he emigrated to Queensland, Australia, and then joined the 9th Battalion, Australian Imperial Force Infantry, during the war effort in 1914.

He initially saw action at Gallipoli then in France after 1916, being involved in fighting at the Somme and Bullecourt. He was killed in action on 21st December 1917 at Ypres, aged 34 years. He is commemorated at the Ypres Menin Gate Memorial (Panel 7 to 31). Pictured is Adam's Australian Attestation paper.

Robert Rollo was born in 1887 in Glasgow. A right-winger, he was initially at Petershill then Clydebank Juniors before joining Hibs in 1907-08. He made 10 first-team appearances and scored one goal.

For the war, Rollo enlisted with the 2nd Battalion Royal Scots Fusiliers after initially joining the 12th Battalion, Lothians. He was badly wounded in Northern France in April 1917 and died from his injuries on 30th April 1917.

He was buried in the Warlincourt Halte British Cemetery, Saulty (X.E.7.). Robert was 30 years old and married to Jeanie Williamson Rollo.

Robert 'Bobby' Wilson was born in 1890 in Chicago, USA. He was signed by Hibs in 1913 from Kirkintilloch Rob Roy amateur side. A right winger, he was nicknamed 'the yank' by both players and supporters. He was well liked and was part of the side that reached the Scottish Cup final in 1914 against Celtic. In fact, newspaper reports state, 'it was through his performances that they reached the final'. After 1915 he is not listed with the squad again until 1918, when he is shown as having played one game against Celtic on 17th August 1918. In all he made over 41 appearances and scored 13 goals.

HIBERNIAN F.C. 1914-15

There is no information of his movements during the war, but it is believed he offered his services along with teammates David Stevenson, James Williamson and Robert Reid, who all enlisted.

Robert died in early November 1918, but from an unspecified illness he had been suffering from and not in action. He was 27-28 years old.

Kilmarnock FC, Division A

(League position: 12th)

James Rae Armstrong was born in 1888 in Dennistoun, Glasgow. He was on the books of Kilmarnock in 1912-13 as an inside forward, and he played two games scoring two goals. He then played at St Mirren the following season, making another two appearances. He was then linked with Girvan Athletic.

Armstrong enlisted with the 5th Cameron Highlanders, serving in France and Flanders. He was killed in action on 11th October 1915 near Rouen, Northern France. He is commemorated at the St Sever Cemetery (A.12.24.). James was 27 years old.

Alexander W. Barrie was born on 18th August 1878 in Camlachie, Glasgow. A centre half, he began at Parkhead Juniors helping them win the Scottish Junior Cup in 1899 before moving to St Bernard's in 1901. He was signed by Sunderland from 1902-07, playing 71 games for them and scoring four goals. A move to Rangers followed, and he made over 11 appearances and scored one goal for them. From 1908-12 he was at Kilmarnock, making 126 appearances in all and scoring six goals. Now aged 34, Barrie had a spell with his last registered club Abercorn.

Barrie enlisted with the 17th Service Battalion (3rd Glasgow), 2nd Battalion Highland Light Infantry and after training served in France and Flanders as a Corporal. He was killed on 1st October 1918 in France, just over a month before the Armistice, and was buried in the Flesquieres Hill British Cemetery (VIII.I.14.). Alex was 40 years old. The inscription reads, *'He was a gallant child, loved and admired by all.'*

James Morton Maxwell (Senior) was born on 26th July 1887 in New Cumnock, East Ayrshire. An outside right, he began with Kilmarnock Shawbank and Petershill. He signed for Kilmarnock from 1904-07 and played 57 games, scoring 15 goals. In 1906 he signed for The Wednesday, playing 27 games and scoring six goals. In 1908 he was at Arsenal, though he was not happy with his treatment there, only managing two games.

He goes off the radar then and reports state that he left the club unannounced and returned north. Various clubs are then mentioned, namely Hurlford, Galston, Carlisle United, Lanemark and then back at Kilmarnock in 1912. He played another eight games there and scored three goals before moving to Nithsdale Wanderers in 1914.

Maxwell enlisted with the 1st Battalion Seaforth Highlanders and served in the Middle East. He was wounded at the Battle of Istanbulat and died on 21st April 1917. James was 29 years old, was married to Helen Maxwell and had two children. He is commemorated at the Basra War Memorial (Panel 37 and 64).

His second son (pictured) who had the same name also became a footballer with Kilmarnock from 1930-34 and was affectionately known as 'Bud Maxwell'. He was a superb centre forward who played 147 games for the club, scoring 120 goals and winning a Scottish Cup Final runners-up medal in 1932. He played for a number of clubs after 1934, having similar success at Preston North End, making 129 games and scoring 60 goals from 1934-38, winning the FA Cup with them in 1938 alongside Bill Shankly. He also represented the Scottish League. Bud served in the Royal Navy during the Second World War. He died in 1990, aged 77 years.

Note: James senior's elder brother, Thomas Maxwell, of the Royal Engineers was killed near Pas de Calais, Northern France, on 24th October 1918, aged 30 years. He was also married.

He was buried in the Terlinchun British Cemetery (VI.C.28.).

Alexander 'Alex' McCurdie was born on 7th January 1895 in Trabboch, Ayrshire. Kilmarnock signed the centre forward in 1913, and he played five games, scoring two goals. He was loaned out to Stevenson United, but returned to the club the next season – 1914-15 – playing another six games. His appearances were always limited as he was a student at Glasgow University.

McCurdie enlisted with the 14th Service Battalion Argyll and Sutherland Highlanders, serving as a Lance Sergeant. He was killed in action during an assault at Beaucamp, Northern France, with 10 of his colleagues, on 24th April 1917.

He was buried in the Fifteen Ravine British Cemetery, Villers-Plouich (II.A.4.). He was 22 years old. Described as 'totally reliable and fearless', he had been recommended for the D.C.M. prior to his death.

Daniel McKellar was born in 1892 in Glasgow. A left winger, he played for Ashfield and Bellshill Athletic before signing for Airdrieonians in 1914, playing three games. He then signed for Kilmarnock from 1914-16 where he played 37 games and scored one goal.

In 1916 McKellar joined the 1st/9th Battalion, Glasgow Highland Light Infantry, serving in France and Belgium. He was killed in action on 13th April 1918 in Belgium and is commemorated at the Ploegsteert Memorial (Panel 9), south of Leper. Daniel was 25-26 years old.

John Dalziel Rollo was born in 1893 from Dreghorn, Ayrshire. A joiner by trade and reserve player at the club in around 1914, he enlisted for the war in 1914 before he had chance to break into the first team.

John was part of the Royal Navy Division, Nelson Battalion, serving initially at Dardanelles, Gallipoli, before going to France, where he was involved in several campaigns. He died from multiple wounds in North East France on 14th February 1917, aged 24 years. He is commemorated at the Varennes Military Cemetery (I.D.33/FR41), the Royal Navy Division Memorial, Horse Guards Parade, London, and the pictured Dreghorn War Memorial.

David Glencross Slimmon M.M. was born on 2nd August 1895 in Kilmarnock. A left back initially playing his football with St Andrews United, he then played for Auchinleck Talbot when they won the Ayr and District Cup. He was on the books of Dumbarton in 1914, where he played one game, before joining Kilmarnock from 1914-16, playing 17 games.

After enlisting with the 419th West Lancashire Field Company, Royal Engineers, he served in Belgium as a Corporal.

He was awarded the Military Medal for an act of bravery reported in the *London Gazette* on 22nd August 1916: 'Slimmon stormed a machine gun nest, allowing his comrades to pass by with safety'.

He was killed in action on 23rd July 1917 at Beaucamps along with 10 of his section. A week later at the third Battle of Ypres, a further 3,500 of his regiment died on the first day of fighting.

He was buried in the Hop Store Cemetery near Eiper (Plot I. Row D. Grave 37). David was 21 years old. (He is not listed on the Scottish War Memorial Roll of Honour.)

Charles Thomas Vickers was born on 12th February 1891 at Hutchestown, Glasgow. An outside left, he played for Kilsyth Emmet before joining Kilmarnock from 1913-15. He played 16 games and scored one goal. He then played for Renton the following season before enlisting.

Vickers joined the Heavy Trench Mortar Battery, Royal Field Artillery, serving in France. He was critically wounded in June 1917 and died at the 23rd Casualty Clearing Station, Lozinghem, on 21st June 1917. He was buried in the Lapugnoy Military Cemetery near Pas de Calais (IV.D.17.). Charles was 26 years old and married to Jessie Ross Vickers.

The pictured Kilmarnock squad is unnamed and may well contain a number of the players detailed in the aforementioned section.

Leith Athletic FC, Division B

(League runners-up)

(The club was finally wound up in 1955 after many attempts to keep them afloat.)

Archibald Cunningham was born on 30th April 1879 in Lasswade, near Edinburgh. A goalkeeper, he was registered with Leith from 1900-03, playing over 30 games for them, and previously played for Bonnyrigg Rose. From here, he then moved briefly to Broxburn Shamrock, then onto Glentoran in 1903-04 in Ireland.

Pictured is the Glentoran squad from that season with Archie Cunningham present. Unfortunately the players are not named. He then returned to Lasswade prior to the war, working as a miner and living in the town with his mother.

Cunningham enlisted with the 1st Battalion Highland Light Infantry and served in France after completing training in Hamilton. He was involved in several heavy engagements and was killed in action on 18th March 1915 in Northern France after the Battle of Neuve Chapelle.

He is commemorated at the Le Touret Memorial (Panel 37 and 38), and also remembered at the Bonnyrigg and Lasswade Memorial. Archibald was 35 years old.

Andrew McDermott was born in 1889 in Edinburgh. A goalkeeper for Newtongrange FC, he was on the books of Leith in 1910-11, playing

Leith Athletic, 1926.

four first-team games. A lithographer by trade, he enlisted with the 1st and 7th Battalion 'C' Coy, Royal Scots, in 1914 and was a Lance Corporal.

Stationed in Turkey, he was wounded in the face during fighting at Dardanelles, Gallipoli, on 28th June 1915. He died from his injuries on 12th July 1915. He is commemorated at the Helles Memorial (Panel 26 to 30), Turkey. Andrew was 26 years old.

Lochgelly United FC, Division B
(League position: 10th)

(The club left the Football League in 1926, entering the Scottish Football Alliance. They were wound up in 1928.)

James Haldane was born in 1898 in Dundee, Scotland. He played for Hearts of Beath, and is listed for one game for Lochgelly in 1914. A pre-war territorial for four years, he enlisted with the 11th Royal Scots on the outbreak of the conflict. He was killed on 27th August 1915. A comrade wrote to his sister with the details of his death: *'He had been attempting to help a wounded colleague from the trenches when he was hit himself and killed instantly. It has cast gloom over a good soldier and all of us. He was well*

liked and buried in the village churchyard. He is lying alongside other heroes who died for the cause, King and country. I am fulfilling his wishes informing you as he and I had agreed between us to let the others family know. This is a terrible war and there will be many sad homes before this has ended. His comrades wish to express their deepest sympathy to you and your family.'

Commemorated at the Cambrin Churchyard Extension (H.11.), Pas de Calais, James was 23 years old.

George Millar was born in 1893 in Lochgelly and was the son of a local councillor. He was signed by the club from amateur football.

Millar signed up for the conflict almost straight away, before the season had started, serving in France with the 1st Royal Highlanders as a Lance Corporal. He was involved in the Battle of Aisne and was killed in action on 28th October 1914 at Yser, Nord, Northern France, on the Belgian border. Just prior to his death, he had written to his father stating he was in good health and missing Lochgelly football club.

He is commemorated at the Menin Gate Memorial (Panel 37), Belgium. George was 21 years old.

- 1908 -

(Greenock) Morton FC, Division A
(League position: fourth)

GREENOCK MORTON A.F.C. 1920-1921

Robert Craig. See Dundee Hibernian
Thomas Gracie. See Hearts
William Pickering. See Burnley
John Young. See Celtic

Motherwell FC, Division A
(League position: 18th)

Frank Davis Kelly was born on 8th December 1892 in Blantyre, South Lanarkshire. His father James ran Blantyre Engineering Company and owned a local pub called Kelly's Corner. He was a footballer himself, captaining the Celtic side in its infancy after 1890, and he gained 16 Scotland caps. He later became President of the Celtic club. Frank was an outside right and played locally for Blantyre St Joseph's and Blantyre Vics, before playing as a trialist for Celtic in 1913. He was on their tour of Germany that year and in all made two appearances before returning to Blantyre. He signed for Motherwell in 1915, playing over 82 games and scoring 16 goals by 1918, including war appearances.

He was loaned to Celtic in 1917-18, playing in the War Fund Shield and Glasgow Charity Cup competitions.

Kelly joined the 9th Cameronian Scottish Rifles and then the 3rd Reserve Battalions, serving with the company in France. He was tragically killed in a train crash near Loiret on 5th May 1919 and was buried in the Montargis Communal Cemetery (Row 8 Grave 23). He was 26 years old.

Patrick Slavin was born on 5th May 1877 in Shotts, Lanarkshire. Another outside right, he began at Fauldhouse Hibs then moved to Celtic in 1897-98 where he played two games and scored one goal. A move to Motherwell followed where he played 12 games and scored three goals. Between 1898 and 1901, he is listed at no less than eight other clubs, with Albion Rovers and Broxburn amongst them. He was then back playing amateur football and was also a freestone quarryman.

Slavin enlisted with the 3rd then 2nd Royal Scots, serving in France as a Sergeant. He was killed during the second battle for the village of Serra on 13th November/ 1916, when during thick fog and bad light the battalion came under sustained fire, with 103 killed and 177 wounded. A later report states, 'as a mission, it had been badly pre-planned prior to its execution'. He is commemorated at the Serra Road 2 Cemetery (I.K.5.). Patrick was 39 years old and married to Mary Slavin.

Alexander White Walker was born on 15th November 1881 in Edinburgh, one of three boys. His elder brother was Robert 'Bobbie' Walker of Hearts, one of their best ever players. Alex began his football career at Hearts as an inside forward from 1899-1902, and he played 14 games and scored three goals. He then transferred to Motherwell, making 18 appearances and scoring one goal. Walker was then at Brentford from 1904-1905, where he played eight games before a serious knee injury seems to have finished his professional career.

He enlisted in Musselburgh with the Royal Scots 3rd/9th Battalion. During training in April 1916 he

Motherwell, 1912.

fell ill, diagnosed afterwards as tuberculosis. After admission to the Second Scottish General Hospital, Craigleith, he died on 12th May 1916 aged 34 years. He was buried in the family plot at Edinburgh Cemetery, North Merchiston (K26).

Partick Thistle FC, Division A

(League position: eighth)

George Allan was born in 1885 in Mauchline, Ayrshire, Scotland. He is recorded as being at Partick from 1906-08 prior to the war. Their records show Allan played 64 games and scored two goals. He is recorded as a half back with a number of appearances as an outside left.

He enlisted with the London Regiment 1st/19th Battalion during early 1916 and was a Second Lieutenant. Whilst on training in Winchester he was receiving instruction on the firing of trench bombs from a spring gun on 14th March 1916 when it failed to ignite. He went to inspect it and as he did the bomb carrier blew up, striking him in the face and causing horrific injuries from which he died a short time later. The instructor later reported a live bomb had mistakenly been loaded instead of a dummy, resulting in a number of casualties. He was buried in the Mauchline Cemetery, Ayrshire (Ref 1028). George was 31 years old.

Thomas Callaghan was born in 1886 in Halesowen, Birmingham. He was described as a fast and pacey winger, and he began his football with local sides Small Heath then Halesowen in 1905. He was signed by Glossop and played over 70 games, scoring eight goals, and he also represented England Juniors in the 1904-05 season. An unsuccessful spell at Manchester City from 1907-09 followed before he moved to Partick, where he had his best spell. In 1911 he was at St Mirren but returned to Partick in 1912 after playing 18 games and scoring three goals for them. Callaghan played 93 games and scored 10 goals in total for Partick.

He enlisted for the war with the Somerset Light Infantry, having moved back to England, living in Birmingham. By 1917 he was serving with the 1st/20th London Regiment in France.

On 20th February 1917 they were involved in an offensive on Hill 60 at Ypres Salient, taking a record number of prisoners and gaining a large amount of intelligence. Although casualties were small, Callaghan was one of the unfortunate six killed.

His Sergeant wrote in a dispatch letter to his brother, *'He was in charge of a gun and stuck to it like grim death, a shell fell on top of him and another man killing them both. I cannot say enough of him. I only wish I was as finer man'.* He was buried in the Chester Farm Cemetery, Vaartstraat (III.G.2.). Thomas was 30 years old.

William John 'Bill' Gray was born on 5th March 1882 in Inverness, Scotland. A half back, he began with Inverness Thistle before signing for Partick in 1900. He was a regular in the side, then he signed for Southampton in 1906, making over 28 appearances for them before an injury forced him out of the team. In 1907 he returned to Partick and in all made over 130 appearances for them, scoring 15 goals.

He enlisted with the 1st/4th (Ross Highland) Battalion, Seaforth Highlanders, attaining the rank of Corporal. He was killed in the Somme offensives on 18th November 1916.

He was buried in the Abbeville Communal Cemetery Extension between Paris and Boulogne (I.F.23.). Bill was 34 years old.

George Strachan Ramsay was born in 1892 in Kilpatrick, West Dumbartonshire. An inside forward, he began at Clydebank Juniors before signing for Queens Park in 1911, playing 48 games for them and scoring nine goals. He went on loan to Rangers in 1912 then moved to Ayr United in 1913-14, where he played 15 games and scored 11 goals. He then signed for Partick and had a good spell there, with 48 appearances and 11 goals by 1917.

Before enlisting he was an apprentice marine engineer. He joined the Royal Air Force, Royal Flying Corps 110 Squadron, ranked as a Lieutenant. Ramsay and his observer, Lieutenant Hartley, had their aircraft, an Airco DH.9, shot down over Bethencourt Bridge during the Battle of Amiens, Northern France, on 8th August 1918. Both men died as a result. George was 27 years old. He is commemorated on the Arras Flying Services Memorial.

Partick Thistle, 1917.

Queens Park FC, Division A

(League position: 20th – not relegated due to league changes and war)

James Alexander was born in 1880, a former student and graduate at Glasgow University. He is listed with one appearance for the club in 1917 against Celtic during the conflict. Additionally, he is registered as a committee member and was also a talented athlete.

Enlisting with the 16th Highland Light Infantry, he was commissioned as a Captain. He was killed in action on 2nd December 1917 near Ypres, Belgium, and is commemorated at the Tyne Cot Memorial (Panel 131 and 132) and Glasgow University Memorial. He was 37 years old.

John 'Doddie' Barbour was born in 1890 in Glasgow. He attended Hutchesons Grammar School and represented Scotland at schools level, scoring in a match against England. He was by trade an auditor, working for a railway company. He was a forward but could play in a number of positions, but additionally mainly as a winger, and he played for Glasgow Perthshire before signing for Queens Park from 1910-13, making 43 appearances and scoring 12 goals, inheriting the nickname Doddie. He was in the squad that toured Holland in 1912. A spell at Dundee in 1912-13 was followed with a move to Preston from 1914-15, where he played 13 games and scored two goals and was involved in their promotion-winning side from the English Second Division.

Barbour enlisted in Glasgow with the 9th Battalion Highland Light Infantry, continuing his football with the Glasgow Highlanders in the army. By 1916 he was a Lance Corporal stationed in France. On 14th July 1916 the Battalion were involved with the 7th Division at High Wood on the Somme, and engaged in an advance on the North West section of the wood. They came up against strong resistance from the Germans, who still held most of the area.

They had to make a short retreat, followed by a 'dig in' for cover. The order was to move forward early the next morning, on 15th July 1916. There had been a great deal of bad and mixed communication, and the battalion by now was trapped by a barrage of artillery and machine gun fire, suffering heavy casualties. At the end of the day 92 Highlanders were dead with 100 more were reported missing, presumed dead, and over 200 were wounded. A report in the *Lancashire Evening Post* stated, '*Lance Corporal Barbour had initially been wounded and reportedly said to a colleague who told him to stay where he was that he would carry on and "Stick to it". John continued to move forward before again being hit. He met his death charging the enemy. George Dickson the ex-Rangers reserve player was at his side when he fell and commented that the ex-Queens Park boy died like a true and gallant soldier'.* The wood was retaken two months later on 15th September.

Commemorated at the Thiepval Memorial (Pier and Face 15C), John was 26 years old and in his informal will left his Preston FC league-winners medal to Gladys Wallace of Newport, Fife.

James Bryce was born in 1884 in Ratho, West Edinburgh. His father ran a local pub, the Bridge Inn. Bryce was a law clerk, later working for Scottish Union and the National Insurance Company. A half back on the club's books from 1907-11, he made 26 appearances.

Bryce enlisted with the 9th Battalion Royal Scots; they later joined up with the 51st Highland Division in France, seeing action at the Somme then moving on to Ypres, Belgium, in 1916. The 9th were relieved from the front line on 14th August, but Bryce transferred to assist the 4th Battalion Seaforth Highlanders with six of his colleagues. After heavy shelling and fighting on their position, he was listed as missing, presumed killed, on 30th August 1916.

He is commemorated at the Ploegsteert Memorial (Panel 1). James was 32 years old.

Macdonald Cameron was born on 18th March 1893 in Partick and was the son of a police superintendent who eventually became chief constable. A goalkeeper described as of magnificent physique, he was signed as understudy to first-team keeper Gordon Kerr from 1913-15, making a number of reserve-team appearances for the 'Strollers'. He worked for the local corporation prior to joining up.

He enlisted with the 6th Battalion Highland Light Infantry, ranked as a Lieutenant. He was killed on 2nd December 1917 in Belgium and is commemorated at the Tyne Cot Memorial (Panel 131-132). Macdonald was 24 years old.

Robert Main Christie was born on 15th November 1865 in Dunblane, Stirlingshire. He could play as a forward, winger or defender and played for Dunblane FC and Edinburgh University whilst studying there. Already highly though of, he was signed by Queens Park in 1883 and selected to represent a Glasgow eleven against Sheffield in London. He was also a Scottish International, making his debut aged just 18 years against England. His younger brother also played for his country and played

for Queens Park in the triumphant 1900 Scottish Cup final. Christie had earlier moved to Glasgow as he was training to be an engineer and architect, which made it easier for him to play for Queens Park.

At the club until 1888, he made over 28 appearances, scoring 15 goals, notably playing in the English Cup final and scoring their only goal in a 2-1 defeat against Blackburn Rovers in 1884. Then in 1886 he was on the winning side playing against Renton in the Scottish Cup final, winning 3-1. He also appeared in two Scottish Cup semi-finals and won the Merchants Charity Cup twice, scoring two goals. Troubled by knee injuries, this forced his retirement from the team and he returned to play for Dunblane, where he remained a member of the club. He was elected president of the Scottish Football Association in 1903. Other interests included golf, and he was a founder member of Dunblane Golf

Club. An excellent curling player, he represented Scotland five times at this sport.

He enlisted with the 10th Company Labour Corps and served with the 13th Battalion Highland Light Infantry, ranked as Major, having previously served in the Boer War as a Captain. On 11th May 1918, Christie was commanding the 101st Labour Company laying cables at Foncquevillers, Somme Valley. They were bombarded by German high explosive shells, spiked with Mustard Gas, which resulted in three officers and 136 men killed. Christie was badly injured and removed to the Red Cross Hospital at Rouen. After three agonising days of pain, he finally succumbed to his injuries on 15th May 1918. He was buried in the St Sever Cemetery (Officers, B.5.6.). Robert was 52 years old and left a wife and five children.

John Clarkson was born on 21st November 1879 in Hamilton. He was a centre half and is listed as playing for the club from 1898-1900 in 14 games, though he remained registered until 1903. He was an engineer by trade.

He enlisted with the Prince of Wales North Staffordshire Regiment and died from wounds received at Ypres on 5th August 1917. John was 38 years old, married to Margaret Clarkson and had a family. He was buried in the Bailleul Communal Cemetery, Nord (III.D.305).

Walter McFarlane Coulter M.C. was born in 1891 in the West Indies to Scottish parents, later attending Glasgow High School. His father had been commissioner of police for the British Virgin Islands, before returning to Scotland. On the books of Queens Park, he made one appearance for the club in 1913, against Rangers at right half. He was also a good cricketer, playing for the Poloc Cricket Club.

He enlisted with the Glasgow Highland Infantry, serving with the 3rd/9th, 3rd/6th and 1st/6th Battalions, commissioned as a 2nd Lieutenant in 1915. He was wounded in the arm in 1916, but thereafter returned to his regiment. In March 1917 he was awarded the Military Cross, *'During action at Bouchavesnes on the Somme, for conspicuous gallantry and devotion to duty during a raid on enemy trenches. He led his men with great dash and the success of the raid was mainly due to his coolness and initiative. He has on many previous occasions done fine work.'* This was recorded in the *London Gazette* on 26th March 1917. Coulter was then promoted to Captain. He was killed in action on 20th May 1917 during an assault on German lines at Arras, which was shambolic, with only a few of the 80 men who were killed ever being recovered; Coulter was not among them. His father asked questions regarding this incident, also enquiring about his son's body. He didn't get a satisfactory answer until 1926. He is commemorated at the Arras Memorial (Bay 8) and the Poloc Memorial. Walter was 26 years old.

William Eadie also Prince was born on 14th June 1882 in Dunblane, Stirlingshire, the youngest of four sons. All four brothers were good footballers and when work took him to Glasgow he joined his brother James at Queens Park from his local amateur side Strathallan. Staying as an amateur, he also played for Dunblane when he could, assisting them in winning the Perthshire Cup in 1906. He managed 21 games

for Queens as a goalkeeper from 1902-05. In 1906 he was at St Mirren, playing in one first-team game. Eadie also made five appearances for Partick Thistle in 1908. He goes off the radar then, probably in amateur football, until 1913 when he is listed at East Fife, playing six games for them, beginning in January of that year.

On 20th March, even though he was on the team sheet for an East Fife game, he set sail on board a ship to Canada to begin a new life there. When war broke out, he enlisted in Quebec with the Canadian Expeditionary Force and was part of the 10th Infantry

Battalion, Alberta Regiment. It is here the confusion begins: He signed his attestation papers three times with the surname Prince, further stating he was born in 1895, some 13 years younger than his actual age. The paper also states he was 5ft 3in, which considering he was a goalkeeper is puzzling, but this could have been a clerical error. He gave his next of kin as his brother David Eadie in Edinburgh.

Serving in Belgium as a Sergeant, he was shot in what was described as 'a hail of bullets' at Langemark, Ypres, on 23rd April 1915. He is listed as killed in action, body not recovered.

William is commemorated on the Menin Gate Memorial, Ypres (Panel 24-28-30), and the Brooding Soldier Memorial to the Canadians at St Julien, where over 2,000 men were killed between 22nd and 24th April 1915 defending the area against German attacks.

William Eadie served as Prince and was 32 years old. Unfortunately, there is no mention of William on the Dunblane Memorial. His father had died and the family had moved to Edinburgh.

Harry Middleton Fletcher was born on  11th May 1878 in Beith, Ayrshire, and was the son of a spirit dealer. A teacher by profession, he was a full back on the clubs books from 1902-09, making 20 appearances.

Fletcher enlisted for the war with the Royal Field Artillery and was commissioned as a 2nd Lieutenant. Previously wounded in 1916, he lost his life in Belgium on 7th June 1917 near Ypres.

He was buried in the Railway Dugout Burial Ground (Transport Farm) Cemetery, Zillebeke. Harry was 39 years old.

Edwin Freeland was born on 3rd June 1878 in  Bridgeton, Glasgow. His father was a newspaper journalist and Edwin was educated at the local Hutcheson Grammar School. After leaving school, he worked as a clerk for a fire insurance company. He was on the books of Queens Park from 1892-94 as a full back, playing four games. After 1894 he emigrated to Canada, working as a bookkeeper in Medicine Hat, Alberta.

He enlisted with the Royal Canadian Regiment 1st and 3rd for the war, fighting in France at the Somme. They were involved in a series of battles for Regine Trench near Grandcourt, east of Beaumont Hamel. He was killed on 8th October 1916 in an unsuccessful attempt to take the ridge, which the Canadians captured and fully cleared on 11th November 1916. He was buried in the Regina Trench Cemetery (I.C.12). Edwin was 38 years old.

Edwin Stanley 'Eddie' Garvie was born on 14th September 1892 in Calton, Glasgow, one of nine children. His father was a successful spirits and wine merchant, and in 1911 they were living in Pollokshields, then Invergowar, Maxwell Park. Garvie was an inside forward or half back signed from 1911-14, making 104 appearances and scoring one goal. He was somewhat of a comedian and known for playing tricks on his teammates. He is  described as the life and soul of any party, and he could also play a number of musical instruments. At the outbreak of war it was reported that he was on the verge of winning his first international cap.

He enlisted with the 5th Battalion Cameron Highlanders, serving in France as a Lance Corporal. They were involved in the Battle of Loos from 25th September 1915, infamously remembered as the first time the British used gas as a weapon. This had a disastrous outcome as the gas lingered where it fell or drifted back towards the British lines. The Highlanders suffered heavy casualties, with 81 killed, 425 wounded and 156 reported missing in action, including Garvie. Of the 72 battalions that attacked that day, 36 were Scottish regiments. It subsequently transpired that Garvie was a prisoner in a German Prison Hospital, with serious wounds received during the offensives. He died from these wounds on 15th October 1915 at Julich bei Aachen, according to the De Ruvigny's Roll of Honour records.

He was buried in the Cologne Southern Cemetery, Germany (VIII.G.24). Edwin was 23 years old. His brother Ernest, a 2nd Lieutenant serving with the Highland Light Infantry, lost his life on 15th June 1918. (He was previously awarded the Military Cross.)

Thomas 'Tom' Haydock was born in 1890 in Darmarnock, near Glasgow. His father ran a cotton-spinning mill in the town. After

graduating from Glasgow University, he was a salesperson for the Clydevale Oil and Colour Company, Bridgeton. He made his debut in 1914, playing 29 games for the club as a centre half in the 1914-15 season.

He initially enlisted in 1914 with the 5th Cameron Highlanders, and was later commissioned as a 2nd Lieutenant with the 7th Battalion Scottish Rifles, part of the 52nd Division. Haydock continued to play for Queens Park until going overseas in 1915.

Initially seeing action in Gallipoli, the Division then moved to Egypt, heavily involved in the British Campaign in Palestine during 1916 and 1917. In November 1917 during a Turkish assault on Umbrella Hill, South West of Gaza, the 7th suffered 103 casualties, and Haydock was badly injured. He returned home to convalesce, during which time he got engaged to a Miss Moore of Carmyle, Glasgow.

Haydock returned to the 52nd in August 1918. They were by now on front-line offensives in Arras, North France. Then on 1st September 1918 the 7th attacked the Hindenburg Line, west of the village of Queant. There was fierce fighting right into the next day, before they made a breakthrough. During the assault, seven officers were wounded, 11 men were killed, and a further 54 regulars were wounded. Haydock was one of the wounded officers and he died from his wounds on 2nd September 1918.

He was buried in the Bac-Du-Sud British Cemetery, Bailleulval, southwest of Arras (III.D.26). Tom was 28 years old.

George Legge was born in 1886 in Shettleston, Glasgow. An electrical engineer by trade, living in Pollokshields, he was on Queens Park books in 1911, playing two games as a forward. Legge enlisted with the Queen's Own Cameronian Highlanders in 1914. He was killed in action on 25th September 1915 during an advance on Auchy-les-La-Bassee at the Battle of Loos, France. He is commemorated at the Loos Memorial (Panel 119-124). George was 29 years old.

John Buchanan Monteith was born in 1883 in Bridgeton, Glasgow. On the club's books in 1911-12 as a full back, he is listed as playing three games.

Monteith was enlisted as a Gunner with the 27th Siege Battalion, Royal Garrison Artillery, serving in France. He was killed in action on 27th September 1918 in Northern France.

He was buried in the Queant Communal Cemetery, British Extension (B.46). John was 35 years old and married to Maggie Finlay Monteith.

Andrew Bowie McCrae was born on 30th December 1886 in Dundee. One of four sons, he was educated at Dundee Grammar School. The family then moved to Crail, Fife, where he gained an MA at St Andrew's University. He then moved back to Dundee, studying law, and after qualifying he worked for Gair and Gibson Solicitors in Falkirk.

A good class amateur footballer and golfer, in 1912-13 he was on the books of Falkirk FC, playing five games and scoring one goal, during which time they won the Scottish Cup in 1913, with a 2-0 victory against Raith Rovers. In 1913-14 he was with Queens Park as an outside right, playing 15 games. He was on the team's 1914 tour of Sweden, scoring one goal in a 2-0 victory against Gothenburg. McCrae then enlisted with the 1st/2nd Lovat's Scouts Yeomanry for the conflict, later becoming part of the Highland Mounted Brigade, 2nd Mounted Division.

Posted to Gallipoli in November 1915, McCrae was now a Lance Corporal. Weather conditions had worsened and summer gave way to snow and blizzards. It was during an assault in terrible conditions at Suvla Bay that Andrew died of wounds sustained on 17th November 1915, aged 28 years. He was buried in the Lala Baba Cemetery, Gallipoli Peninsula (I.D.7), and he is commemorated at the Crail and Eilan Dolan Memorials, Scotland, and also remembered at his educational institutions.

Alex McLean was born in 1879 in the Glasgow area. A commercial clerk by occupation, he was registered as a player with the club from 1900-02, making 10 appearances, and he was also used in the reserves. McLean later became the club's honorary secretary. He enlisted with the Cameronians Scottish Rifles in 1915, but he was discharged through illness in 1917 with tuberculosis. Alex died in Glasgow Ruchill Hospital on 29th October 1917, aged 38 years.

John James Ormiston was born on 4th November 1880 in Glasgow. He was educated at Queens Park School, then the Royal Technical College, which is now part of Strathclyde University. A right half, he was at Queens Park from 1899-1903, where he played 34 games.

In 1911 he was known to be living in the Vancouver area of Canada. Ormiston enlisted as a Private with the Canadian Central Ontario Regiment, though under the name Armstrong for unknown reasons. He was killed in action on 1st March 1917 and buried in the Villers Station Cemetery, Northern France (VII.D.15). John was 36 years old.

John Stevenson is listed as being a player with Queens Park from 1907-09, playing 11 games and scoring two goals as an inside forward. Not much information is available regarding him. It is believed he enlisted with the Highland Light Infantry, serving in France. A John Stevenson from Rutherglen, Glasgow, is on the Glasgow Memorial. He was killed on 28th November 1917, aged 31 years, and he is also commemorated on the Cambrai Memorial, Nord.

John Wilkinson was born in 1886 in Partick, Glasgow. He was a coal salesperson living in the Hyndland area of the city, near to the main school in the area. A goalkeeper, he was with Queens Park from 1908-09, making four appearances.

He enlisted with the 4th Battalion Argyll Sutherland Highlanders. A 2nd Lieutenant, he later transferred to the 12th part of the 77th Brigade, 26th Division. After training, he was stationed in Turkey, where they were mainly used in the Salonika region. On 18th September 1918 they were involved in attacks against Bulgarian Forces on the Macedonian Border, near 'Pip Ridge', a vulnerable position on the border itself.

The 12th became involved in heavy fighting and came under considerable bombardment. An eyewitness account of the action is on record:

'It was now the turn of the Scotsmen - Fusiliers, Rifles and Highlanders of the 77th Brigade, undismayed by the dreadful evidence of havoc, ran forward among the Welsh and Bulgarian dead. Fighting on into a

maze of enemy entanglements, the Scotsmen were being annihilated, their flanks withering under a terrible enfilade. We gained only the unimportant ruins of Doiran Town and a cluster of small hills immediately above it, never of any value to the enemy or strongly defended. The fortress of Grand Couronne was unshaken, with crumpled bodies of men and a litter of awful wreckage below it. The Royal Scots Fusiliers lost 358, the Argylls 299 and the Scottish Rifles 228 men.'

John was amongst the casualties. He was buried in the Dorian Military Cemetery (V.F.17). He was 32 years old and his date of death is listed as 19th September 1918.

James Gilmour Wilson was born in Kilwinning, Ayrshire, in 1895. He was the son of Alexander Wilson, the owner of the Eglinton Arms Hotel. He was a student at Kilwinning Higher Grade School and then Irvine Royal Academy, before joining the firm of accountants Carstairs

Queens Park has outstanding historical research records of their involvement in the Great War. At the time of press, over 216 players, reserve players, former players and members from the club are on the pictured remembrance plaque. They remain registered to date as an amateur club. The team picture displayed is the 1913-14 squad.

in Charing Cross, Glasgow. A left back initially with Kilwinning Rangers, he is listed at Queens Park in 1914-15. There is some confusion thereafter with his player records, but it is believed he played over 46 games, though he is also shown as playing two games in 1917-18.

Wilson enlisted with the 2nd Battalion Royal Scots Fusiliers, Black Watch 1st/7th Fife Battalion, serving in France, including at the Somme after 1915. He returned home in late 1916/early 1917 to train for his commission as a 2nd Lieutenant.

On returning to France, he was again with the Royal Scots. He was shot by a sniper on 15th December 1917 serving in Belgium during the Passchendaele offensive. He is commemorated at the Ypres Menin Gate Memorial (Panel 19 and 33). James was 22 years old.

Raith Rovers FC, Division A

(League position: 19th – not relegated due to league changes and war

Thomas Cranston was born in 1891 in Ardrossan, North Ayrshire. An outside right, he began with local amateur side Ardrossan Celtic, then signed for Raith in 1912, with 33 games and five goals. He was in the side that lost 2-0 in the Scottish Cup final in 1913 to Falkirk. He then spent time at Third Lanark from 1913-14, playing seven games for them before returning to Raith in the same year, playing another 23 games and scoring three goals.

During season 1914-15 Cranston was at Clyde FC, making over 22 appearances for them and scoring five goals. It was from here that he enlisted with the 2nd Battalion Black Watch, Royal Highlanders. After training, he served in Mesopotamia. He was killed in Iraq on 13th January 1916.

He was buried in the Awara War Cemetery, Tigris. (XIX.D.15). Thomas was 24 years old and married to Agnes Calvert Cranston.

James Burton Gibson was born on 24th June 1889 in Kirkcaldy, East Ayrshire. He studied at St Andrews University and played for the

college football team there, qualifying as a teacher from his studies.

Gibson signed for Raith in 1912-13, playing 17 games and scoring two goals as a half back. He then emigrated to New Zealand where he taught at the State Boys High School in Napier.

Gibson enlisted with the New Zealand Expeditionary Force, Auckland Regiment. James was badly injured in fighting at Gallipoli and removed to HM Hospital Ship *Salta*, but unfortunately he died from his wounds on 5th September 1915, aged 26 years. He was buried at sea the following day and is commemorated on the Lone Pine Memorial (Ref 72), Gallipoli, Turkey.

George McLay M.M. was born in 1889 in Crossgates, Fife. A big tough half back, he began his career at Glencraig Celtic before signing for Raith from 1910-15, making over 80 appearances and scoring five goals.

McLay enlisted with the 16th Royal Scots (McCrae's) and saw action in France and Flanders, surviving the Somme. By 1917 he was a Sergeant in Belgium, involved in fighting at Poelcapelle. He was killed during an offensive push at Passchendaele on 27th October 1917. The nature of his death was recorded: *'He had become entangled in barbed wire and been shot several times, it was during this time that he was shot again in the forehead and killed.'* Having previously shown great bravery, he was posthumously awarded the Military Medal. He is commemorated at the Tyne Cot Memorial (Panel 11 to 14 and 162). George was 28 years old.

James Scott was born in Airdrie in 1895. He attended Airdrie Academy before training as a wire rope maker, like his father. A renowned and talented footballer, playing for Craigton Thistle and Petershill, Raith snapped him up in 1913. He played as a forward and was described in news reports as, *'Raiths Opportunist, a most finished player and consistent goal scorer, the best they had ever had'*. He played 59 games and scored 29 goals before enlisting.

Like his colleague, he joined the 16th Royal Scots, stationed in France after training. He was killed on 1st July 1916 during the first day of fighting at the Somme.

The record states, '*during an attack on German trenches near La Boisselle, Scott was one of the first to mount an enemy trench but was shot in the stomach and neck by machine gun fire, he was seen to fall to the ground.*'

Commemorated at the Thiepval Memorial (Pier and Face 6D and 7D), James was 20-21 years old and married to Catherine Scott. (It is believed he was buried with others in unmarked graves at the Gordon Dump Cemetery in La Boisselle.)

James Colin Todd was born in 1895 in Edinburgh. An outside forward, it is believed he joined Raith from Musselburgh in 1914-15, playing 22 games and scoring one goal. He was highly thought of and prior to enlisting was attracting considerable interest from the Hearts club.

He enlisted with the 16th Royal Scots. On 12th March 1916 during fighting at Armentieres, France,

Raith Rovers FC, 1913.

he was hit in the chest by shell fragments and carried into a dugout. Todd died a short time later. He was buried in the Erquinghem-Lys Church Extension (I.H.13), Nord. James was 20 years old.

(The Edinburgh-based club Raith Rovers, like Heart of Midlothian, are synonymous with their links to the 16th Royal Scots.)

Rangers (Glasgow) FC, Division A

(League position: third)

RANGERS F.C.

Names (left to right)—Back Row—H. Lock, J. Hempsey, J. Muir.
Middle Row—W. Struth, J. Hendry, P. Pursell, T. Kelso, R. Brown, J. Logan, H. Muir, A. Craig, G. Dickson, J. Paterson, T. Gilchrist.
Front Row—W. Reid, A. S. Duncan, J. Bowie, T. Cairns, A. Bennett, J. Gordon, A. Smith.

Rangers FC, 1914.

Alexander Barrie. See Kilmarnock FC
David Murray. See Leeds City
James Spiers. See Bradford City
Walter Tull. See Northampton Town
(Note, John Clarke enlisted with the Royal Irish Rifles and is listed as a casualty. Information shows him as wounded but not killed.)

St Bernards FC, Division B

(League position: third – the club was dissolved in 1943 due to financial difficulties)

Frederick James Albert was born in 1892 in Canterbury, Kent, and his family then moved to Edinburgh during his childhood. He was a centre forward, initially playing for Corstorphine Rangers. A St Bernards player from 1911-13, he made 22 appearances and scored 15 goals. His best statistics were in the Scottish Cup, in which he scored eight of his goals in nine games.

In 1913 he emigrated to Australia on a ship named *Ballarat*, which docked in Sydney. It is believed he settled in a town called Minmi, near Newcastle, in New South Wales, and he is listed as married. In 1916 Albert was with the 36th Australian Infantry on board Troop Ship *Benalla A24* on route to France and Flanders.

```
36th.  A.I.F.              Albert. F.J. 2520.
                             A Coy.
                               12/16 / .
                             K. 10/12/17
                             Det. D/B.

   "I knew Albert well.  He was killed by a shell on the
Passchendaele Ridge, and I spent several hours in the shell hole
where his body was lying.  We had to fall back from this position
and I feel sure that there was no burial and that no information
on this point can be looked for."

        Eyewitness:   I saw the body.

        Description:

          Informant:    Cpl. W.M. Connor 2549.
                          36 A.I.F.  A Coy.
                          Beaufort War Hospital,
                                Bristol.
```

He was killed in action on 12th October 1917 when a shell exploded next to Frederick, literally blowing him apart on Passchendaele Ridge, Belgium, in no man's land. He was 25 years old and is commemorated at Tyne Cot Cemetery Memorial and the Australian War Memorial, Commemorative area 126.

John Ferguson was born in 1892 in Glasgow. He was brought up by his aunt in Aberfoyle, Stirlingshire, and he played a prominent role with the local Callander High School football team as an inside or centre forward. Whilst at Edinburgh University studying art, he signed for local club St Bernards.

JOHN FERGUSON.

He was to become a vital part of the team from 1910-11 until the 1913-14 season, making over 124 appearances in total and scoring 41 goals. In 1913 they held a dinner in his honour. This was for services to the club, presenting him with a gold chain and medal.

Other clubs were now after his signature and Third Lanark managed to secure him during the 1913-14 season, though he was still allowed to represent St Bernards in the Consolidation Cup. Newcastle and Hearts had been chasing his signature, but the Lanark manager Edward Tarbat did a crafty bit of work. After an evening at Glasgow Empire, he took Ferguson for dinner and persuaded him to sign.

He played 31 games and scored six goals for them before the war, when he enlisted with the 4th Battalion Cameronians, Scottish Rifles, serving as a 2nd Lieutenant.

On 23rd October 1916 the Scottish Rifles had taken Zenith Trench near Flers, Orne, in North Western France. When ordered to take a further trench called Orion, they came under a severe and vicious counter attack forcing them back. Ferguson's Captain then penned the following report:

'John succeeded in entering the hostile trench with a Sergeant and his Servant. He then bombed along the trench until wounded, when he moved across the open, continuing bombing. Again wounded and finally blown up by a bomb. He had succeeded in putting three machine guns out of action and cleared a length of over 200 yards of the trench and it was wholly on account of his gallantry that the company on our left succeeded in their attack. His was the bravest act I have seen in eighteen months on the front line, and John will probably get a posthumous V.C. All the men in the company and officers in the battalion adored him.

Allow me to offer my deepest sympathy in your great loss. I know it is poor consolation for the loss of a son, to know he did his duty brilliantly and well, but such as it is you have. I personally deeply regret the loss of John as a friend and an officer.'

John never received any awards, and he is only mentioned in dispatches. His body was lost on the battlefield after the explosion. He was commemorated at the Thiepval Memorial (Pier and Face 4D). John was 24 years old.

John Fleming was born in 1890 in Slamannan, Stirlingshire. He started out as an inside forward with Musselburgh, Armadale Thistle and Bonnyrigg Rose Athletic before signing for St Bernards in 1909-11, playing 53 games and scoring 17 goals.

He signed for Newcastle in 1911 for £250, and despite scoring four goals in a friendly game he only managed four games before moving to Spurs for £300 in 1913-15, where he played 19 games and scored three goals for them. In 1915 he was back in Scotland at Rangers prior to the war, where he played four games and scored one goal.

Fleming enlisted with the Queen's Own Cameron Highlanders 8th Reserve Battalion. A Lance Corporal stationed at Richmond Camp, Yorkshire, John fell seriously ill with pneumonia. He died in hospital on 21st March 1916, aged 26 years. He was buried in the Inveresk Parish Churchyard, East Lothian (B.784).

John Frail was born in 1882 in Burntisland, Fife, near Dumfermline. An outside right, he is listed with a number of clubs including Lochgelly United and Hibernian. His main success was at St Bernards where he played 17 games and scored one goal.

A miner by trade, he had somewhat of a reputation as a difficult man who liked a drink, which probably restricted his football career, due to his unreliability. This also affected his marriage.

When war broke out he joined the 1st Battalion, 42nd Foot, Black Watch, Royal Highlanders and this seemed to suit his strong outgoing character. He was listed as missing, believed killed in action, in Northern France on 9th May 1915, though there was initially confusion as one report stated he was in hospital.

He is commemorated at the La Touret Memorial (Panels 24 to 26). John was 33 years old, married to Sarah Frail and had two children. She received £3.10/4d in 1916 and an additional £3 gratuity in 1919.

James Hastie was born in 1892 in Edrom, Berwickshire. A full back, he was with Selkirk FC for five seasons followed apparently by a year with Stockport County, though not as a first-team player. (He is not listed in their records.) In 1914 he was at St Bernards, making one first team appearance in September, followed by a trial match for Glasgow Rangers. He worked for the Power Station Company in Edinburgh prior to the war.

Hastie had previous territorial reserve experience, enlisting with the King's Own Scottish Borderers, followed by the 1st Battalion, 3rd Reserve Gordon Highlanders. He is listed as killed in action on 14th December 1914 near Ypres, Belgium. He is commemorated on the Menin Gate Memorial (M.R.29 Panel 38). James was 22 years old.

Gordon Hossack was born on 26th June 1883 in the St Machar area of Aberdeen. A full back, he was listed at St Bernards from 1904-1906, making 44 appearances in total, scoring two goals. He is known to have been with Bo'ness FC in 1910-11 (front second from left, image courtesy of his grandson Gordon Hossack). He was living in the town working as a comb maker.

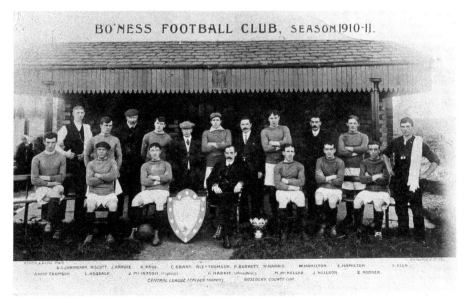

Hossack enlisted in Glencorse, Midlothian, with the 4th Battalion Black Watch, Royal Highlanders, serving in France. He was shown as missing, killed in action, on 25th September 1915 during fighting near Loos. Gordon was 32 years old, and he is commemorated at the Loos Memorial (M.R.19 Panel 78 to 83) and the Bo'ness War Memorial. He was married to Jane Hossack and had two sons, James and Robert. (James served with the Royal Scots Fusiliers in World War Two.)

Alexander Kay was born in 1879 in Edinburgh. A full back, he began at Dalry Primrose then signed for St Bernards in 1898-1900, making 69 appearances. The following year he was at Partick Thistle where he played 33 games. During the 1901-02 season he was at Sheffield United and played six games for them. He seems to leave the professional circuit after this, though there is mention of him playing at West Ham United.

Kay enlisted with the 11th Service Battalion Rifle Brigade 'C' Company, serving in France. He was killed at the Somme on 15th February 1917.

He is commemorated at the Thiepval Memorial (Pier and Face 16B and 16C). Alex was 38 years old.

St Bernards, 1914-15.

David Brunton McDougall was born in 1894 in Leith, Edinburgh. An inside or centre forward, he began his career at Bonnrigg Rose Athletic. He signed for St Bernards in 1914-15, playing 24 games and scoring 11 goals. He was in the team that won the Scottish Qualifying Cup in the same season. From 1916-18 he was on the books of Hibernian, making eight appearances for them.

McDougall enlisted with the 6th Service Battalion King's Own Scottish Borderers. He is listed as killed in action near Ploegsteert, Belgium, on 18th August 1918.

He is commemorated at the Ploegsteert Memorial (Panel 5). David was 24 years old.

St Johnstone FC, Division B
(League position: eighth)

(Most of their first-team players enlisted; therefore, they ceased activities until 1918-19.)

David McWalter was born in 1891 in Luncarty, Perth and Kinross. A right winger with the local side, he joined St Johnstone in 1912-13, making 55 appearances and scoring 11 goals before he enlisted after 1914.

After joining the Royal Garrison Artillery as a gunner, he was killed in action on 2nd February 1918 in Greece. He was buried in the Sarigol Military Cemetery, Kriston (D.622). David was 27 years old and married to Margaret McWalter.

Thomas Fletcher Moncrieff was born in 1886 in Glencarse, Perthshire. A student at the Perth Academy, he was a half back listed with St Johnstone from 1911-12, playing two games.

After enlisting with the Royal Army Service Corps Moncrieff, he served in Belgium. He was killed in action on 26th April 1918. He was buried in the Haringhe Bandaghem Military Cemetery, Poperinge (V.A.1), and is commemorated at the Perth Academy Memorial. Thomas was 32 years old.

Bertram Sampson was born on 17th January 1886 in Perth, Scotland. A centre or half back, he was signed by the club in around 1905 from local amateur football, he was a fixture with St Johnstone until after 1911-12. By trade, he worked at the Pullers dye works, Perth. Given a trial at Rangers, he preferred to stay with the Saints, gaining the club captaincy. Sampson played over 121 games and scored four goals, and he was then given a benefit match.

He enlisted with the 1st and 7th Black Watch Royal Highlanders, serving in France and Flanders. He was wounded in the neck by shrapnel in 1916 and sent home, though he returned to the front after convalescing. He was killed at the Battle of Arras on 23rd April 1917. He buried in the Brown's Copse Cemetery, Roeux, France (III.B.29). Bertram was 31 years old, married to Marjory Sampson and had six children.

His brother **Frank** died on 28th July 1918 at the Battle of Tardenios, Marne, France. He was 36 years old and buried in the Chambrecy British Cemetery (VIII.C.10). (They are pictured together; Bertram is on the right.)

NOTE: The Official St Johnstone club history book refers to three other players as casualties of the Great War. There are a number of other soldier deaths with the same or similar names. Therefore, with the lack of personal information and regiment details to hand, we are unable to confirm any death records.

John Cameron. This surname is in the club records until 1914. Statistics show about 30 games played under this name in a number of positions, though he will have played considerably more games. (Player details were not recorded as meticulously until after 1910.) He was given a

St.Johnstone's Football Team, Perth, 1911.

benefit match on 5th April 1911 against Clyde, and his last recorded game was in the 1914-15 season. There is a Cameron pictured in the 1911 team photo (middle right player).

William MacPherson was listed at the club from 1911-12, playing 10 games and scoring four goals as a forward. (Cameron and McPherson are apparently mentioned in the local *Evening Telegraph*, dated 30th May 1919, as being casualties of the war.)

Charles Scott a full back at the club in the 1914-15 season, played 31 games and scored one goal. There is mention of the Rangers football club as well, though this is a different player and there is no listing shown with them.

St Mirren FC, Division A
(League position: ninth)

James Rae Armstrong was born in 1888 in Dennistoun, Glasgow. He was a student at the local Whitehall School. An inside right on the books of Kilmarnock from 1912-13, he made two appearances and scored two goals. He was then with St Mirren in 1914 and had two registered first-team games with them.

Armstrong then enlisted with the 5th Battalion Queen's Own Cameron Highlanders, serving in France. James died from wounds on 11th October

1915 in the 5th General Hospital near Loos, aged 27 years. He was buried in the St Sever Cemetery, Rouen (A.12.24.), and is also remembered on the Whitehall School Memorial. His brother Robert Rae Armstrong served with the Canadian Army Service Corps.

James Brannick was born in the Cheetham area of Manchester. An inside right, he is shown on Everton's books from 1912-13, playing three first-team games and scoring two goals. He was not a regular first-team choice, though in his time there he was top scorer in their reserve team with 30 goals. In 1914 he signed for St Mirren, the *Daily Record* reporting the transfer, stating Brannick was 22 years old. Released in 1916 after 38 games and 11 goals, he enlisted back in Cheetham with the 11th Lancashire Fusiliers. He was stationed in Flanders and listed as killed in action on 10th August 1917 near Ypres, Belgium. He is commemorated at the Ypres Menin Gate Memorial (Panel 33). This would make James 25 years old, though the War Graves Commission lists him as 32 years old.

His brother **Richard Brannick** served with the 8th Royal Lancaster Regiment. He was also a casualty, killed in Belgium on 13th October 1915. He was buried in the Ploegsteert Wood Military Cemetery and was married to Mary Brannick.

George Elmore was born in 1880 in Witton, Cheshire. A much travelled forward who could play in a number of positions, he began at Witton Villa then Witton Albion, followed by Northwich Victoria in 1897 and Broadheath in 1902.

Signed by West Brom in 1902-03, he struggled to gain a place, only managing four games and one goal. Bristol Rovers signed him in 1903, where he made 21 appearances and scored five goals. From 1904-07 Altrincham was his club of choice, where he was top scorer several times and, as reported, '*stood out as a*

player who was too good for the Manchester league, which they dominated with him up front'. Glossop signed Elmore in 1907-09, his stats there being 35 games and 14 goals. A further move followed to Blackpool in 1909-10, where he played 34 games and scored six goals. A change of scenery followed with a transfer north of the border to Partick Thistle in 1910-12, where he played 66 games and scored22 goals. It is then that St Mirren move in for him, where he played 70 games and scored 20 goals. A short return to Witton followed in 1914, before St Bernards used his services in 1915, where he played six games and scored two goals. As the war was escalating, he assisted Broxburn United before eventually enlisting.

Elmore joined the 15th Service Battalion Royal Scots, Lothian Regiment, where he was a Lance Corporal. He was killed on the first day at the Somme – 1st July 1916. His body was lost during one of the assaults. George was 36 years old, and is commemorated at the Thiepval Memorial (Pier and Face 6D and 7D).

Thomas 'Tom' Alexander Jackson was born in Thornliebank, Glasgow, on 12th November 1878. A right back or centre half, he joined St Mirren from Thornliebank amateurs in around 1896 and remained with the club until 1910-11. A regular in the side, he made over 200 appearances and scored  three goals. He was also a Scottish international, playing six games from 1904-07, one as captain against Wales in 1905. As a pastime, he gained a reputation as an excellent bowls and billiards player. He moved on to St Johnstone from 1910-12, playing 43 games for the club before finishing his career assisting Bathgate FC in the West Lothian area to build their reputation. (They eventually gained promotion to the Scottish League Division Two in 1921.)

Jackson enlisted with the Argyll and Sutherland Highlanders, serving in France. He was killed in action on 9th October 1916 in the Somme area. He was buried in the Adanac Military Cemetery, Miraumont (VI.H.6). Thomas was 39 years old.

Archibald McLardie was born in 1889 in Paisley, Glasgow. A pupil at Paisley Grammar, he eventually qualified as a lawyer. He played football for the grammar school and the John

LIEUT. ARCHD. M-LARDIE 5th A.D.S.H.

St Mirren, 1916-17.

Neilson Institution. He was listed on the books of St Mirren from 1910-12, playing five games for them before being released, leaving him to continue his main occupation. It is believed he was briefly on the books of Queens Park.

He received his commission as a 2nd Lieutenant in June 1915 before arriving with the 1st/5th Argyll and Sutherland Highlanders in Gallipoli. McLardie is recorded as being killed by a bomb with five others on Christmas Day 1915. He was buried in the Pink Farm Cemetery, Helles (III.D.13), and is commemorated on the Paisley Grammar School Memorial. Archie was 26 years old.

Third Lanark FC, Division A
(League position: 16th)

(The club was dissolved in 1967 and reformed in 1996, though after several attempts to reignite their previous league status they remained in the Greater Glasgow Premier League.)

James Blyth Galloway was born on 3rd July 1893 in Buckhaven on the Fife coast. A centre forward, he played for Haywood Juniors, though

Third Lanark had him on their books from 1913-18. He played seven games for them and scored one goal. By trade, he was an architect.

INDEX Nos. GALLOWAY, 2nd Lt. James Blyth. Royal INDIA 23-58 Field Artillery. Died of pneumonia 17th Nov., PUNJAB AND 1918. Age 25. Son of David B. and Eliza DELHI Galloway, of 11, Queen's Park Avenue, Crosshill, Glasgow. Born at Buckhaven, Fife. 8. 3.

Galloway was already a territorial reservist and enlisted with the Royal Field Artillery and was a 2nd Lieutenant serving in India. James contracted pneumonia and succumbed to the illness on 17th November 1918, after the armistice. He was buried in the Kasauli Cemetery in the Himachal Pradash state province (Plot 8. Grave 3).

George Gibb was born in 1892 in Wishaw, 15 miles south of Glasgow. He was a full back who could also play at half back.

GIBB, Lce. Serjt. George, 332096. 9th Bn. Highland Light Inf. Died of wounds 7th June, 1917. Age 25. Son of George and Mary Gibb, of 12, Bridge St., Motherwell. Native of Motherwell. XXV. G. 4.

Initially he was with Cambuslang Rangers before signing for Third Lanark in 1914-15, making 38 appearances before enlisting.

Gibb enlisted with the 9th Glasgow Battalion Highland Light Infantry. Serving in France as an Acting Lance Sergeant, George died from wounds near Etaples, Northern France, on 7th June 1917, aged 25 years. He was buried at the Etaples Military Cemetery (XXV.G.4.).

Vale of Leven FC, Division B

(League position: 14th – not relegated due to league changes and war)

(Formed in 1872, they continued in the Scottish League until 1938, when financial constraints forced them from the main league. They reformed in 1939 as a new club in the Scottish Football Alliance.)

John Wilson was born in 1889 in Blackford, Perthshire. In 1912-13 he was shown as a defender at the Dumbarton football club, playing 11 games and scoring three goals. He was then listed at Vale of Leven, with 13 appearances for them and one goal.

WILSON, Pte. John, 916. 1st Bn. Black Watch. Died of wounds 20th Sept., 1914. Age 25. Youngest son of John and Christina Wilson; husband of Catherine B. Rushton (formerly Wilson), of 3, Appin Terrace, Slateford Rd., Edinburgh. Born at Blackford, Perthshire. 19. I. A. 9.

Wilson joined the 1st Battalion Black Watch Royal Highlanders, serving in Northern France. He was badly wounded and removed to the Hotel Majestic Military Hospital, Paris. John died from his wounds on 20th September 1914, aged 25 years. He was buried in the City of Paris Cemetery, Bagneux (19.I.A.9.), and commemorated on the Blackford War Memorial. Ironically, his wife Catherine gave birth to their daughter in Edinburgh on the same day he died.

LEAGUE TEAMS FROM WALES

Barry Town FC, Southern League Division Two
(League position: ninth)

(They were elected into the league in 1913-14. After 1920, they competed initially in the Welsh Section of the Football League.)

James Wightman M.C. and D.S.O. was born in 1893 in Whitehaven, Cumbria. An exemplary scholar, he studied at Carmarthen College where he qualified as a teacher. It was from here he met and later married Eleanor Gertrude Morris in 1915 (pictured). A footballer who was gaining a reputation as a reliable solid player, he was soon on the books of Barry Town, gaining the captaincy in 1914. By occupation, he was a teacher in Troedyrhiw, near Merthyr Tydfil.

He was determined in his obligation to his country and joined the East Surrey Regiment at the outbreak of war. Gaining rapid promotion, he was soon a Captain then Major in the 8th Service Battalion, involved in fierce fighting at the Somme, France. On 30th September 1916 he was awarded the Military Cross during an assault at Schwaben Redoubt, Thiepval Ridge. The citation granted in November 1916 read, *'For conspicuous gallantry in action. He led a bombing party with great courage and determination, and repulsed the enemy. He acted as leading thrower and threw bombs for two hours. He had previously done fine work.'*

The East Surrey had earlier been involved in a piece of elaborative publicity on the first day of the Somme on 1st July 1916 when they

Barry Town FC, 1914.

kicked two footballs into no man's land to encourage an advance. By March 1918, after being involved in numerous bloody battles throughout 1917, the battalion were being used as part of the defence against the German Spring Offensive at St Quentin, with heavy fighting again taking place. He is mentioned in dispatches and awarded the Distinguished Service Order for his bravery during this offensive near Arras on 4th April 1918. Whilst leading a further assault, a defective grenade caused him serious injury. He was removed to a field hospital and he died from his wounds on 9th April 1918. He was buried in the Picquigny British Cemetery (G.12). James was 25 years old.

His brother John Wightman of the Military Corps (also received the Military Cross) lost his life, killed on 4th April 1918, the same day James received his wounds. He is commemorated at the Pozieres Memorial, aged 23 years. After receiving this heart-breaking news, their parents commissioned a tiled floor in the St James Church, Whitehaven, in their memory. It is located in the choir vestry.

Cardiff City FC, Southern League Division One
(League position: third)

Wally Stewart (possibly Walter) is in Cardiff's first professional squad in 1910-11, though he was not a regular first teamer, and there is no other information about him. He has nine known recorded games and scored four goals, playing in a number of positions (listed as a centre forward). This is the only season he was with the club. No information thereafter xan be found on his football career.

Cardiff have him recorded as killed in 1916 during fighting in the Dardanelles region. There is insufficient information on Wally to trace his service records and death.

Thomas 'Tom' William Witts was born in Durham, Northumberland, in 1895. Playing as a full back, he was living in Cardiff when they signed him in around 1913 until 1914-15, though he was mainly used in the reserves. Witts made one recorded first-team appearance. However, full records are not available for this period.

Witts enlisted in Northumberland with the Durham Light Infantry 1st/6th then 15th Battalion, Royal Engineers, and was appointed as a

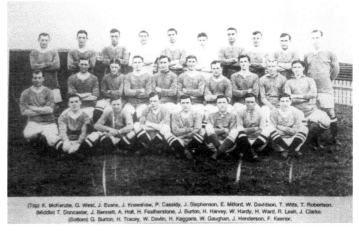

Cardiff City FC, 1914.

Lance Corporal. He is recorded as dying from wounds on 9th November 1918, two days before the Armistice, in Northern France. He was buried in the Caudry British Cemetery, Nord (I.A.7). Thomas was 23 years old and married to Beatrice Witts; they had three children, his third child being born six months after his death. Sadly, one of his son's third birthday was on the day he died.

Ebbw Vale FC, Southern League Division Two
(League Position 13th – not relegated due to war)

No players listed. After the war, the club went into the Welsh League Section in 1920-21. (The team pictured is from the early 1920s.)

Llanelly Town FC, Southern League Division Two
(League position: eighth)

(They joined the league in 1912-13 and moved into the Welsh Section in 1920-21. They changed their name to Llanelli in 1963.)

Thomas Pryce Hamer was born in 1883 in Llanidloes, Montgomeryshire. He was a local celebrity and a wealthy industrialist. He played as a

centre half for Llanidloes Town and in 1910 gained a Welsh international amateur cap against England in a 6-0 defeat at Huddersfield. It was after this that he went onto the books of Llanelly for two seasons prior to the war.

In 1915 he was commissioned as a Lieutenant in the 14th Royal Welsh Fusiliers, then 11th Service Battalion South Wales Borderers, attached to the 38th Division. By December that year he was serving in the trenches at Armentieres, France. June 1916 saw them at the Somme. An order to clear and capture Mametz Wood began on 7th July 1916, and it took until the 14th to take and clear. Hamer lost his life on the first day of the assault, and they were unable to recover his body. He is commemorated at the Thiepval Memorial (Pier and Face 4A) and on the Carmarthenshire War Memorials site. Thomas was 33 years old.

(No Llanelly team photographs can be sourced for that era.)

Merthyr Town FC, Southern League Division Two

(League position: third, in restructured First Division 1919-20 – voted out of the Football League in 1930)

• MERTHYR TOWN, A.F.C. 1911-12. •

G. MACEY, W. DAVIES, C. CRAIG, D. LEWIS, J. WHITE, W. SAVAGE, T. JONES, W. HOLMES, (D. DAVIES)
(W. FISHER) J. DODDS, H. DRAPER, G. GATES (CAPT) F. COSTELLO, J. LOWE, F. TAYLOR.

Jabez Cartwright. See Bolton Wanderers
Frederick Costello. See Southampton
William Kirby. See Portsmouth

Mid Rhondda FC, Southern League Division Two

(League position: 12th – not relegated due to war – the club was dissolved in 1928)

No players listed.

Newport County FC, Southern League Division Two

(League position: 10th in restructured First Division 1919-20)

Robert Henry Hammett was born in 1897 in Monmouth, one of three children. A promising centre forward, he made one appearance at the end of the 1913-14 season on 30th April 1914 in a 1-0 win against Llanelly. He was described as full of promise, but he then enlisted with the 16th Service Battalion Royal Warwickshire Regiment.

He was wounded serving in the Somme region in France and was removed to the Vacquemont 15th Field Hospital on 28th July 1916, also suffering from shell shock. Hammett was repatriated back home to Cardiff Western General Hospital. He died from his wounds and blood poisoning on 25th September 1916. He was buried in the Newport Christchurch Cemetery (X753) and remembered on the town cenotaph. Robert was 19 years old.

Albert Edwards was a half back initially at Swindon Town, and he is shown on the Queens Park Rangers F.C. site as being a victim of the Great War. He is listed with them from 1902-06, playing 17 games and scoring one goal. It is also recorded that he played for Bristol City and Newport County. (Insufficient information is available to check further regarding war service.)

Newport County FC, 1913-14.

It appears the Edwards played for Bristol City some six years later, in 1912-13, with four games, and then Newport County from 1913-15, where he played 59 games and scored six goals. It is not the same man as the one who played for Queens Park Rangers as he appears much younger. The images of them in team photographs differ considerably, giving circumstantial proof for this. (Furthermore, the QPR man appears to be registered on a team image as A.E. Edwards in 1906). Albert Edwards, the Newport player, apparently joined the Welsh Regiment in Newport, Monmouthshire, in 1917. (No definitive death record has been sourced. He is in the team photograph in 1913-14, back row second from the left, and was playing for the club up to end of 1915.) He does not appear as a war casualty in Newport County records.

Pontypridd FC, Southern League Division Two
(League position: 11th)

(League members from 1911-1926. The club then left the league and during this period they were runners-up in the Welsh Cup three times and Welsh Champions in 1923-24.)

No players listed.

The Dragons, Pontypridd FC, 1921.

Swansea Town FC, Southern League Division Two

(League position: fourth in restructured First Division 1919-20)

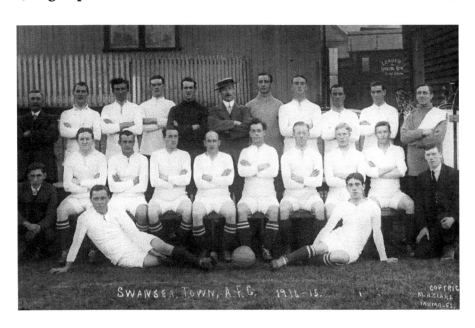

(In 1969 the club changed its name to Swansea City after Swansea was given a city status).

Spencer Bassett. See Exeter City
Joseph Bulcock. See Crystal Palace
Edward Mitchell. See Reading

Ton Pentre FC, Southern League Division Two

Ton Pentre FC, 1906.

(League position: sixth)

(The club were league members from 1909-1923, when the decline of the coal industry in the area forced their withdrawal for financial reasons. They elected to join localised Welsh League football.)

No players listed.

LEAGUE TEAMS FROM IRELAND

Although the Irish League consisted of only eight sides, the Irish national side won the home international championships in 1914. Some of the country's top players were playing outside Ireland at this time. Pictured is the international squad for that year.

Belfast Celtic FC
(League winners 1914-15)

(Team photograph in 1911. The club was dissolved in 1949.)

Back Row : C. Murphy, R. Barr (Secretary), E. Magee, D. McCloskey, P. Dobbin.
Middle Row: J. McIlvenney (Trainer), W. Anderson, G. McGivern, L. Murphy, A. Davidson, G. McClure, W. Moore, J. Connor.
Front Row: J. McAnerney, I.F.A., N. Clarke, P. McCann, M Hamill, C. Crothers (Captain), W. Briggs, J. Davidson.
T. McCann, I.F.A.

Bernard Donaghy. See Hibernian

Bohemian FC

(League position: eighth)

Sidney Kingston Gore was born in 12th July 1889 in Barry Dock, Glamorganshire, one of six children. His father was a doctor and, after relocating, Gore attended Harvey Grammar School in Kent. He joined the British Army stationed in Dublin and represented them at both football and cricket.

He is said to have been a member of the Bohemians club during his time in Dublin, and is described as a centre forward of great skill and ball control. In 1914 he captained the army side to a 4-1 victory against the Irish Team in the Herald Hospital Charity Cup, scoring two of the goals. Gore was later honoured and presented with the Independent Trophy. He was the last Englishman to get this award, due to Britain's fracturing relationship with Ireland, which changed dramatically after the war.

A Second Lieutenant in the 1st Battalion Royal West Kent Regiment, he served in France, seeing particularly heavy fighting at Neuve Chapelle in the Artois region. On 28th October 1914 with his regiment partially surrounded and being one of only three surviving officers, Gore led his company forward into enemy territory as cover for others attempting to withdraw. He was killed instantaneously during this confrontation, the report stating he was, 'shot in the head'. He was buried the next day in an unmarked grave, the location of which was then lost.

He is commemorated at the Le Touret Memorial (Panel 30-31) and All Souls Church, Cheriton, Kent. Sidney was 25 years old.

Harold Alexander De Barbizon Sloan was born on 25th August 1882 in Catleknock, County Dublin, the third of four sons. He was related to the prominent Rathbone family who were also residing with them. The Rathbones owned and ran a long-established candle-making company in Dunsinea, Dublin, with a number of the Sloan family working for the firm. Sloan himself was educated at the local high school, but dropped out in the sixth form to join the civil service in 1899.

H. A. Sloan
Bohemian F.C. Dublin. Irish International

The Bohemians club, which started in 1890, was establishing its reputation around 1900 and had the strength in numbers to form a reserve side. Sloan fast established himself with the club around this

Bohemian FC, 1908 and 1918.

time as a fast, two-footed forward with good pace, thereafter breaking into the first eleven.

In 1901 the club's new ground at Dalymount Park opened, with Sloan scoring the opening goal in a 4-2 victory against Shelbourne. The ground then became the home venue for the Republic of Ireland's home fixtures for a large part of the 20th century. In 1902 the Bohemian club joined the Northern Irish-club dominated Irish Football League. By this time, Sloan had already helped them win five Leinster Senior Cups and the Leinster League three times.

In 1903 the Irish team was using the ground for home international matches and Sloan gained his first international cap against England in a 4-0 defeat. In the same year Distillery beat Bohemians 3-1 in the Irish Cup final at the Dalymount ground.

In 1907-08 he won the Irish Cup with the club in a 3-1 victory against Shelbourne in a replay after an initial draw. The following season they reached the final again, though lost out to Cliftonville 2-1, again in a replay, with Sloan now the club captain. He continued to play for Bohemians until around 1911 when he retired. Internationally he had made eight appearances for his country with five goals, including a hat trick against Wales. He also gained two amateur caps and represented the Irish League side on two occasions.

Although Sloan did not initially join the conflict, by 1916, with pressures regarding the war mounting, both he and his brother Norman signed up. Through the Inns of Court Regiment, Harold was commissioned as a Second Lieutenant in the 198th Royal Garrison Artillery, serving in France from November 1916.

Harold's death on 21st January 1917 was at the Somme, but the exact circumstances or cause are unknown. He was buried in the Guards Cemetery, Combles, Somme, France (I.B.4.). A letter to his wife on 16th February 1917 informed her of the fact that a 'Durable Wooden Cross' had marked the grave. Harold Sloan was 34 years old and married to Mabel Sloan, and they had one son, Harold Fitzgerald. Unfortunately, he too lost his life in action during the Second World War, serving as a Surgeon Lieutenant in the Royal Navy Reserve when the Germans attacked the ship HMS *Javelin* in 1940. Harold's brother Norman survived the Great War.

Cliftonville FC

(League position: seventh)

Hiriam Walton Harvey McKee was born on 16th September 1877 in Belfast. A right half, he was on the books of local club Cliftonville aged just 16 years in 1893, when they reached the Irish Cup final but lost to Linfield 5-0. In 1895, still just 17, he earned a cap for the national side. They were on the end of a 9-0 drubbing by England. He did gain two more in the same year, but was not selected thereafter. Outside the game, he was a trained accountant, and after finishing with Cliftonville he emigrated to Canada around 1909. His younger brother was goalkeeper Fred McKee, who played for Cliftonville, Linfield, Bradford City and Celtic. He represented his country on five occasions.

Hiriam enlisted with the 183rd Battalion, Canadian Infantry, in May 1916 and was in France within months. By November 1916 he returned home seriously ill and unfortunately died on 29th November 1916 in Brandon Hospital. (The cause is not specified.) He was buried in the Brandon Cemetery, Manitoba (S.16.B.). Hiriam was 39 years old.

Cliftonville FC, 1909.

James McManus was born in 1879 in Larne, County Antrim. He is isted on the club's books prior to the war. A Sergeant in the 12th Battalion Royal Irish Rifles, he was wounded on the first day of the Somme, on 1st July 1916, and removed to the Rouen Military Hospital. He died on 14th July 1916 and buried in the St Sever Military Cemetery (A.26.10). James was 37 years old.

Glenavon FC
(League position: sixth)

Samuel Alexander was born in 1899 in Lurgan, County Armagh. He was shown as being a Glenavon player prior to joining the army in around 1907.

Alexander was with the East Lancashire Regiment 'A' Coy, 1st Battalion in 1914, serving in France. He was killed by a sniper in Belgium on 24th November 1914, whilst he was looking through an observation loophole. The incident was included in the report by his commanding officer.

Buried in the Lancashire Cottage Cemetery, Comines-Warneton (I.A.14), Samuel was 25 years old. (He was also remembered on the Lurgan Memorial.)

Moses Cummins from Lurgan was a keen all-round sportsman was a Glenavon player prior to the war. He enlisted with the Royal Irish Rifles and was a Lance Corporal. He and his three brothers all served. He was killed in action on 19th July 1915 and buried in the 'Y' Farm Cemetery, Bois-Grenier, France (K.37). His age is unknown. He is remembered

In the midst of the battlefield's glory
There died a Lurgan soldier true,
And I mourn his loss all over,
For he is one for which we only have a few.

But I hope he rests in Heaven,
For he was a good living lad;
But he's gone from me forever,
That's why today I feel so sad.

So now you town-folk of Lurgan,
You can see he is not forgot,
For its men like him we want today,
And of him I thought a lot.

on the Lurgan Memorial. The following is a poem published in *Lost Words the Great War Poets of Portadown and Lurgan.* It is written in honour of Moses and others who fell in battle. They had all been part of the local 'Hill Street Brass Band', including Samuel Alexander.

Richard 'Dick' Irwin was born in May 1885 in Donagheloney, County Down, one of four children. He was a weaver by trade and a

Drill Sergeant in the Waringstown Company of the Ulster Volunteers. An all-round sportsman, he played in goal for Waringstown and Woodview, then Glenavon reserves, plus he made a number of appearances for the first team. His other passion was cricket, playing for the Waringstown club, appearing in the 1911 final against North Down.

Irwin joined the Royal North Irish Horse in 1908 and was then with the Royal Irish Fusiliers during the war. He was killed in action in Northern France on 3rd November 1917 during an attack on a German gun position.

He was buried in the Neuville-Bourjonval British Cemetery, Pas de Calais (E.17), and remembered on the Lurgan Memorial. Richard was 32 years old, married to Margaret and had a daughter, Sadie.

William Kelly was born in 1880 in Bathgate, Glasgow. A goalkeeper with the club before the war, Kelly enlisted with the 36th Ulster Division, 9th Battalion Royal Irish Rifles. Like many others, he was killed on the first day of the Somme on 1st July 1916. Information reads, '*Corporal Kelly was engaged in an attack at Schwaben Redoubt and killed after breaking through enemy lines, possibly by friendly fire*'.

He was buried in the Ancre British Cemetery, Beaumont-Hamel (VIII.A49). William was 36 years old and married to Ellen Kelly, and they had a daughter also named Ellen, born in 1916. (He is remembered on the Lurgan Memorial.)

John 'Toby' Magill was born in County Armagh in 1892. On Glenavon's books prior to the conflict, he also played for Queens Park Swifts. He was mainly a reserve. Of note, a J. Magill is in the Glenavon FC club history book and team photographs in 1897-98 and 1912-13, making him considerably older.

Our Magill enlisted with the 1ˢᵗ Battalion Royal Irish Fusiliers. He was killed in France near the Belgian border on 27ᵗʰ April 1915, aged 23 years. His two older brothers also served in the war with the 2ⁿᵈ Battalion Royal Irish Rifles.

He was buried in the Bailleul Communal Cemetery, Nord (B.26). He is remembered at the Lurgan Memorial.

Thomas James Mitchell was born in 1895 in County Armagh. He was on Glenavon's books, mainly as a reserve player. Mitchell enlisted with the 2ⁿᵈ Battalion Royal Irish Rifles alongside his friend William Weir, both serving in France.

Wounded in action on 2ⁿᵈ October 1915, Weir died from his injuries, aged 20 years. He was buried in the Etaples Military Cemetery near Boulogne (IV.F.15). Thomas continued with his duties, though his friend's death had affected him. Sadly, he also died from wounds received in action on 16ᵗʰ July 1917, aged 22 years. He was buried in the Bailleul Communal Cemetery, Nord (III.D.25). Both are remembered on the pictured Lurgan Memorial.

Joseph O'Neill was born in 1892 in County Armagh. A regular member of the Glenavon team prior to the war, he was nicknamed 'Coxy'. He was described as a feared centre forward with good speed and strength, an accomplished goal scorer with a ferocious shot. Prior to enlisting, he was attracting the attention of several Scottish clubs.

He enlisted with the 8ᵗʰ Battalion Duke of Cornwall's Light Infantry, ranked as a Sergeant. He was killed on 4ᵗʰ September 1917 in Northern Greece and buried in the Dorian Military Cemetery (VI.C.34). Joseph was 25 years old. He is remembered on the Lurgan Memorial.

James Tipping from Waringstown, County Down, was a Glenavon team regular and regarded as a skilful defender. He was with the club prior to the war. James enlisted with the 1ˢᵗ Battalion Royal Irish Rifles, serving in France.

He was killed in the Somme offensive on 1st April 1917 and buried in the Fins British Cemetery, Sorel-le-Grand, Somme region, (VI.F.14). He is remembered on the Lurgan Memorial.

John Walker from Lurgan was on the books of the club before the war. He enlisted with the 2nd Battalion Royal Irish Rifles in Ballykinlar, County Down, and was killed in France on 16th July 1916, though he was initially reported missing during the Somme offensive. (His wife was informed of the official death date during March 1917. Lord Derby later wrote to her expressing his and the King's sympathies.) He is commemorated on the Thiepval Memorial (Pier and Face 15A and B). John was married to Rose Ann Walker and is remembered on the Lurgan Memorial.

James Weir from Lurgan was born in 1895, one of nine children. He was described as a popular character, all-round sportsman and a player with Glenavon. Enlisted with the 1st Battalion Royal Irish Rifles serving in France, he was killed in action on 14th March 1916. He was buried in the Rue-Du-Bois Military Cemetery, Fleurbaix (I.B.24). James was 21 years old. Some of his fellow comrades penned the following poem in his memory:

Although his hands we cannot clasp,
His face we cannot see,
Just let this little token tell,
We still remember thee.

We often think of days gone by,
When we were all together;
But the shadow o'er his life has cast,
Our loved one gone forever.

It is hard to be a mother,
And see her loved one go,
To a foreign land to take his stand,
Against the cruel foe.

It is hard to be a father also,
But still their poor hearts break;
But we will sleep with a rest and give him
our best,
For our King and country's sake.

John Wilson was born in 1891 in Lurgan and came from a family with a military background. His father served 23 years in the army, and John and his four brothers all served. Before the war he was on the books of

Glenavon, 1913.

Glenavon. He was killed in action on 24th January 1915 in Belgium, serving with the 2nd Battalion Royal Irish Fusiliers, attempting to assist his platoon leader Lieutenant Hatch. (He was hit in the back by shrapnel whilst jumping to his assistance.) He is commemorated at the Memorial to the Missing at Menin Gate, Ypres (Panel 42), and the Lurgan Memorial. John was 24 years old. His brother Allen was a Sergeant Major in the same battalion.

Glentoran FC

(League runners-up)

Archibald Cunningham. See Leith Athletic

Bernard Donaghy. See Hibernian

Linfield FC

(League position: third)

William James Creevey was born in 1890 in the Shankhill Road area of Belfast. A fitter by occupation, he was on the books of Linfield in 1910-11. His previous clubs were Ligoneil and Glentoran. He was a fast speedy winger, playing 12 games for Linfield Swifts and four for Linfield, scoring one goal.

Creevey enlisted with the Royal Irish Rifles, then the 15th Battalion Royal Ulster Rifles, serving as a Corporal. After contracting pneumonia in France, he returned home. He died in Hartlepool Hospital on 28th June 1917. He was buried in Hartlepool New Cemetery (row V, grave 5). William was 27 years old.

David Drennan from Whiteabbey, Belfast, was born on 17th June 1877. Playing as a goalkeeper, he started out with the local club Woodvale before signing for Cliftonville. He signed for Linfield in 1899-1903, where he played 13 games. A move to Willowfield followed before he returned to Cliftonville in 1903-04. It is believed he spent some time at the Distillery club. By occupation, Drennan worked for the G.P.O. though he was living in Canada at the time of his enlistment in 1915.

Drennan enlisted with the 11th Battalion Royal Irish Rifles, serving in France and Flanders. He was killed in action on 1st September 1916 near the Belgian border. He was buried in Ration Farm Cemetery, La-Plus Douvre Annex, Belgium (Plot 2-Grave 4. HC27). David was 37 years old, married to Mary Drennan and had four sons.

John Edmondson was born in Belfast in 1873. On the club's books in the early 1900s, he then enlisted with the Royal Irish Rifles for the conflict.

Recorded as being back home prior to his death from war-related illness, he died on 5th November 1918, aged 45 years. He was buried in the Belfast City Cemetery (H3.610). John was married to Margaret Jane Edmondson.

James Quinn Forbes was born in 1899. His family lived in Forfar, Scotland. (He is listed on the Linfield FC Memorial). Quinn joined the 4th Gordon Highlanders during the war and was stationed in Northern France as a Lance Corporal. Quinn's death was recorded as 25th July 1918. He was buried in the Soissons Cemetery (M.R.18), which is to the north east of Paris. James was 19 years old.

William Hall was listed on the Linfield FC Memorial, serving with the 2nd Battalion Royal Irish Rifles. He was killed in action near Ypres on 20th July 1915 and is commemorated at the Ypres Menin Gate (Panel 40). No other details are known.

Leslie Houston was born in Ahoghill, County Antrim. He was on the books of Linfield but was mainly a player with Linfield Swifts and South End Rangers, with whom he played in the Irish Junior Cup final from 1910-11. By occupation, he worked for the Lancashire Chemist's Shop in the area.

He enlisted in August 1914 with the Royal Inniskilling Fusiliers, serving in Northern France. He was badly wounded and removed to the 2nd Clearing Station Hospital near Bailleul, where he died from his wounds on 31st October 1914. He was buried in the Bailleul Communal Cemetery (J.2). Leslie left a wife and four children.

His brother (pictured) was the more famous **John Houston**, who also played for Linfield, as well as Everton and Partick Thistle, among others. He also earned six international caps for Northern Ireland. He served with the Royal Irish Rifles, commissioned as a Lieutenant, receiving the Military Medal. John survived the conflict.

The pictured team photo of South End Rangers has Leslie in the front row, fourth player from the left.

Thomas Johnston was born in Larne, County Antrim, in 1888, one of four brothers and eight sisters. He is on the books of Linfield from 1907-09, playing two games and scoring two goals as a centre forward, though he remained on the Larne FC team books. After 1909 he was with the Distillery club. His brother Walter (Wattie) was a more regular player with Linfield, winning a league and cup medal with them in 1908-09.

Thomas enlisted with the Royal Irish Rifles, ranked as Sergeant. There are two reports, one stating he was seriously ill from wounds to the stomach, the other saying he was killed in action (both from October 1916). The death location is still not clear. The Antrim Masonic Lodges hold Thomas's records. He was 27-28 years old. (He is listed on the Linfield FC Memorial.)

Thomas William King was born on 4th August 1879 in Winchcombe, Gloucestershire, one of two children. On the club's books in 1909-10. He had been in Belfast from 1901 due to his rugby skills. A good sportsman, he was an excellent cricketer as well, representing Gloucestershire as an all-rounder. He was also a coach at Cliftonville and a professional at Holywood Cricket Club. King played football as a centre or half back, playing 22 games for Linfield.

He served with the 1st and 5th Gloucester Regiment during the conflict. He was killed in Belgium near

Ypres on 7th August 1917. He is commemorated on the Ypres Menin Gate Memorial (MR.002) and the Winchcombe and Linfield Memorials. Thomas was 38 years old.

Wesley Maultsaid was born on 27th August 1888 in Londonderry, Northern Ireland, one of eight children. He played for Linfield Swifts and Institute. Prior to the war, he had also gained a junior international cap. He was educated at the Foyle College, Londonderry.

Maultsaid and his brother David enlisted with the Royal Inniskilling Fusiliers, then the Irish Rifles, commissioned as a 2nd Lieutenant. His cousin Jim was the company war artist, and he had two books published about his experiences after the war had ended. Wesley's brother Arthur played for Linfield in 1921-22 in the team that won seven trophies.

Severely wounded on 11th November 1916 near Sanctuary Wood, Ypres, Belgium, Wesley died from his wounds the next day. He was buried in the cemetery there (II.J.21). He was 28 years old. He is also commemorated on the Foyle College Memorial.

Isaac McConnell from Belfast, was born in 1872 and was on the books of the Linfield club during the early 1900s. He enlisted with the Corps of the Royal Engineers, serving in Belgium as a Lance Corporal. He was killed on

9th July 1917 and buried in the Irish New Farm Cemetery (XVII.E.6). Isaac was 45 years old, married to Jeannie and had a son, James.

James Wilfred McConnell M.M. enlisted aged 15 years in June 1916 with the Royal Army Service Corps, giving the wrong information about his age. The youngest known person serving in the war at that time, he eagerly wanted to follow his father into service. He was later awarded the Military Medal for rescuing colleges whilst under fire in France and Flanders, though he was still only 16 years old. After his father's death, a terrible twist of fate followed. James was involved in a road traffic accident in Bangor, Ireland, on 20th August 1919. Knocked off his pedal cycle, he suffered severe head injuries, dying at the scene. He was 18 years old. He was buried in Belfast City Cemetery (J.78).

Richard 'Dick' Moore was born in Shankhill, Belfast, on 18th January 1867, the son of a rope merchant. His career as a soldier with the Irish Rifles and Fusiliers spanned more than 21 years. A respected and talented half back, he attended the Model School in Belfast then the Intermediate school in Lisburn. Best remembered for his exploits with Linfield, he also played for Dundalk and Dundalk Rovers. He was with Linfield in 1890-91 when they won the Irish League and Cup, and he also won the Leinster Cup with Dundalk in 1896-97. Moore gained three international caps in 1891 and represented the Ulster select side.

As his footballing career was ending, he was by now a Colour Sergeant with the Royal Irish Rifles and after leaving the forces he became a labourer. Moore then re-enlisted in 1914 and was immediately accepted back into his regiment as a Quartermaster Sergeant. He was now 46 years old. After three years' service in 1917, on the recommendation of Colonel Sharman Crawford, he transferred to the 2nd Garrison Battalion, Royal Irish Fusiliers, as a 2nd Lieutenant.

Stationed in Salonika, Greece, in late 1918, Moore was seriously ill during October and admitted to hospital with dysenteric symptoms. He died in the 42nd hospital on 29th October 1918. He was buried in the

Greetings from Belfast. LINFIELD FOOTBALL TEAM, 1915-16

Kirechkoi-Hortakoi Military Cemetery near Thessalonica (Grave 400). Richard was 50 years old and married to Ellen Moore.

James Walker was born in 1892 in Dunadry, County Antrim. He was on the books of Linfield in 1913-14. He enlisted with the Royal Irish Rifles for the conflict, serving in France.

He was killed at Forceville, near Arras, on 6th May 1916 and buried at Forceville Communal Cemetery (I.C.14). James was 24 years old. (James is the uniformed soldier pictured in the Linfield team photograph at the end of the Linfield section.)

(There are two other names on the Linfield FC Memorial. 1. **Captain G. Gibson** Royal Irish Rifles 1918. 2. **Private Turner** 1917. No football-related information found.)

Lisburn Distillery FC

(League position: fourth – club known as Distillery until 1999)

William Brolly from Dungeiven, County Derry, is listed with the Distillery club from 1913-14 before enlisting with the 1st Battalion Royal Inniskilling Fusiliers in Londonderry during the war.

He was listed as missing, presumed dead during fighting at Scimitar Hill, Gallipoli, on 21st August 1915 and commemorated at the Helles Memorial (Panel 98 to 102). (He is also in the 1914 team photograph at the end of the Lisburn section.)

Samuel Long was born in Belfast and was a playing member of the Distillery club before emigrating to South Africa.

He enlisted with the 5th Regiment South African Infantry and was killed in action at Kangata, German East Africa, on 20th June 1916.

Samuel was buried in the Dar Es Salaam War Cemetery (Grave 3.J.5), Tanzania.

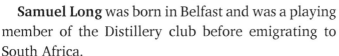

John Spencer Dunville V.C. (2nd Lieutenant) is listed on the Distillery Roll of Honour plaque. He was a member of the club, not a player. His father, Colonel John Dunville Senior, was the founder member. He ran Dunville's, one of the largest whiskey distilleries of the 20th Century. His son received a posthumous Victoria Cross for conspicuous bravery near Epehy, France, on 24th

June 1917, serving with the 1st Royal Dragoons. He placed himself between the enemy and his men, enabling vital work to be carried out, and although severely wounded he directed operations successfully. John died from his wounds the following day on 25th Junev1917, aged 21 years. He was buried in Villiers-Faucon Communal Cemetery (Plot A21), Somme. (His medal is displayed in the Household Cavalry Museum, London.)

Donald Sloan was born on 31st July 1883 in Rankinston, Scotland, one of twelve children, though two died in infancy. He was signed by Everton in 1906 from Belfast Distillery as a back-up for first-team keeper Billy Scott. Sloan had already represented the Irish League side. He stayed at Everton for two seasons, making six appearances,

D. SLOAN, Belfast Distillery.

before moving across Stanley Park to Liverpool for £300, where he made six appearances for them. In 1909 he returned to Distillery as player-coach, helping them to win the Irish Cup. In total he played over 124 games.

On outbreak of war, he joined the 8th Black Watch Royal Highlanders and fought in France. He was killed on New Year's Day 1917 near Arras, when he was sheltering in a dugout with four colleagues and a shell exploded directly on top of them, killing all five men. He was buried in the Faubourg D'Amiens Cemetery (III.A.32). He was 33 years old, married to Edith Sloan and had four children. Three of his brothers, Robert, William and Thomas, also died in the conflict. (They are all remembered on the Rankinston Memorial in East Ayrshire, which their father unveiled in 1921.)

The other name on the Distillery Plaque is **David Drennan** (See Linfield FC). Pictured is an old Distillery team image from 1913-14.

Shelbourne FC
(League position: fifth)

Frederick 'Fred' Morrow was from Dublin and was born in 1896. He was a centre forward though small in stature for that role, standing at

Shelbourne FC 1914-15

just about 5ft 5in in height. He began at local club Tritonville FC before signing for Bohemians aged 17 years in 1913. He then moved to Linfield before moving again to Shelbourne in 1914-15, playing six games and scoring two goals.

BOMBARDIER F. MORROW.

Morrow enlisted with the Royal Horse and Field Artillery, serving in France as an Acting Sergeant, as did his teammate and former Manchester United player Oscar Linkson. He was seriously wounded near Bailleul, Nord, France, and he died shortly after; the date was 27th September 1917. He was buried in the Outtersteene Communal Cemetery Extension, Bailleul (I.C. 8). Fred was 21 years old.

APPENDIX 1

Football League tables for 1914-15

English League One and Two

		P	W	D	L	F	A	Pts
1	Everton	38	19	8	11	76	47	46
2	Oldham Athletic	38	17	11	10	70	56	45
3	Blackburn Rovers	38	18	7	13	83	61	43
4	Burnley	38	18	7	13	61	47	43
5	Manchester City	38	15	13	10	49	39	43
6	Sheffield United	38	15	13	10	49	41	43
7	Sheffield Wednesday	38	15	13	10	61	54	43
8	Sunderland	38	18	5	15	81	72	41
9	Bradford Park Avenue	38	17	7	14	69	65	41
10	West Bromwich Albion	38	15	10	13	49	43	40
11	Bradford City	38	13	14	11	55	49	40
12	Middlesbrough	38	13	12	13	62	74	38
13	Liverpool	38	14	9	15	65	75	37
14	Aston Villa	38	13	11	14	62	72	37
15	Newcastle United	38	11	10	17	46	48	32
16	Notts County	38	9	13	16	41	57	31
17	Bolton Wanderers	38	11	8	19	68	84	30
18	Manchester United	38	9	12	17	46	62	30
19	Chelsea	38	8	13	17	51	65	29
20	Tottenham Hotspur	38	8	12	18	57	90	28

		P	W	D	L	F	A	Pts
1	Derby County	38	23	7	8	71	33	53
2	Preston North End	38	20	10	8	61	42	50
3	Barnsley	38	22	3	13	51	51	47
4	Wolverhampton W.	38	19	7	12	77	52	45
5	Arsenal	38	19	5	14	69	41	43
6	Birmingham	38	17	9	12	62	39	43
7	Hull City	38	19	5	14	65	54	43
8	Huddersfield Town	38	17	8	13	61	42	42
9	Clapton Orient*	38	16	9	13	50	48	41
10	Blackpool	38	17	5	16	58	57	39
11	Bury	38	15	8	15	61	56	38
12	Fulham	38	15	7	16	53	47	37
13	Bristol City	38	15	7	16	62	56	37
14	Stockport County	38	15	7	16	54	60	37
15	Leeds City	38	14	4	20	65	64	32
16	Lincoln City	38	11	9	18	46	65	31
17	Grimsby Town	38	11	9	18	48	76	31
18	Nottingham Forest	38	10	9	19	43	77	29
19	Leicester Fosse**	38	10	4	24	47	88	24
20	Glossop	38	6	6	26	31	87	18

Southern League One and Two

	P	W	D	L	F	A	Pts
Watford	38	22	8	8	68	46	52
READING	38	21	7	10	68	43	49
Cardiff City	38	22	4	12	72	38	48
West Ham United	38	18	9	11	58	47	45
Northampton Town	38	16	11	11	56	51	43
Southampton	38	19	5	14	78	74	43
Portsmouth	38	16	10	12	54	42	42
Millwall	38	16	10	12	50	51	42
Swindon Town	38	15	11	12	77	59	41
Brighton & Hove A.	38	16	7	15	46	47	39
Exeter City	38	15	8	15	50	41	38
Queen's Park Rgs.	38	13	12	13	55	56	38
Norwich City	38	11	14	13	53	56	36
Luton Town	38	13	8	17	61	73	34
Crystal Palace	38	13	8	17	47	61	34
Bristol Rovers	38	14	3	21	53	75	31
Plymouth Argyle	38	8	14	16	51	61	30
Southend United	38	10	8	20	44	64	28
Croydon Common	38	9	9	20	47	63	27
Gillingham	38	6	8	24	43	83	20

	P	W	D	L	F	A	Pts
Stoke	24	17	4	3	62	15	38
Stalybridge Celtic	24	17	3	4	47	22	37
Merthyr Town	24	15	5	4	46	20	35
Swansea Town	24	16	1	7	48	21	33
Coventry City	24	13	2	9	56	33	28
Ton Pentre	24	11	6	7	42	43	28
BRENTFORD	24	8	7	9	35	45	23
Llanelly	24	10	1	13	39	32	21
Barry	24	6	5	13	30	35	17
Newport County	24	7	3	14	27	42	17
Pontypridd	24	5	6	13	31	56	16
Mid Rhondda	24	3	6	15	17	40	12
Ebbw Vale	24	3	1	20	23	88	7

1914/15

SCOTTISH FOOTBALL LEAGUE CHAMPIONSHIP TABLES - SEASON

DIVISION 1 1914/15									
Club	P	W	D	L	F	A	W	D	L
		Home					Away		
Celtic	38	18	1	0	56	10	12	4	3
Hearts	38	17	1	1	50	13	10	6	3
Rangers	38	11	1	7	37	23	12	3	4
Morton	38	13	4	2	43	17	5	8	6
Ayr United	38	13	3	3	29	12	7	5	7
Falkirk	38	10	5	4	31	19	6	2	11
Hamilton Academical	38	9	3	3	37	26	7	1	11
Partick Thistle	38	10	3	6	36	22	5	5	9
St. Mirren	38	9	4	6	31	25	5	4	10
Airdrieonians	38	9	4	6	35	28	5	3	11
Hibernian	38	9	5	5	36	27	3	6	10
Kilmarnock	38	12	2	5	39	24	3	2	14
Dumbarton	38	9	3	7	29	30	4	5	10
Aberdeen	38	7	7	5	21	14	4	4	11
Dundee	38	8	4	7	24	21	4	5	10
Third Lanark	38	7	8	4	32	22	3	4	12
Clyde	38	8	4	7	27	24	4	2	13
Motherwell	38	7	5	7	31	30	3	5	11
Raith Rovers	38	5	8	6	31	27	4	2	13
Queen's Park	38	3	2	14	14	39	1	3	15

DIVISION 2 1914/15									
Club	P	W	D	L	F	A	W	D	L
		Home					Away		
Cowdenbeath	26	12	0	1	33	5	4	5	4
St Bernards	26	13	0	0	43	10	5	1	7
Leith	26	10	2	1	35	10	5	5	3
East Stirling	26	11	2	0	33	12	2	3	8
Clydebank	26	9	2	2	46	16	4	2	7
Dunfermline Athletic	26	9	1	3	34	18	4	1	8
Johnstone	26	10	2	1	27	13	1	3	9
St. Johnstone	26	9	3	1	38	19	1	3	9
Albion Rovers	26	7	4	2	27	15	2	3	8
Lochgelly United	26	6	3	4	26	19	3	0	10
Dundee Hibernians	26	7	2	4	31	23	1	1	11
Abercorn	26	5	4	4	25	21	0	3	10
Arthurlie	26	4	2	7	19	24	2	2	9
Vale of Leven	26	4	5	4	22	23	0	0	13

Irish League Table

Club	P	W	D	L	GF	GA	Pts
Belfast Celtic	14	10	3	1	24	7	23
Glentoran	14	9	3	2	27	10	21
Linfield	14	6	5	3	27	18	17
Distillery	14	7	1	6	23	16	15
Shelbourne	14	6	3	5	17	12	15
Glenavon	14	3	5	6	24	28	11
Cliftonville	14	4	1	9	13	29	9
Bohemians	14	0	1	13	10	45	1

Cup Finals information:

The English FA Cup final in 1914-15 was played at Old Trafford on 24th April, 1915, with an attendance of 49,557. The two sides competing for the trophy were **Sheffield United** and **Chelsea**, with the Sheffield team winning the day 3-0, with goals from Simmons, Fazackerley and Kitchen.

The Scottish Cup final in 1913-14 was between the dominant **Celtic** side and **Hibernian**. The initial game was played at Ibrox Park, Glasgow, on 11th April 1914, with an attendance of 56,000, which resulted in a 0-0 draw. The replay was again at Ibrox five days later on 16th April, before 40,000, and resulted in a 4-1 victory for Celtic. Celtic scorers were McColl (2), Browning (2). Hibernian's consolation goal came from Smith. (There was no final in 1915 as both the English and Scottish competitions were suspended until 1920.)

The Irish Challenge Cup continued throughout the conflict. (Winners were: 1914 – Glentoran, 1915 – Linfield, 1916 – Linfield, 1917 – Glentoran, 1918 – Belfast Celtic.)

Appendix 2

Known medal honours
  Victoria Crosses 5 (Two none player related, club members)
  Military Medals 13
  Military Crosses 7
  Military Cross-with Bar 2
  Distinguished Conduct Medal (D.C.M.) 4
  Distinguished Service Order 2
  Croix de Guerre 2 (French bravery award for acts of heroism)
  Russian Medal of St George 1
  Recommended for Military Cross 1 (Not given)
  Recommended for D.C.M. 1 (Not given)
  Sourced reports for those Mentioned in Despatches 3 (One for V.C.).

William Angus V.C. A special mention is made here for the Celtic FC man, awarded the Victoria Cross for rescuing his Commanding Officer under intense fire at Givenchy-les-la-Bassee, France, during which time he received over 40 wounds. Thankfully, he survived and made a remarkable recovery, though he did lose the sight in his left eye and part of his right foot. He died in 1959, aged 71.

Appendix 3

The war officially ended, as previously mentioned, in November 1918, and a great sadness was felt throughout the football community. It would be well over another year before life began to return to some kind of normality; family and community wounds would take much longer. Football resumed fully in 1918-19 with a large void left by the deaths of many top-flight players. Their memorials, graves and crosses are scattered across the globe.

It is now over 100 years since this conflict ended and now, as then, it is just as important to reflect on their sacrifice and maintain the memory. The passage of time should never diminish this and this compendium will assist in ensuring that doesn't happen. We should also celebrate their lives and the pleasure they gave to thousands of people through their sport.

War and violence still affects many people to the present day. This has also directly affected one of my relatives.

Her daughter Emma was the partner of David 'Jaffa' Atherton, aged 25 years. They have one daughter called Millie. In civilian life they lived in Kearsley, near Bolton.

He was with the 1st Battalion Grenadier Guards stationed in Afghanistan, serving with the Anti-Tank Section, Number 3 Company. He had been in the army since 2002 and had already served in Bosnia and Iraq. The company had encountered Taliban fighters near the village of Mirmandab, and David successfully engaged them with an Anti-Tank missile, enabling his comrades to advance. He was unfortunately shot and killed during this engagement. It was Thursday 26th July 2007. He was laid to rest in Manchester in full uniform with military honours. Emma and Millie, after counselling, have managed to move on with their lives, though they visit David's grave regularly and his memory is still very much a large part of their lives.

This tragic story, though, does not end here. His mother, Gill Atherton, ran a shop in the Stretford area of Manchester called 'Jaffs', which she opened in his memory in 2009. She had also devoted much of her time to helping other bereaved families after her son's death, though she suffered terribly from depression.

Her body was discovered on 11th April 2012 in the flat above the café by her daughter, David's sister Kelly. She stated, 'mother was never the same person and could not come to terms with David's death'. She was buried alongside her son. Gill was 47 years old. (Pictured together opposite).

In conclusion, the world and football has moved on at a tremendous pace since 1918. It will be a distant memory for many and sadly completely unknown to some of the younger generation. I hope this book has given a reasonable insight into the history of football and the impact the war had on sport during this period. The Great War is still a major topic of discussion and debate today, with many lessons learned and, without doubt, many mistakes were made. Of all the recorded victims, many thousands more were lost to the battlefields. As late as 1937-38 thousands of bodies were being interred to a recognised grave. Yet even as these recovery operations continued, more dark clouds were again gathering and another chapter in history was about to be written, which would be equally devastating.

Jeff Williamson

ND - #0252 - 270225 - C0 - 234/156/21 - PB - 9781780915777 - Gloss Lamination